DICTIONARY
of
ROYAL
BIOGRAPHERS

DICTIONARY
of
ROYAL
BIOGRAPHERS

John Van der Kiste

A & F

First published by A & F 2015

A & F Publications,
South Brent, Devon, England TQ10 9AS

ISBN-13: 978-1517115272
ISBN-10: 1517115272

Typeset 11pt Baskerville
Printed by CreateSpace

CONTENTS

PREFACE

My fascination with Kings and Queens, and their lives as well as those closest to them, began not very long after I learned to read. An obsession with historical dates, and almost all things biographical, followed not long afterwards. I remember spending hours poring over the *Dictionary of National Biography*, as it was then, during my teens in the public and also the school library, which made it more or less a dream come true some twenty years or so later when I was asked to contribute to the revised work, the *Oxford Dictionary of National Biography*. In the natural course of things, this extended to a desire to learn something about the royal biographers themselves.

A few enquiries from friends online confirmed my belief that nothing of the kind existed, and more gratifyingly still, that I was not alone in my interest. If I was to fill the gap, several people would be interested in a copy of the result, and so the work you have in front of you came about.

Naturally, parameters have to be set. My aim has been to cover biographers writing about British and European royalty from the Norman conquest, or to coin a phrase, '1066 and all that' onwards. To qualify, authors included must have had at least one work translated into and published in English. In a very few cases, editors of particularly relevant journals, such as Paul Minet, founder and editor of *Royalty Digest* for its fourteen-year existence whose only published books were on the bookselling trade, have also been included. The two earliest biographers covered, Robert Huish and Agnes Strickland (or rather the Strickland family), were born in the 18th century.

The line between history and royal biography is a blurred one. Do the writers of lives, or rather lives and times, of Norman and Plantagenet Kings of England – or in fact, more or less any monarchs up to, say, Hanoverian times - qualify as the former or the latter? For the sake of this book and in the interests of making this work more comprehensive, I have counted them as biographies. Authors of books on the institution of monarchy have with some misgivings been excluded.

As was self-evident when I began working on it, such a book could turn into a never-ending task. I have endeavoured to include the authors of what I consider all the major lives of some of those most written about, but the number of published books about Queen Victoria, Queen Elizabeth II and Diana, Princess of Wales is considerable. Some readers may question my inclusion of several writers whose books clearly come from what might be called 'the tabloid journalism school'. Nevertheless I have mentioned these as well if only as a matter of record, secure in the knowledge that the more gossipy scribes of the 1990s onwards had their parallels nearly a century earlier, as a glance through these pages will reveal.

The ill-fated Emperor Maximilian of Mexico may have been a monarch outside Europe, but as a Habsburg and brother of the Emperor of Austria, for these purposes he counts as European. Some might contend that Napoleon Bonaparte was not royal or really imperial at all, but it was difficult to omit him, or rather his biographers, if only as he rapidly became royally connected by marriage. Biographies of royal claimants, such as Perkin Warbeck and Anna Anderson, are excluded.

What about members of royalty who wrote and published their memoirs? After initially planning to leave them out, I changed my mind. However I am acting on the assumption that users of this book will probably be sufficiently acquainted with the basic facts on the lives of Queen Victoria and her eldest grandson, German Emperor William II, not to need yet another recital of these. My entries on them in this book, therefore, place the emphasis on their careers as published authors, such as they were. Writers of letters, such as George III and the Empress Frederick, edited by others have thus been excluded as authors, although there are naturally entries for her editors, namely Sir Frederick Ponsonby, Arthur Gould Lee, and Sir Roger Fulford, who are royal biographers in their own right.

Should those who are closest to royalty also be included, or to put it another way, to what extent are biographies of Dorothea Jordan, Baron Stockmar and Rasputin biographies of the crowned heads with whom they are so closely associated? There is no watertight answer, and in some cases arbitrary decisions have had to be made.

Titles of books and date of first publication are listed at the end of each entry. In some cases, royal biographies formed only a small output of a writer's work, and a few prolific authors only published one such title in their entire careers, but they still have their place in these pages. I have of necessity refrained from adding a complete list of their other publications. Regarding some of the most prolific wordsmiths, such as Marjorie Bowen, Barbara Cartland and Ursula Bloom, to have added all their novels in addition to the very small number of biographies they wrote would have bulked these pages out unnecessarily. Also in the interests of space, a few lengthy sub-titles have been curtailed at the author's discretion. Where it is considered helpful, the subject of a biography has been added in square brackets after the title when the identity of the person written about would be otherwise unclear.

As far as possible, when an author has revised or published different editions of what is basically the same biography, I have tended to list just the first. There have however been instances where a writer has produced a totally new book on a particular royal person many years after the first, often for a different publisher. Elizabeth Longford is a good example; best known for *Victoria RI*, she brought her writing career to a close some years later with a 'pocket biography' of the same sovereign. Where I have not been able to see both separate books myself, I have erred on the side of caution and listed both, on the assumption that both are different titles albeit with the same author and same subject.

The amount of information available on each relevant author is inevitably very varied. Some of those still living have their own websites, while other illustrious names of the recent past were well covered by generous obituaries in *The Times, Daily Telegraph, Guardian* and other papers shortly after death, and in some cases have an entry in the *Oxford Dictionary of National Biography*. (Some of them, the present author included, wrote one or more articles for the latter publication themselves). At the other extreme, a very few (living and dead) have left seemingly almost no trace online or elsewhere other than copies of the books they wrote and published and perhaps their dates of birth and death, while a few others whose primary careers were in the academic world have a record of the universities or similar institutions they taught at, but nothing more. Titles for each author have been checked as far as possible against the British Library online catalogue. 'Additional' forenames which an author did not normally as part of his or her professional name have been added in brackets, as have maiden names and the original names of those who wrote under pseudonyms. Nationalities and lifespan dates are given where known.

I should add that this was never intended to be a consumers' guide, with one- to five-star gradings for books, recommendations as to the best, and the like. Entries are basically written from a neutral point of view. Where critical comments are added, these are the opinions of others, not mine, and sources have been quoted where possible. In the course of forty years or so of working and researching in libraries, writing and reviewing, I have seen and handled many but by no means all of these titles, and am not in a position to pass judgment on more than a small proportion. Finally, it is as well to remind users that a number of titles listed in the following pages, particularly older volumes long since out of copyright, may be hard to find in their physical form but are often freely and almost instantly accessible online.

I would like to thank everybody on the Facebook Royal Pages, who sustained me in my belief that this was a book which would indeed have its place. My particular gratitude goes to Deb Wilson, who responded to several queries about elusive names with some invaluable digging for and supply of facts. I am also very grateful to the royal biographers themselves whom it has been my pleasure to know and meet personally or be in contact with from time to time, and who have been kind enough to approve and make suggestions and improvements to the entries I already had for them, even if they almost invariably requested that their year of birth was not mentioned. It has been a salutary reminder that, despite checking and re-checking facts from online and print sources, it is all too easy to make mistakes – or rather terminological inexactitudes. Finally, as ever my greatest thanks are to my wife Kim for her tireless support as ever, not least through the death and speedy replacement of two of my computers.

There may be occasional inconsistencies in the use of royal forenames, some given in their original European spelling, others Anglicised. I have tried to strike a balance between the form which is more familiar and acceptable to an English-reading audience, and the style by which a person may be better known.

Errors and omissions will inevitably remain. I would welcome any corrections, and further biographical details, including missing years of birth and death, that readers might have and can supply particularly about those writers whom I have only been able to list by name alongside their relevant titles, as a second edition may be feasible in time.

In conclusion, this volume is respectfully dedicated to the memory of Theo Aronson, one of the most loved and respected royal biographers of the late twentieth century, a good friend always ready with encouragement and advice, and a lasting inspiration. It is a happy coincidence that, on checking the proof, I find that he has what must surely be one of the longest entries, if not the longest, in the whole book.

John Van der Kiste
August 2015

ROYAL BIOGRAPHERS

A

ABBOTT, John (Stevens Cabot) (1805-77), American historian, biographer and pastor, born in Brunswick. He was a member of the ministry in the Congregational Church in Massachusetts, until retiring in 1844 to devote himself to writing.

History of Napoleon Bonaparte (1855); *The History of Frederick II, Called Frederick the Great* (1871)

ACTON, Sir Harold (Mario Mitchell), CBE (1904-94), British writer and scholar, born into a prominent Anglo-Italian-American family near Florence. Educated in England and Switzerland, he read Modern Greats at Christchurch, Oxford, where he helped to found an avant-garde magazine *The Oxford Broom*, and publish a first volume of poems. He was a special constable during the General Strike of 1926. After publishing further poems, novels, and a translation from the Italian, he wrote several titles about the Italian nobility and royalty. He divided his time between England, France and Peking, leaving the latter on the outbreak of the Second World War when he returned to England and joined the Royal Air Force. After the war he lived again in Florence.

The Last Medici (1932); *The Bourbons of Naples (1734–1825)* (1956); *The Last Bourbons of Naples (1825–1861)* (1961)

AIRY, Osmund (1845-1928), British historian, was born at the Royal Observatory, Greenwich, his father Sir G.B. Airy being Astronomer-Royal. He studied at Trinity College, Cambridge, and then taught successively at Blackheath Propriety School and Wellington College until 1878. In that year he was appointed Inspector of Schools, and Divisional Inspector from 1904 until his retirement in 1910. He published history textbooks and works on mathematics as well as books on 17th century subjects, and was a contributor to *Encyclopedia Britannica* and *Dictionary of National Biography*.
Charles II (1904)

ALBERT, Harold A. (real name Harold Albert Kemp) (1909-97), British author, began his career as a journalist for the *Evening News* and *Daily Mirror*, personally interviewing both Hitler and Mussolini. A lifelong pacifist, during the Second World War he was imprisoned as a conscientious objector. After the war he turned to writing biographies, while maintaining that he was the literary manager of biographer Helen Cathcart. The books were aimed at a women's audience, so he felt a woman's name as author was necessary. Under this byline he approached editors with articles and manuscripts, and arranged serialisations of his work, while rejecting requests for interviews, lectures and book signings on the grounds that Mrs Cathcart was a shy recluse, interested only in promoting her subject, not herself. He never disclosed her age or details of her private life, beyond allowing a rumour that she had been a member of the staff of King George V to circulate unchallenged. Journalists who visited him at his home suspected that she did not exist. He carried out his research in the London Library and from letters written in her name asking sources for supporting evidence, anecdotes and stories. Suspicious journalists visited him at his home to try and get him to admit as much, but failed. Occasionally, 'Helen Cathcart' acknowledged the kind help of Harold Albert in her prefaces. The name was initially used for articles and then books about the royal family and about individuals, alongside histories of Sandringham and the Queen's racehorses. He also ghosted two books by Queen Alexandra of Yugoslavia, based on conversations with her and on press reports. Ironically the book of which he was proudest, and his most substantial, was a life of Queen Victoria's half-sister Feodora, one of two titles published under his own name. After the market for more deferential biographies declined from the 1980s and early 1990s, he wrote a column, again under the byline, for *Majesty* magazine. He planned to reveal the secret in an autobiography which he never managed to write. Following his death, a notice identified him simply as 'Harold Albert, author and famed royal biographer under the name of Mrs Helen Cathcart'.

As Harold A. Albert: *The Queen and the Arts* (1963); *Queen Victoria's Sister: The Life and Letters of Princess Feodora* (1967)

As Helen Cathcart: *The Queen and the Turf* (1959); *HRH Prince Philip, Sportsman* (1961); *Her Majesty* (1962); *The Queen Mother* (1965); *Princess Alexandra* (1967); *Lord Snowdon* (1968); *The Married Life of the Queen* (1970); *The Duchess of Kent* (1971); *Anne and the Princesses Royal* (1973); *Princess Margaret* (1974); *Prince Charles: The Biography* (1976); *The Queen in Her Circle* (1977); *The Queen Mother Herself* (1979); *The Queen Herself* (1982); *The Queen Mother: Fifty Years a Queen* (1986); *The Queen and Prince Philip: Forty Years of Happiness* (1987); *Charles, Man of Destiny* (1988); *Anne, the Princess Royal: A Princess for our Times* (1988)

ALEXANDER, John T., PhD., MA, BA, American biographer and specialist in Russian history, Professor Emeritus in History, University of Kansas.
Catherine the Great: Life and Legend (1989)

ALFORD, Stephen (1970-), British historian and biographer, studied at the University of St Andrews, then moved in 1997 to the University of Cambridge as a British Academy Post-doctoral Research Fellow in the Faculty of History and a Junior Research Fellow of Fitzwilliam College, was elected Ehrman Senior Research Fellow in History at King's College, Cambridge in 1999, and joined the Cambridge Faculty of History as an Assistant Lecturer, a Lecturer and a Senior Lecturer. In 2000 he was elected a Fellow of the Royal Historical Society, then left Cambridge to become Professor of Early Modern British History, Leeds, in 2012.
Edward VI: The Boy King (2014)

ALLEN, Walter Gore (1911-60), British local historian and biographer, died shortly before the publication of his last book, a biography of William IV.
King William IV (1960)

ALLFREY, Anthony (Rodney) (1930-2010), British biographer, was born in London and educated in England, America and France. While living in Portugal he produced a monthly economic newsletter. He was a contributor to the *Dictionary of National Biography*.
Edward VII and his Jewish Court (1991)

ALLMAND, Christopher (Thomas) (1936-), British academic historian, was Professor of Medieval History until retirement in 1998, subsequently Honorary Senior Fellow at University of Liverpool, and editor of the seventh and final volume of the New Cambridge Medieval History.

Henry V (1997)

ALMEDINGEN, E.M. (Marta Alexandrovna Almedingen, later Edith Martha Almedingen) FRSL (1898–1971), Russian-born novelist, biographer and children's author of Russian origin, born in St Petersburg. She settled in England in 1922, and became a British citizen.
Empress Alexandra, 1872-1918: A Study (1961); *Emperor Alexander II* (1962); *Catherine the Great: A Portrait* (1963); *An Unbroken Unity* (1964)

AMES, Winslow (1907-90), American art historian, was born in Chile and grew up on Staten Island. A graduate of Phillips Andover Academy and Columbia College, he was Director of the Lyman Allyn Museum in New London, Connecticut, the Springfield Art Museum in Springfield, Missouri, and the Gallery of Modern Art in New York City. He also taught Art History at several universities and wrote widely on the decorative arts and genealogy.
Prince Albert and Victorian Taste (1967)

ANDERSON, Christopher (1949-), American biographer, studied at University of California, Berkeley. He joined the staff of *Time* Magazine as contributing editor in 1969, and was senior editor of *Time Incorporated's People Magazine* from 1974 to 1989. He has also contributed to *The New York Daily News*, *Life*, and *Vanity Fair*. As an author he wrote initially on subjects including psychology and true crime, later turning to royal and celebrity biographies.
Diana's Boys: William and Harry and the Mother They Loved (2001); *After Diana: William, Harry, Charles, and the Royal House of Windsor* (2007); *William and Kate: A Royal Love Story* (2010)

ANDREWS, Allen (1913-?), British author, born at Greenwich, writer of several works of popular biography and history.

The Follies of King Edward VII (1975); *The King Who Lost America: George III and Independence* (1976)

ANOLIC, Tamar, American author, born at Rockaway, New York. She studied Law in New York, and then became an Attorney with US Customs and Border Protection at Washington, DC.
The Russian Riddle: Grand Duke Serge Alexandrovich of Russia, 1857-1905 (2013)

ARENGO-JONES, Peter.
Queen Victoria in Switzerland (1995)

ARKELL, R.L. (*née* Ruby Lillian Percival) (1908-83), British biographer, born in India. She was the wife of palaentologist William Joscelyn Arkell.
Caroline of Ansbach, George the Second's Queen (1939)

ARMITAGE-SMITH, Sir Sydney (1876-1932), British civil servant and historian, born in London. He read History at New College, Oxford, joined the Civil Service, worked in the Treasury, became Private Secretary to the Chancellor of the Exchequer, and was a treasury representative at the Paris Peace Conference. In addition to his acclaimed biography, he also edited two volumes of John of Gaunt's Register for the Royal Historical Society. On his death, a fellow historian called it a source of regret that the calls of public service prevented him from continuing his researches into medieval history. (*The Times*, 3.11.1932)
John of Gaunt (1904)

ARONSON, Theo (Theodore Ian Wilson) (1929–2003), South African-born British biographer, born in Kirkwood, South Africa, the son of a Latvian Jewish storekeeper. He studied Art at Cape Town University, where he acted with

Nigel Hawthorne, then worked as a commercial artist in Johannesburg. Moving to England, where he spent the rest of his life, he had been fascinated by royalty since seeing King George VI, Queen Elizabeth, and Princesses Elizabeth and Margaret at a siding near Kirkwood on their 1947 visit to South Africa, and was greatly impressed by the Queen's charm and skill with the crowds. He was further inspired to write royal biographies after visiting the mausoleum of Emperor Napoleon III at St Michael's Abbey, Farnborough. At first he specialised largely in 19th and early 20th century British and European royalty, but after a change of publisher, he 'was persuaded that dynastic studies were no longer required, so he began to write studies of the more recent history of the British royal family.' (*The Times*, 20.5.2003) In the introduction to his memoirs, which turned out to be his last book, he acknowledged that during his thirty-five year career as a writer, 'various Kings, and their families, have proved to be devilish good subjects for me', and that being 'something of an outsider, unrestricted by the British class system' (*Royal Subjects*, 2000, ix-x) had proved something of an advantage for him in that he was granted almost unprecedented access to royal circles.

The Golden Bees: The Story of the Bonapartes (1964); *Royal Vendetta: The Crown of Spain 1829-1965* (1966); *The Coburgs of Belgium* (1969); *The Fall of the Third Napoleon* (1970); *The Kaisers* (1971); *Queen Victoria and the Bonapartes* (1972); *Grandmama of Europe: The Crowned Descendants of Queen Victoria* (1974); *Royal Ambassadors: British Royalties in Southern Africa 1860-1947* (1975); *A Family of Kings: The Descendants of Christian IX of Denmark* (1976); *Victoria and Disraeli: The Making of a Romantic Partnership* (1978); *Kings Over the Water: Saga of the Stuart Pretenders* (1979); *Princess Alice, Countess of Athlone* (1981); *Royal Family: Years of Transition* (1983); *Crowns in Conflict: The Triumph of the Tragedy of European Monarchy 1910-1918* (1986); *The King in Love: Edward VII's Mistresses:*

Lillie Langtry, Daisy Warwick, Alice Keppel and Others (1988); *Napoleon and Josephine: A Love Story* (1990); *Heart of a Queen: Queen Victoria's Romantic Attachments* (1992); *The Royal Family at War* (1994); *Prince Eddy and the Homosexual Underworld* (1996); *Princess Margaret: A Biography* (1997); *Royal Subjects: A Biographer's Encounters* (2000)

ARTHUR, Sir George (Compton Archibald), MVO (1860-1946), biographer, succeeded his father as 3rd Baronet in 1878. Joining the army in 1880, he was gazetted Second Lieutenant in the Second Life Guards. He fought in the Egyptian campaign and was at the battle of Tel-el-Kebir in 1883, the Nile expedition of 1884-5, and saw action in the Second Boer War. He was appointed Private Secretary to Lord Kitchener during the First World War, and after the latter's death he was attached to General Headquarters in France from 1917 to 1918. He turned to writing, specialising in royal and military biographies, and a memoir, after the war.
Queen Alexandra (1934); *Queen Mary* (1935); *King George V* (1936); *Seven Heirs Apparent* (1937); *Concerning Queen Victoria and her Son* (1945)

ASHDOWN, Dulcie M. (1946-), British biographer.
Queen Victoria's Mother: Victoire, Duchess of Kent (1974); *Queen Victoria's Family* (1975); *Royal Children* (1979); *Princess of Wales* (1979); *Victoria and the Coburgs* (1981); *Royal Weddings* (1981); *Royal Paramours* (1987); *Royal Murders: Hatred, Revenge and the Seizing of Power* (1998); *Tudor Cousins: Rivals for the Throne* (2000)

ASHDOWN-HILL, (Louis) John (Frederick), FSA, BA, MA, PhD (1949-), read History and French at University of East Anglia, and Linguistics and Medieval History at University of Essex. An independent historian with particular interest in King Richard III and the house of

York, he taught languages including English, French, Spanish, Italian and modern Greek and also Classical Civilisation in Britain and overseas, before giving up teaching in favour of historical research. In 2003 colleagues in Belgium asked him to seek the mitochondrial MTA sequence shared by Richard III and his brothers and sisters, and he spent a year tracing the all-female line of descent from the King's eldest sister, Anne, to Joy Ibsen, a Canadian resident. Two years later he announced the discovery of the family's Mitochondrial DNA sequence, and in 2006 he gave a presentation on the subject of his DNA research to the Richard III Society in London. Three years later he was involved in the Looking for Richard Project, relating to the exhumation of Richard III's body, and in 2012 the search for the King's remains began with the excavation of the Social Services Department car park in Leicester. On the first day of the dig, bones found were subsequently proved by DNA research to be those of the King.

Richard III's Beloved Cousyn: John Howard and the House of York (2009); *Eleanor The Secret Queen: The Woman Who Put Richard III on the Throne* (2010); *The Last Days of Richard III and the Fate of His DNA* (2013); *Royal Marriage Secrets: Consorts and Concubines, Bigamists and Bastards* (2013); *The Third Plantagenet: George, Duke of Clarence, Richard III's Brother* (2014); *The Dublin King: The True Story of Lambert Simnel and the Princes in the Tower* (2015); *The Mythology of Richard III* (2015)

ASHLEY, Maurice (Percy), CBE, DLitt (1907–94), British historian, was educated at Oxford. In 1929 he was appointed literary assistant to Winston Churchill while the latter was writing a biography of the Duke of Marlborough. He joined the *Manchester Guardian* in 1933, then moved to *The Times* in 1937 as foreign sub-editor, and *Britain Today* as editor 1939-40. During the war he served with the Grenadier Guards, and then the Intelligence

Corps. After the war he joined *The Listener* as Deputy Editor, becoming Editor in 1958 until retiring in 1967 and then Research Fellow at Loughborough University until 1970. He wrote over thirty works of history and biography.

The Life and Times of William I (1973); *The Life and Times of King John* (1973); *Rupert of the Rhine* (1976); *The Battle of Naseby and the Fall of King Charles I* (1992)

ASPINALL, Arthur (1901-72), British historian, was born at Stainland, near Halifax. He studied History at the Victoria University of Manchester, becoming a Lecturer at the University of Rangoon from 1925 to 1931, and at the University of Reading from 1931 until his retirement in 1965. He devoted much of his working life to the editing and publication of documentary sources of the later Hanoverian period, particularly the letters of Kings George III and George IV. Once the work was completed he planned to re-edit the earlier correspondence of George III, but was prevented by failing eyesight. He also edited and published the correspondence of Princess Charlotte and of Mrs Jordan, mistress of the Duke of Clarence. His editing of the latter was criticized by her modern biographer, who claimed that he made some unacknowledged omissions, mistook some dates, and found her 'an unsympathetic character' (Tomalin, *Mrs Jordan's Profession*, 1994, xix–xx).

The Letters of King George IV, 1812–30, 3 vols (ed.) (1938); *Letters of the Princess Charlotte, 1811-1817* (ed.) (1949); *Mrs Jordan and her Family: Being the Unpublished Correspondence of Mrs Jordan and the Duke of Clarence, later William IV* (ed.) (1951); *The Later Correspondence of George III, 1783-1810,* 5 vols (ed) (1962-7); *The Correspondence of George, Prince of Wales, 1770-1812,* 8 vols (ed.) (1963-70)

ASQUITH, Annunziata (1948-), British biographer. A descendant of the Edwardian Prime Minister Herbert Henry Asquith, she was a former model for Burberry Group PLC, and partner of Patrick, 5th Earl of Lichfield.
Marie Antoinette (1974)

ASTON, Sir George (Grey), KCB (1861-1938), British officer and author, educated at Royal Naval College, Greenwich, and joined the Royal Marine Artillery in 1879. He served in the Sudan in 1884 and the second Boer War, and held several important posts, including that of aide-de-camp to King George V from 1911, rising to the rank of Major-General by the time he retired in 1917. He published several books on military history, military and naval biographies, and on fly fishing. His official biography of the Duke of Connaught, published while the Duke was still alive, was 'read and passed for publication' by his comptroller.
His Royal Highness the Duke of Connaught and Strathearn (1929)

AYLING, Stanley (Edward) (1909-98), biographer, born in Lambeth, London, was a historian and biographer specialising in 18th century England.
George the Third (1972)

B

BAGLEY, John J. (Joseph) (1908-89), historian and biographer, was a part-time tutor at the Extra-Mural Department of Liverpool University. During the Second World War he worked at RAF Cranwell, instructing signals officers in Mathematics, and leading Adult Education classes in Current Affairs organized by the Adult Education department, Nottingham University. He became Senior Lecturer in History at Liverpool University in 1960 and Reader in History in 1967 until his retirement eight years later. In addition to medieval studies he also wrote extensively on Lancashire local history.
Margaret of Anjou, Queen of England (1948); *Henry VIII* (1962)

BAKER-SMITH, Veronica P.A., British biographer, was born in Derbyshire, and read History at the University of Wales. She lived in the Netherlands for some time, where she undertook major research in private papers in the Koninklijk Huisarchief for her first book.
A Life of Anne of Hanover, Princess Royal (1995); *Royal Discord: The Family of George II* (2008)

BALDWIN, David, historian and biographer, Fellow of the Royal Historical Society, who formerly lectured at the Universities of Leicester and Nottingham, specialising in late medieval English history and biography. In 1986, a quarter of a century before King Richard III's body was discovered and excavated in Leicester, he forecast where the remains would be found.

Elizabeth Woodville (2004); *The Kingmaker's Sisters: Six Powerful Women in the Wars of the Roses* (2006); *The Lost Prince: The Survival of Richard of York* (2007); *Richard III* (2012); *Henry VIII's Last Love: The Extraordinary Life of Katherine Willoughby* (2015)

BALFOUR, Michael (Leonard Graham), CBE (1908-95), British historian and civil servant, born in Oxford, was Director of Public Relations and Information Services, Control Commission, in the British Zone of Allied-occupied Germany 1945-47, Chief Information Officer at the Board of Trade 1947-64, and Professor of European History at the University of East Anglia 1966-74. He was the author of several books on modern German and British history.

The Kaiser and his Times (1964)

BALFOUR, Neil (Roxburgh) (1944-), British merchant banker, financier, politician and author. He was called to the bar in 1968 but did not practise law, and instead joined Baring Bros & Co. He married Princess Elizabeth of Yugoslavia, daughter of Prince Paul, in 1969, but they were divorced in 1978. He was Conservative Member of the European Parliament for North Yorkshire from 1979 to 1984, and stood unsuccessfully four times for election to the House of Commons.

Paul of Yugoslavia: Britain's Maligned Friend [with Sally MacKay] (1980)

BARBER, Richard (William), FRSL, FSA (1941-), British historian specialising in medieval history and literature, particularly Arthurian legend. For some years he worked in publishing, initially at Macmillan and at George Bell &

Sons. In 1969 he helped to found The Boydell Press, and in 1972 D.S. Brewer, the two firms later merging as Boydell & Brewer, with him as group managing director until 2009. He was also Honorary Visiting Professor in History at the University of York.

Henry Plantagenet (1964); *Edward, Prince of Wales and Aquitaine: A Biography of the Black Prince* (1976); *The Life and Campaigns of the Black Prince: From Contemporary Letters, Diaries and Chronicles* (1997); *The Black Prince* (2003); *Edward III and the Triumph of England: The Battle of Crécy and the Company of the Garter* (2013); *Henry I: A Prince among Princes* (2015)

BARKELEY, Richard (real name Richard Baumgarten) (c.1900-61), was born in Austria of a Jewish family, lost several relatives in concentration camps during or after World War Two, and moved to England. He undertook regular lecture tours in Germany after the war as part of an extension programme of the Workers' Educational Association, as there was a demand for German speakers knowledgeable about British institutions. He published two biographies and left a sequel to the second, *Sarajevo and Madeira*, about the end of the Habsburg monarchy in Austria, unfinished at his death.

The Empress Frederick, Daughter of Queen Victoria (1956); *The Road to Mayerling: The Life and Death of Rudolph, Crown Prince of Austria* (1958)

BARLOW, Frank, CBE, FBA, FRSL (1911–2009), studied History at Oxford. He was Professor of History at the University of Exeter from 1953 until he retired in 1976 and became Emeritus Professor.

William I and the Norman Conquest (1965); *Edward the Confessor* (1970); *William Rufus* (1983)

BARRY, Stephen P. (1949-86), British biographer, and former valet to Charles, Prince of Wales for twelve years until his retirement in 1981, shortly after the Prince's wedding. His two volumes of memoirs appeared in America, where they allegedly made him about $1,000,000, but not in Britain as publishers decided not to handle them out of deference to the palace. He died of AIDS.

Royal Service: My Twelve Years as Valet to Prince Charles (1983); *Royal Secrets: The View From Downstairs* (1986)

BATTISCOMBE, Georgina (*née* Esther Georgina Harwood), FRSL (1905-2006), British biographer, was born in London. Her father was George Harwood, Liberal MP for Bolton, and she once considered pursuing a political career herself. Her husband Christopher was Secretary to the Sultan of Zanzibar, where they lived for several years. From 1943 onwards she wrote and published biographies of Charlotte Mary Yonge, Gladstone, Elizabeth Wordsworth, and the Spencer family at Althorp, as well as a book of verse. She was inspired to write her best-known title, on Queen Alexandra, as she had also suffered from otosclerosis from an early age. As a royal biographer she was appalled by the way in which members of the Royal Family were frequently treated, decrying the sensational and the scandalous, considering many royal biographies ill-informed, and noting that 'so often the unfortunate royalties do not even receive common politeness from those who write about them' (*Daily Telegraph*, 2.3.2006). Keenly interested in the conservation of ecclesiastical buildings, from 1958 to 1981 she was a member of the Oxford diocesan advisory committee for the care of churches.

Queen Alexandra (1969)

BAUER, Ludwig (1878-?), Austro-Swiss journalist and writer, worked as a journalist in Vienna, writing particularly on travel and theatre. A pacifist by nature, because of his opposition to the First World War he moved to Switzerland. His best-known book, translated into English as *War Again Tomorrow* (1932), warned of the dangers of another world war.

Leopold the Unloved, King of the Belgians and Money (1934)

BAXTER, Stephen B. (1929-), American historian and biographer, specialising in 17th and 18th century history. He studied History at Harvard University and Trinity College, Cambridge, then worked at Dartmouth College and University of Missouri.

William III (1966) UK/*William III and the Defense of European Liberty, 1650-1702* (1966) US

BEECHE, Arturo, Costa Rican author based in the San Francisco Bay area, California, founder and editor of *European Royal History Journal*, founded in 1997, and publisher of Kensington House Books.

King Michael I of Romania – A Tribute (2001); *A Poet Among the Romanovs – Prince Vladimir Paley* (ed.) (2004); *The Grand Duchesses: Daughters and Granddaughters of Russia's Tsars,* (ed.) (2004); *Ella: Grand Duchess Elisabeth Feodorovna of Russia* (ed.) (2005); *My Fifty Years: The Memoirs of Prince Nicholas of Greece* (ed.) (2006); *Gilded Prism: The Konstantinovichi Grand Dukes & the Last years of the Romanov Dynasty* (ed.) (2006); *The Royal Hellenic Dynasty* [with HRH Prince Michael of Greece] (2007); *The Gotha: Still a Continental Royal Family,* Vol 1 (2009); *Royal Gatherings, Vol. 1: 1914-1939* [with Ilana Miller] (2012); *Dear Ellen: Royal Europe Through the Photo Albums of Grand Duchess Helen Vladimirovna of Russia* [with HRH Princess Elizabeth of Yugoslavia] (2012); *The Grand Dukes: Sons and Granddaughters of Russia's Grand Dukes* (ed.) (2013); *The Other Grand Dukes: Sons and Grandsons of Russia's Grand Dukes* (ed.) (2013); *The Coburgs of Europe* (2013); *Russia and Europe – Dynastic Ties* [with Galina Korneva & Tatiana Cheboksarova] (2013); *Apapa: King Christian IX and his*

Descendants [with Coryne Hall] (2014); *Grand Duchess Marie Pavlovna* (ed.) (2014); *The Nassaus of Luxembourg* [with Kassandra and Sabrina Pollock] (2014); *Maria Pia - Queen of Portugal* (ed.) (2015); *Royal Exiles in Cannes - The Bourbons of the Two Sicilies of the Villa Marie-Thérèse* [with David McIntosh] (2015); *I did it my way ... The Memoirs of HH Prince Andreas of Saxe-Coburg and Gotha* [with HH Prince Andreas of Saxe-Coburg and Gotha] (2015); *The Royal House of Savoy* (ed.) (2015); *The Royal House of Bavaria* [with Coryne Hall] (2015); *The Grand Ducal House of Hesse and by Rhine* [with Ilana Miller] (2015); *Royal Gatherings, Vol. 2: 1914-1939* [with Ilana Miller] (2015)

BEER, Peter J., British biographer.
The Playboy Princes: The Apprentice Years of Edward VII and Edward VIII (2014)

BEIK, Paul (Harold), Ph.D. (1915-2002), American historian and biographer, specialist in 18th and 19th century French history, born in Olivet, Michigan, read History at Columbia University and became a Professor at Swarthmore, Pennsylvania, retiring in 1980.
Louis Philippe and the July Monarchy (1965)

BELLER, Steven (1958-), British historian and authority on modern Austrian and Jewish history and anti-Semitism, born in London, visiting scholar at Washington University and Research Fellow at Peterhouse College, Cambridge.
Francis Joseph (1996)

BELLOC, Hilaire (Joseph Hilaire Pierre René) (1870-1953), was born in La Celle-Saint-Cloud to a French father and English mother, but was moved to England at the age of two after his father died. Although he became a naturalised British subject in 1902, he retained French citizenship. One of the most prolific authors of his time, his works included history, biography, fiction and poetry. Once when asked why he wrote so much, he replied, 'Because my children are howling for pearls and caviar.' He was Liberal MP for Salford from 1906 to 1910.

James the Second (1928); *Charles I, King of England* (1933); *William the Conqueror* (1933); *Monarchy: A Study of Louis XIV* (1938); *The Last Rally: A Study of Charles II* (1939)

BENGTSSON, Frans Gunnar (1894-1954), Swedish writer, born in Tossjö, Skåne. He began his writing career as a poet and then essayist. His biography of Charles XII was published in Sweden in 1932 but not in English translation for another twenty-eight years.

The Life of Charles XII [of Sweden] (1960)

BENNETT, Daphne (*née* Daphne Meyler) (1912-96), British biographer, was inspired to write biography relatively late in life by the widely contradictory assessments by others of the Empress Frederick's personality, resulting in her first book. When unacknowledged extracts from her first book appeared in Princess Michael of Kent's (q.v.) *Crowned in a Far Country*, angered by the latter's statement in a radio interview, 'what does it matter', she sued for plagiarism in 1986, resulting in an out-of-court settlement of £8,000. After two subsequent royal biographies she also wrote lives of Margot Asquith and Emily Davies. Her husband was the military historian Ralph Bennett.

Vicky, Princess Royal of England and German Empress (1971); *King Without a Crown* (1977); *Queen Victoria's Children* (1980)

BENSON, E.F. (Edward Frederic) (1867-1940), was one of the most prolific writers of his time with over a hundred volumes, including novels, short stories, works of non-fiction and plays to his credit. His father, Edward White

Benson, was headmaster of Wellington College and Chancellor of Lincoln Cathedral.

King Edward VII (1933); *Queen Victoria* (1935); *The Kaiser and English Relations* (1936); *Queen Victoria's Daughters* (1938) US/ *The Daughters of Queen Victoria* (1939) UK

BENSON, Ross (1948-2005), British journalist and biographer, born in Scotland, educated in Africa, Australia and Holland and at Gordonstoun, where he was in the same class as Prince Charles. After leaving school, he worked for *London Life* magazine. He first joined the *Daily Mail* as a reporter in 1967. In 1971 he moved to the *Sunday Express* and then the *Daily Express*, as foreign editor, US correspondent, chief foreign correspondent, special feature writer and from 1987 editor of a gossip column. As an old classmate of the Prince of Wales, he claimed to have more information than most during the speculation about the Waleses' marriage. In 1993, after the publication of Andrew Morton's (q.v.) *Diana: Her True Story*, he attempted to redress the balance in *Charles: The Untold Story*, which one reviewer called an 'impertinent project...but not impertinent enough to do any good'. Some doubted whether he was as close to royal sources as he claimed. His wife Ingrid (Seward, q.v.) said he had been previously 'frozen out of royal circles' after writing a piece for *Woman's Own* about the Prince's days at Gordonstoun. On the day he left the *Daily Express*, 31 August 1997, Diana, Princess of Wales was killed, and the paper asked him to return for a week to cover the aftermath of her death and funeral, to which he agreed, prior to rejoining the *Daily Mail*. He also wrote biographies of George Best and Paul McCartney. He died suddenly after watching Chelsea FC's Champions League victory over Barcelona at Stamford Bridge.

Charles: The Untold Story (1993)

BERNARD, George, *see* LOACH, Jennifer

BERNIER, Olivier, Franco-American biographer and historian, born in the United States of French parents and educated in Paris, at Harvard, and the Institute of Fine Arts, New York University. After being director of exhibitions at the Martha Jackson Gallery, New York, he became a private art dealer in 1968. In 1977, he began writing French history and biography. He also contributed regularly to the *New York Times* and various arts and history magazines.

Louis the Beloved: The Life of Louis XV (1984); *Secrets of Marie Antoinette* (1985); *Words of Fire, Deeds of Blood: The Mob, the Monarchy, and the French Revolution* (1989)

BERRY, Wendy (1932-), British biographer and former royal housekeeper to Charles and Diana, the Prince and Princess of Wales, from 1985 to 1993. She allegedly breached a High Court injunction by publishing a book in America purporting to quote verbatim arguments between her former employers, and which earned her about £200,000. The Prince described her actions as 'morally and legally indefensible', but it was later confirmed that he had instructed his lawyers not to take legal action to have her jailed for contempt of court, and that she 'was told she would face no further action provided she makes no new attempt to betray his trust' (*Daily Telegraph*, 8.10.2000).

The Housekeeper's Diary: Charles and Diana Before the Break-Up (1995)

BERTRAM, Werner.
A Royal Recluse: Memories of Ludwig II of Bavaria (1936)

BINGHAM, Caroline (*née* Caroline Margery Conyers Worsdell) (1938-98), British biographer and historian, was born at York, read History at Bristol University, and was a Research Fellow of Royal Holloway and Bedford New

College from 1985 to 1987. Her books reflected a lifelong interest in medieval and Scottish history.

The Making of a King: The Early Years of James VI and I (1968); *The Life and Times of Edward II* (1973); *The Crowned Lions* (1978); *James VI of Scotland* (1979); *James I of England* (1981); *Darnley* (1995)

BIRD, Anthony, British author of biographies and books on motoring.

The Damnable Duke of Cumberland: A Character Study and Vindication of Ernest Augustus, Duke of Cumberland and King of Hanover (1966)

BLACK, Jeremy, MBE (1955-), British historian, graduated from Queens' College, Cambridge, taught at Durham from 1980 as Lecturer and then Professor, and was appointed Professor of History at University of Exeter in 1996. He published over 90 books, mostly on 18th century British politics and international relations. A senior fellow at the Center for the Study of America and the West at the Foreign Policy Research Institute, he lectured extensively in Australia, Canada, Denmark, France, Germany, Italy, New Zealand, and the USA, where he held visiting chairs at West Point, Texas Christian University, and Stillman College. A past Council member of the Royal Historical Society, he was on several editorial boards including the *Journal of Military History*, the *International History Review*, and *History Today*, and was editor of Archives. He was awarded an MBE in 2000 for advisory work on stamps to the Royal Mail, which involved selecting topics covering British history, writing briefings for the stamp designers, and writing text for the presentation packs.

George III: America's Last King (2006)

BLED, Jean-Paul (1942-), French biographer and historian, studied History and Politics at Nantes and Strasbourg, and was Professor at the Sorbonne.
Franz Joseph (1992)

BLOCH, Michael (1953-), British biographer, was trained for the law. From 1979 he assisted Maître Suzanne Blum, the Parisian lawyer of the Duke and Duchess of Windsor. He is the author of several books on the Windsors as well as other works of non-fiction.
Wallis and Edward: Letters 1931-37 (ed.) (1986); *Operation Willi: The Plot to Capture the Duke of Windsor, July 1940* (1986); *Duke of Windsor's War* (1986); *The Secret File of the Duke of Windsor* (1988); *The Reign and Abdication of Edward VIII* (1990); *The Duchess of Windsor* (1996)

BLOOM, Ursula (1892-1984), British novelist and biographer, born in Springfield, Chelmsford. She wrote over 500 books, mostly historical and romantic novels written under pseudonyms, including Sheila Burns, Mary Essex, Rachel Harvey, Deborah Mann, Lozania Prole and Sara Sloane, as well as her own name.
The House of Kent (1969); *The Duke of Windsor* (1972); *The Great Queen Consort* [Mary, Queen of George V] (1976)

BLUCHE, François (1925-), French historian and biographer, born in Ganges, was Professor of Modern History at University of Besançon, then at the University of Paris-Nanterre. In addition to his own French historical studies, in 1998 he produced a volume, *Le Journal secret de Louis XIV*, 'reconstructed from historical sources' to read as if they were the King's diaries. They were erroneously used by biographer Veronica Buckley (q.v.) as a primary source for one of her own works, which had to be recalled from publication and corrected.
Louis XIV (1991)

BLUNT, Wilfrid (Jasper Walter) (1901-87), British biographer, born in Ham, Surrey, and studied at Worcester College, Oxford. After a year he went to l'Atelier Moderne, Paris, intending to become an artist. Following a period as an engraving student at the Royal College of Art, London, he taught art and drawing at Haileybury College, Hertfordshire, and at Eton College. Retiring from the latter in 1959 he became curator of the Watts Gallery in Compton, near Guildford, Surrey, retiring in 1983, and also took up writing, largely biographies, as a past time. His younger brother was the noted art historian and spy Anthony Blunt.
The Dream King: Ludwig II of Bavaria (1970)

BOCCA, Geoffrey (1924-83), British biographer and novelist, who spent most of his working life in the United States.
Elizabeth and Philip (1953); *The Woman Who Would be Queen: A Biography of the Duchess of Windsor* (1954) US/*She Might Have Been Queen: A Biography of the Duchess of Windsor* (1955) UK; *The Uneasy Heads: A Report on European Monarchy* (1959) UK/*Kings Without Thrones: European Monarchy in the Twentieth Century* (1959) US

BOLITHO, Hector (Henry) (1897–1974), British author, was born in Auckland, New Zealand, where he accompanied Edward, Prince of Wales on his empire tour in 1920. Moving to Sydney, he became editor of the *Shakespearean Quarterly* and literary editor and drama critic of the *Evening News*. After travelling for several years throughout Africa, Canada, America and Germany, he settled in Britain in 1924, working as a freelance journalist. In World War Two he joined the Royal Air Force Volunteer Reserve as an intelligence officer and edited the *Royal Air Force Weekly Bulletin*, later the *Royal Air Force Journal*, and the *Coastal Command Intelligence Review*. He made several lecture tours of America between 1938 and 1949. He wrote about sixty books, including biographies, novels, plays and memoirs, as well as editing several volumes of royal and court letters.

With the Prince in New Zealand (1920); *The Letters of Lady Augusta Stanley* (ed.) (1927); *The Later Letters of Lady Augusta Stanley* (ed.) (1929); *Albert the Good, A Life of the Prince Consort* (1932); *The Prince Consort and his Brother* (1934); *Victoria, the Widow and her Son* (1934); *King Edward VIII: His Life and Reign* (1937); *Royal Progress* (1937); *George VI* (1937); *Victoria and Albert* (1938); *Further Letters of Queen Victoria* (ed.) (1938); *Roumania under King Carol* (1939); *The Reign of Queen Victoria* (1948); *A Century of British Monarchy* (1951); *Their Majesties* (1951); *Albert, Prince Consort* (1964)

BORMAN, Tracy, British biographer and historian, born at Scothern, Lincoln and taught history at Hull University. She had a successful career in heritage and worked for a range of historic properties and national heritage organisations, including the Heritage Lottery Fund, The National Archives and English Heritage. In 2013 she was appointed Joint Chief Curator of Historic Royal Palaces. As a writer she appeared on TV and radio, and was a regular contributor to BBC History and other history magazines.

Henrietta Howard: King's Mistress, Queen's Servant (2008); *Elizabeth's Women: The Hidden Story of the Virgin Queen* (2009); *Matilda: Queen of the Conqueror* (2011)

BOTHAM, Noel (1940-2012), British journalist and author, born in York, served an apprenticeship with the Croydon Advertiser, and was thereafter on the staff of the *Daily Sketch* and *News of the World*. He also ran one the French House, a pub in Soho. His two royal biographies are regarded as somewhat sensationalized; in one obituary

he was described as 'the epitome of a Fleet Street scandalmonger and happy to be regarded as such' (*Guardian*, 23.11.2012).
Margaret: The Last Royal Princess (2002); *The Murder of Princess Diana* (2008)

BOWEN, Marjorie (*née* Campbell, Mrs Gabrielle Margaret Vere Constanza by first marriage, surname Long by second) (1885-1952), British author of fiction, including historical fiction, romance, mystery and horror, biography and history, born on Hayling Island, studied at the Slade School of Fine Art and later in Paris. A prolific writer, her lifetime output extended to about 150 titles, mostly under the pseudonym of Marjorie Bowen, with a few published as Joseph Shearing, George R. Preedy, John Winch, Robert Paye and Margaret Campbell.
William III and the Revolution of 1688 (1934); *Mary Queen of Scots: Daughter of Debate* (1936); *Crowns and Sceptres: The Romance and Pageantry of Coronations* (1937); *In the Steps of Mary Queen of Scots* (1952); *William III and the Revolution of 1688 and Gustavus Adolphus II (1594–1632): elected King of Sweden, of the Goths and Vandals* (1988)

BOWER, Leonard and BOLITHO, Gordon.
Otho I, King of Greece (1939)

BOWLE, John (Edward) (1905-88), British historian, read History at Balliol College, Oxford, then taught at Westminster School and Eton College. During the Second World War he worked for the Air Ministry and the Foreign Office, then lectured at Wadham College, Oxford, from 1947 to 1949. He was Professor of Political Theory at the College of Europe, Bruges, from 1950 to 1967, then a visiting lecturer at Columbia and Indiana Universities, and colleges at Los Angeles and Massachusetts.
Henry VIII (1964); *Charles I* (1975)

BOWMAN, William Dodgson (1865-1951), British author, born at Whitehaven.
The Divorce Case of Queen Caroline (1930)

BRADBURY, Jim (1937-), British historian and biographer specialising in the medieval period, formerly lectured in History at Brunel University.
Philip Augustus, King of France 1180-1223 (1997); *Stephen and Matilda: The Civil War of 1139-53* (2005); *The Capetians: Kings of France 987-1328* (2007)

BRADFORD, Sarah (*née* Sarah Hayes, Sarah Bradford by first marriage, Sarah Ward, later Viscountess Bangor by second) (1938-), British author, born in Bournemouth, and studied at Oxford. She worked at Christie's Auctioneers in the manuscript department, and then became a writer, mostly of biographies, her non-royal subjects including Benjamin Disraeli and Sacheverell Sitwell. She was an assistant screenwriter on *The Borgias* TV series in 2011.
Princess Grace (1984); *George VI* (1989) UK/ *The Reluctant King* (1989) US; *Elizabeth: A Biography of Her Majesty the Queen* (1996); *Diana* [Princess of Wales] (2006); *Queen Elizabeth II: Her Life in Our Times* (2011)

BRANDI, Karl (Maria Prosper Laurenz) (1868-1946), German historian, born in Meppen, Lower Saxony. He became Professor of Medieval and Modern History at the University of Göttingen in 1902, and later Rector, retiring in 1945.
The Emperor Charles V: The Growth and Destiny of a Man and of a World-Empire (1949)

BRANDRETH, Gyles (Daubeney) (1948-), British writer, broadcaster and actor, born in Wuppertal, Germany. He moved to England with his parents at the age of three. He

studied at New College, Oxford, and has appeared on various light entertainment and panel radio and TV shows, including *Countdown*, *Have I Got News For You*, and *Wordaholics*. He was Conservative MP for the City of Chester from 1992 to 1997. In addition to royal biographies he has also written a life of Sir John Gielgud, several books of word games, and fiction.
Philip and Elizabeth: Portrait of a Marriage (2004); *Charles and Camilla* (2006)

BRIFFAULT, Frederic T.
The Prisoner of Ham: Authentic Details of the Captivity and Escape of Prince Napoleon Louis (1846); *Prince Louis Napoleon Bonaparte* (1852)

BROOKE, John (1920-) British historian, specialising in royal and political 18th century history. He studied history at Manchester University, and later became Senior Editor of the Royal Commission on Historical Manuscripts. His biography of King George III included a Foreword by Charles, Prince of Wales.
King George III (1972)

BROOK-SHEPHERD, (Frederick) Gordon, CBE (1918-2004), British biographer and historian, read History at Cambridge, and served on various campaigns during World War Two, becoming an Intelligence officer in the War Office, specialising in resistance movements in Europe, and ending up as Lieutenant-Colonel on the staff of the British High Commissioner in Austria. In 1948 he was appointed the *Daily Telegraph* correspondent in Vienna, writing under the name Gordon Shepherd. On the launch of the *Sunday Telegraph* in 1961 he was appointed Diplomatic Correspondent and then Deputy Editor. He wrote several books on 20th century Austrian affairs, including a number of biographical studies of the last of the

Habsburgs, his last title being one of Archduke Otto, MEP for Bavaria and a close friend.

The last Habsburg [Charles of Austria-Hungary] (1968); *Uncle of Europe: The Social and Diplomatic Life of Edward VII* (1975); *Victims at Sarajevo: The Romance and Tragedy of Franz Ferdinand and Sophie* (1984); *Royal Sunset: The Dynasties of Europe and the Great War* (1987); *The last Empress: The Life and Times of Zita of Austria-Hungary* (1991); *Uncrowned Emperor: The Life and Times of Otto of Austria-Hungary* (2003)

BROUGH, James (1918-2001), British biographer, born in London. After leaving school he went to work as a Fleet Street reporter and became the *Daily Mail* foreign correspondent. His first major assignment was covering the death of Franklin D. Roosevelt. He stayed in the United States, and worked as an editor and freelance contributor in New York, contributing to *Ladies' Home Journal*, *McCalls'* and *Cosmopolitan* among others.

The Prince and the Lily: The Story of Edward VII and Lily Langtry (1975); *Margaret, The Tragic Princess* (1978)

BRYAN, J. (Joseph) III, *see* MURPHY, Charles J.V.

BRYANT, Sir Arthur (Wynne Morgan), CH, CBE (1899-1985), British historian and journalist. His university studies were interrupted by service in World War One. In 1917 he joined the Royal Flying Corps as a pilot officer, returning to Oxford in 1919 to study Modern History and later Law. In 1923 he became headmaster of the Cambridge School of Arts, Crafts, and Technology. From 1927 to 1936 he lectured in history at Oxford. In 1936, he took over G.K. Chesterton's 'Our Note Book' column for the *Illustrated London News*, which he wrote until his death almost half a century later. He contributed regularly to London papers and magazines, and wrote scripts for historical radio broadcasts and radio plays for the BBC. He

wrote over forty books, and lectured throughout Great Britain, America and Europe.
King Charles the Second (1931); *George V* (1936)

BUCHWALDT, Randi, *see* **ROSVALL, Ted**

BUCKLEY, Veronica (1956-), British biographer, born in Christchurch, New Zealand, read French and Philosophy at Canterbury University, and Cultural and Social History at University of London. She worked firstly as a musician, and as a technical writer and information management specialist in information technology, then undertook doctoral research in Modern History at Oxford University before becoming a writer. The first edition of her second title about Françoise d'Aubigné, Marquise de Maintenon, had to be recalled and reprinted because one of her prime sources consisted of quotes from journals said to be of Louis XIV himself, but were only found in 1997, nearly three hundred years after they were supposedly written, and were apparently the work of French historian François Bluche (q.v.), dating from the mid-1990s.
Christina, Queen of Sweden: The Restless Life of a European Eccentric (2004); *Madame de Maintenon: The Secret Wife of Louis XIV* (2008)

BUISSERET, David (1934-), British historian, born at Totland Bay, Isle of Wight, read History at Corpus Christi College, Cambridge. During national service he served with the army in Egypt, and then as a pilot with the RAFVR. He has contributed to *American Historical Review*, *English Historical Review*, and *Journal of Modern History*. He taught at the University of the West Indies from 1964 to 1980, was Director of the Hermon Smith Dunlap Smith Center for the History of Cartography at the Newberry Library, Chicago, from 1980 to 1995, then held a professorship in South-Western Studies and the History of Cartography, University of Texas, until retirement in 2006. *Henry IV* (1984)

BURG, Katerina von (1932-98), British biographer.
Ludwig II of Bavaria: The Man and the Mystery (1989); *Elizabeth of Austria: A Life Misunderstood* (1995)

BURNE, A.H. (Alfred Higgins), DSO (1886–1959), British military historian, was educated at the Royal Military Academy, Woolwich, and was commissioned into the Royal Artillery in 1906. During the First World War he was awarded the DSO, and during the Second, he was Commandant of the 121st Officer Cadet Training Unit, reaching the rank of Lieutenant-Colonel. An authority on the history of land warfare, he was Military Editor Chambers Encyclopedia from 1938 to 1957, and a contributor to the *Oxford Dictionary of National Biography*.
The Noble Duke of York: The Military Life of Frederick, Duke of York and Albany (1949)

BUXHOEVEDEN, Sophie (1883-1956), Danish by birth, was chosen by Empress Alexandra as an honorary lady in waiting in 1904, and she became an official lady in waiting in 1913. Her father Carlos Buxhoeveden was the Russian minster in Copenhagen during the First World War. She followed the imperial family to Siberia after the Tsar's abdication and the revolution in 1917, and was released by the Bolsheviks, probably because they believed she was Swedish and they did not imprison foreign nationals for fear of reprisals from neutral nations. She escaped from Russia and spent the rest of her life in exile successively in Copenhagen, Germany and London, where she became a lady-in-waiting for the Tsarina's eldest sister Victoria, Marchioness of Milford Haven, and where she died. She wrote and published three books, one a biography of the

Empress and two memoirs about her life in Russia. Between them they are generally regarded as giving as good a picture as any others of the final days of the Romanovs, their family life and imperial Russia.

The Life and Tragedy of Alexandra Feodorovna (1928); *Left Behind: Fourteen Months in Siberia During the Revolution* (1929); *Before the Storm* (1938)

BYRNE, Conor, British biographer, read History at the University of Exeter.

Katherine Howard: A New History (2014)

C

CADBURY, Deborah, British author and TV producer, read Psychology at Sussex University and Linacre College, Oxford, then joined the BBC as a documentary maker and producer.

The Lost King of France: Revolution, Revenge and the Search for Louis XVII (2003); *Princes at War: The British Royal Family's Private Battle in the Second World War* (2015)

CALLOW, John, BA, MA, British author, screenwriter and historian, specialising in 17th century history and politics, witchcraft, and popular culture. He studied at Lancaster University and has lectured there, at Goldsmiths College, at the Peace Institute, Ljubljana, and the Ho Chi Minh Political Academy in Vietnam. He has appeared on television programmes and radio shows for RTE, BBC, ITV, the Canadian Broadcasting Corporation, BBC Radio 3, Radio 4, Radio Ulster, Sky, Sky Living, Russia Today, Yesterday and the BBC World Service. He was formerly Director of Archives at the Marx Memorial Library, London, and has been a National Officer for the GMB Union and a visiting tutor at the University of Suffolk.

The Making of King James II: The Formative Years of a Fallen Saint (2000); *King in Exile: James II, Warrior, King and Saint* (2004); *James II: The Triumph and the Tragedy* (2005)

CAMMAERTS, Emile, CBE (1878-1953), Belgian biographer, historian, writer on art and literature, poet and translator, was born in Brussels. He settled in England in

1908, but remained a Belgian citizen throughout his life. His account of Leopold II, published during the Second World War, was described in his obituary as 'a sober and persuasive vindication' (*The Times*, 3.11.1953).

Albert of Belgium: Defender of Right (1935); *The Keystone of Europe: History of the Belgian Dynasty, 1830-1939* (1939); *The Prisoner at Laeken: King Leopold: Legend and Fact* (1941)

CAMPBELL, Lady Colin (*née* George William Ziadie) (1949-), was born in Jamaica, with a genital defect which led to her being initially registered at birth as a boy. She had corrective surgery at 21, legally changed her name to Georgia, and was issued with a new birth certificate. She married Lord Colin Campbell, son of the 11th Duke of Argyll, in 1974, left him after nine months and divorced him after fourteen. Her biographies have been criticised for startling and sometimes unverified claims about some of their subjects.

Diana in Private: The Princess Nobody Knows (1992); *The Royal Marriages: What Really Goes On in the Private World of the Queen and her Family* (1993); *The Untold Life of Queen Elizabeth the Queen Mother* (2012); *The Real Diana* (2013)

CANNADINE, Sir David (Nicholas), British historian (1950-), British historian, born in Birmingham, worked at the Institute of Historical Research, University of London, from 1998 to 2003, and then as Professor at Princeton University. He has also been general editor of the Penguin History of Europe series, and from 2014 Editor of the *Oxford Dictionary of National Biography*.
George V: The Unexpected King (2015)

CAREY, Agnes, British biographer, whose book was based on the ten months she spent in 1886 at Farnborough in the household of the widowed ex-Empress.
The Empress Eugenie in Exile (1922)

CARLTON, Charles, British historian. Born in England, he read History at Cardiff University and the University of California, Los Angeles, then became a part time soldier in the Territorial Army, serving as an officer in the Welsh Regiment, the Special Air Service Regiment and the Intelligence Corps. He later became Professor Emeritus of History at North Carolina State University.
Charles I: The Personal Monarch (1995)

CARSON, Annette, British historian, studied at the Royal College of Music, worked as a Programme Manager for Thames TV, and in public relations and advertising as a copywriter. She then turned to writing books and articles on flying, rock music and history, and has contributed to *Encyclopædia Britannica*. As a 15th century specialist she was invited by Philippa Langley to become a historical consultant on the 'Looking For Richard' project, a team of historians and researchers who conceived and organised the search for Richard III's lost grave, which resulted in finding the King's remains at Leicester on 25 August 2012.
Richard III: The Maligned King (2008); *Finding Richard III: The Official Account* (2014); *Richard of Gloucester: Protector and Constable* (2015)

CARTER, Miranda (1965-), British historian and writer, read History at Exeter College, Oxford. She has also published fiction and a biography of Anthony Blunt, and is married to the novelist John Lanchester.
The Three Emperors: Three Cousins, Three Empires and the Road to World War One (2009)

CARTLAND, Dame Barbara, DBE, CstJ (*née* Mary Barbara Hamilton) (1901–2000), British novelist and biographer, born at Edgbaston, Birmingham, began her writing career as a society reporter and writer of romantic fiction. A prolific author, in 1983 alone she wrote 23 novels, and holds the Guinness World Record for the most novels written in a single year. Towards the end of her life, her publishers estimated that since her writing career began in 1923, she had produced 723 titles altogether, including five royal biographies. She was a friend of Earl Mountbatten of Burma, and through her daughter Raine McCorquodale, the step-grandmother of Diana, Princess of Wales, although it was reported that they did not get on particularly well. Cartland was alleged to have said that 'The only books Diana ever read were mine, and they weren't awfully good for her' (*Daily Mail*, 15.8.2013).

The Outrageous Queen [Christina of Sweden] (1956); *The Scandalous Life of King Carol* [Carol II of Roumania] (1957); *The Private Life of Charles II* (1958); *The Private Life of Elizabeth, Empress of Austria* (1959); *Josephine, Empress of France* (1961)

CASSELS, Lavender Mary Jean (1916-96), British biographer, noted for her studies of the last years of the Habsburgs in Austria.

Clash of Generations: A Habsburg Family Drama in the Nineteenth Century (1973); *The Archduke and the Assassin: Sarajevo, June 28th, 1914* (1984)

CATHCART, Helen, *see* ALBERT, Harold A.

CECIL, Algernon (1879-1953), British author of royal and political biographies. Grandson of the second Marquess of Salisbury, father of the late 19th century Prime Minister, he read Modern History at New College, Oxford. He was a contributor to *The Times* and the *Dictionary of National Biography*.

Five Stuart Princesses: Margaret of Scotland, Elizabeth of Bohemia, Mary of Orange, Henrietta of Orleans, Sophia of Hanover (1908); *Queen Victoria and her Prime Ministers* (1952)

CECIL, Lamar (real name William R. Kenan, Jr), was Emeritus Professor of History at Washington and Lee University, and author of biographies and histories on imperial Germany themes.
Wilhelm II, Vol 1: Prince and Emperor, 1859-1900 (1989); *Wilhelm II, Vol 2: Emperor and Exile, 1900-1941* (1996)

CHAMBERLIN, Frederick, FR. HistS, FSA (1870-1943), American historian, born in North Allington, Massachusetts. He studied at Harvard University and the University of Paris, then became Paris correspondent of *Boston Herald*, and *New Orleans Picayune*, and special correspondent of the *Boston Globe, New York Sun* and *Harper's Weekly*, writing mainly about art, the stage and music. He returned to America in 1895, graduated in Law and practiced in corporation and investment cases until 1912, when he settled in London, where he spent the rest of his life apart from a short time in Palma, Majorca.
The Private Character of Queen Elizabeth (1921); *The Sayings of Queen Elizabeth* (1923); *The Private Character of Henry VIII* (1932); *Elizabeth and Leicester* (1939)

CHAMBERS, James, British biographer and historian, born in Northern Ireland, and educated at Harrow and Christ Church, Oxford. After reading for the Bar he researched and wrote documentary film scripts and worked in film production, as well as writing books. He was the husband of Josephine Ross (q.v.).
The Norman Kings (1981); *Charlotte and Leopold: The True Story of the Original People's Princess* (2007)

CHAMIER, (Jacques) Daniel (Barbara Chamier) (1885-?), British biographer and historian, born in India, the daughter of a general. She had already published books in India on political law and procedure when, it is thought, she was approached by monarchist circles in Germany to

write a life of the former German Emperor, it was translated into German by the daughter of a former Prussian minister and the niece of a Prussian general, then sent to ex-Emperor William and corrected by him before publication. (Röhl, *Wilhelm II: Into the Abyss of War and Exile, 1900-1941*, 1218-9)
Fabulous Monster [Emperor William II] (1934)

CHANCELLOR, Frank (Francis Beresford) (1897-1972), British biographer, born in London.
The Prince Consort (1931)

CHANCELLOR, John (1927-2014), British biographer and publisher, was born in London. After working briefly in insurance he found his vocation in publishing, working with Purnell's where he helped to establish the successful partwork series, *Knowledge, New Knowledge*, and *Discovering Art*. He then worked for Sidgwick & Jackson, then set up his own business, Kew Books, thus named as he lived in Kew Green at the time, and for a while dealt in antiquarian books. His younger brother Alexander was successively editor of the *Spectator* and *The Oldie*.
The Life and Times of Edward I (1981)

CHANDLER, David (Geoffrey) (1934-2004), British historian and expert on Napoleon and his era, served in the army, reaching the rank of captain. He later taught at the Royal Military Academy, Sandhurst. In addition to biographies of the Emperor and military histories of the age, he also wrote extensively about the Second World War.
Napoleon (1973)

CHAPMAN, Hester W. (Wolferstan) (1899-1976), British biographer and novelist, born in Dorset, had no formal academic education, but wrote several highly-regarded and very successful books on Tudor and Stuart royalty as well as historical fiction. During the Second World War she sometimes worked on the telephone switchboard at the offices of her publisher, Jonathan Cape. Her biography of Edward VI was awarded the W.H. Heinemann Foundation Prize in 1958.

Mary II, Queen of England (1953); *The Last Tudor King: A Study of Edward VI* (1958); *The Tragedy of Charles II* (1964); *The Sisters of Henry VIII* (1969); *Caroline Matilda, Queen of Denmark, 1751-75* (1971); *Lady Jane Grey* (1972); *Anne Boleyn* (1974)

CHAPMAN-HUSTON, Desmond (real name Wellesley William Desmond Chapman-Huston Mountjoy) (1884-1952), Irish biographer and editor. He lived in Bavaria for several years, and wrote as well as collaborated with and helped to edit and write introductions to memoirs of several members of European royalty and nobility, including the diaries of Princess Frederick Leopold of Prussia (q.v.), Daisy, Princess of Pless, and Princess Pilar of Bavaria (q.v.). He also wrote essays and verse under the name of Desmond Mountjoy.

Bavarian Fantasy: The Story of Ludwig II (1955)

CHARLOT, Monica (*née* Monica Huber), OBE (1933–2005), historian and political scientist, was born at St Pancras, London, of Anglo-Swiss parentage. She studied French at Bedford College, then moved to Paris where she was employed as 'English assistante' in a French *lycée*. She moved to Algeria when her husband Jean (1932–1997), a French political scientist, was called up to serve there during the civil unrest. After they returned to France she divided her time between teaching and studying political and social history. She published several books and contributed to a number of collective works on various aspects of British politics and society. Ironically none of her titles were translated into English with the exception of

her biography of Queen Victoria, which covered her life to 1861. A second volume had been planned but was never completed. From 1984 to 1991 she was Director of the Maison Française at Oxford, and was honoured for her services by British and French governments.
Victoria: The Young Queen (1991)

CHARTERIS, Sir Evan (Edward) (1864-1940), English biographer, barrister and arts administrator, was gazetted to a commission in the Coldstream Guards, then went to Balliol College, Oxford, and was called to the Bar from the Inner Temple in 1891. He served as a Staff Captain in the Army in the First World War, and was made King's Counsel in 1919. He was Chairman of the Trustee of the National Portrait Gallery and of the Tate Gallery Board, and a Trustee of the National Gallery and the Wallace Collection.
William Augustus, Duke of Cumberland, His Early Life and Times (1913); *William Augustus, Duke of Cumberland and the Seven Years' War* (1925)

CHEBOKSAROVA, Tatiana, *see* BEECHE, Arturo E.

CHEETHAM, Anthony, British historian, biographer and publisher. He read History at Balliol College, Oxford, and originally specialised in the 15th century. He later founded the publishing houses Orion and Century, then became Chairman and Chief Executive of Random House from 1989 to 1991. Later he co-founded Quercus, and then Head of Zeus.
The Life and Times of Richard III (1972)

CHENEVIX TRENCH, Charles (Pocklington), MC (1914-2003), born at Simla, India, studied at Oxford. On the outbreak of World War Two joined the Indian cavalry regiment, serving in Persia, Iraq and Syria, and was awarded the MC. After the war he served in India until Partition, then became a district commissioner in Kenya. Following independence in 1963, he returned to England and taught English, Swahili, Urdu, history, symbolic logic and polo at Millfield for six years. His cousin, Anthony Chenevix-Trench, was a contemporary Headmaster of Eton. He retired to concentrate on writing, including a monthly article for *Blackwood's Magazine*, under the pseudonym 'The Looker On', book reviews for the *Irish Times* and the *Irish Independent*, and books on British India, and 17th and 18th century history.

The Royal Malady [George III's illness] (1964); *George II* (1973)

CHOMET, Seweryn (1930-2009), born in Drohobycz, Poland, Polish physicist, author, journalist, historian, publisher, prolific translator of Russian scientific journals into English. He came to England after the Second World War, having hidden from persecution after his parents were forcibly taken by the Russians to serve as doctors in the army. They later joined him and set up a medical practice in London. He studied Physics at King's College, London, and later became a Lecturer there for over twenty years until retirement in 1987. He was also a writer, contributing restaurant reviews to *New Law Journal* as well as scientific articles to *The Times*, and was reputed to hold the world record for the greatest number of letters (around a hundred) published in the latter. His several books included one royal biography.

Helena: A Princess Reclaimed (1999)

CHRIMES, S.B. (Stanley Bertram) (1907-84), British historian, studied History at King's College, London and Trinity College, Cambridge. Recognised as one of the leading constitutional and administrative historians of his generation, he was Head of the Department of History

from 1953 to 1974 and subsequently Emeritus Professor at University College, Cardiff.
Henry VII (1972)

CHRISTIE, Mabel E. (Mabel Elizabeth Seebohm), (1884-1971), British historian, born in Bedford.
Henry VI (1922)

CHRISTMAS, Walter (real name Walter Christmas-Dirckinck-Holmfeld) (1861-1924), Danish author of fiction, non-fiction and plays. He spent much of his active life in the Danish navy, which he joined at the age of 14. He took part in expeditions to Greenland, the Caribbean and South America, and up the Amazon River, to investigate whether it would be possible to establish a Danish shipping route on the river, a project that failed because of a lack of potential investors. In 1895 he joined the Greek navy and took part in the war against Turkey. Four years later he took part in an attempt to sell the West Indies to Germany, and when it failed, he tried to sell the islands to America, but was suspected of trying to bribe American officials and politicians. Although acquitted by an American commission of inquiry, the move left him in severe financial straits, and he turned to writing to make money. He retired from the Navy in 1916 due to ill-health. It was alleged that he was an undisclosed secret agent of the British intelligence service, and while serving as a naval officer in Skagen during the First World War had forwarded navy coastguard reports to MI6.
King George of Greece (1914)

CLARK, Chris (Sir Christopher), PhD (1960-), Australian historian working in England, well known for his published work on Prussian and modern European history. He studied History at universities in Sydney, Berlin and Cambridge. After being a member of Pembroke College,

Cambridge from 1987 to 1991, he became Professor in Modern European History at the University of Cambridge and Fellow of St Catherine's College, where he was appointed Director of Studies in History. He was knighted for his services to Anglo-German relations in 2015. Living in West Berlin between 1985 and 1987, almost the last years of the divided Germany, gave him an insight into German history and society. His book on the last German Emperor aimed 'to offer correctives to many of the traditional positions' in the less sympathetic three-volume biography by John C.G. Röhl (q.v.).
Kaiser Wilhelm II: A Life in Power (2000)

CLARKE, Stephen (1958-), British writer, born in St Albans, grew up in Bournemouth, and read French and German at Oxford University. He worked for HarperCollins as a bilingual lexicographer, then moved to Paris, and in his words 'is doing his best to live the *entente cordiale*'. Although best known for his comic 'Merde' novels, he has also written a lighthearted biography of King Edward VII.
Dirty Bertie: An English King Made in France (2014)

CLAY, Catrine, British television producer and historian. Working for the BBC, she produced several documentaries for the History Unit. Both her listed books were TV tie-ins for accompanying series and documentaries.
Princess to Queen [Queen Elizabeth II] (1996); *King, Kaiser, Tsar: Three Royal Cousins Who Led the World to War* (2006)

CLITHEROW, Mary (1764-1847), British writer of letters. She, her younger brother James, whose family seat was at Boston House, Brentford, Middlesex, and his wife Jane were close friends of William and Adelaide, Duke and Duchess of Clarence, later King William IV and Queen Adelaide. Sometimes known as 'the Boston House Trio',

they were the only untitled people to attend the Queen's birthday party in 1833, and Mary left a large quantity of correspondence describing their visits to St James's, Brighton and Windsor Castle.
Glimpses of King William IV and Queen Adelaide, in Letters of the Late Miss Clitherow, of Boston House, Middlesex, with a Brief Account of Boston House and the Clitherow Family (1902)

COCKERILL, Sarah, barrister and historian, read Law at Oxford, and became a barrister and QC specialising in commercial law.
Eleanor of Castile: The Shadow Queen (2014)

COLE, Hubert (Archibald Noel) (1908-84), British biographer, born in London.
The Black Prince (1976)

CONSTANT, Stephen.
Foxy Ferdinand, 1861-1948, Tsar of Bulgaria (1979)

COOK, Andrew (1959-), British biographer and historian.
Prince Eddy: The King Britain Never Had [Albert Victor, Duke of Clarence] (2006); *The Murder of the Romanovs* (2010)

COOKE, Sir Clement Kinloch, 1st Baronet, KBE (1854-1944), British journalist and politician, born in Brighton, read Mathematics and Law at St. John's College, Cambridge. He was called to the bar in 1883 by the Inner Temple, joined the Oxford Circuit, and became Treasury prosecuting counsel for Berkshire. Later he became a legal adviser to the House of Lords Sweating Commission and private secretary to the Earl of Dunraven and Mount-Earl, Under-Secretary of State for the Colonies, from 1885 to 1887, and examiner under the Civil Service Commission for factory inspectorships. He was a contributor to and staff writer on various journals including *English Illustrated*

Magazine, the *Observer*, the *Pall Mall Gazette*, and the *New Review*, on imperial and colonial subjects, and founded the *Empire Review* in 1901. Turning to politics, he became a member of the London County Council in 1907, was Unionist MP for Devonport from 1910 to 1923, and Unionist MP for Cardiff East from 1924 to 1929. While serving in parliament he was Chairman of the Naval and Dockyards Committee, and the Expiring Laws and Continuance Act Committee.

A Memoir of HRH Princess Mary Adelaide, Duchess of Teck, Based on her Private Diaries and Letters (1900); *Life of Her Majesty Queen Mary* (1911)

CORNFORTH, John (Lewley), CBE (1937-2004), British architectural historian, was born at Haywood Abbey, Staffordshire. He wrote extensively on the history of the English country house and was a member of the staff of *Country Life* from 1961 to 1993, serving as architectural editor from 1967 to 1977. As a member of the Historic Buildings Committee of the National Trust and the Historic Buildings Council for England, he helped to create new British galleries at the Victoria and Albert Museum.

Queen Elizabeth the Queen Mother at Clarence House (1986)

CORPECHOT, Lucien (1871-1944), French journalist and author, contributor to journals including *Le Figaro*, *L'Echo de Paris*, and *La Revue Universelle*.

Memories of Queen Amelie of Portugal (1915)

CORTI, Egon Caesar Conte (1886-1953), Austrian biographer and historian, born in Zagreb, Croatia, was an officer in the imperial Austro-Hungarian military staff. After the First World War he devoted himself to writing, and most of his titles were translated into several languages.

Leopold I of Belgium (1923); *The Downfall of Three Dynasties* (1934); *Elizabeth, Empress of Austria* (1936); *Ludwig I of Bavaria*

(1938); *Alexander von Battenberg* (1954); *The English Empress: A Study in the Relations between Queen Victoria and her Eldest Daughter, Empress Frederick of Germany* (1957)

COUGHLAN, Robert (1914-92), biographer, has also written on William Faulkner and Maurice Utrillo.
Elizabeth and Catherine: Empresses of all the Russias (1974)

COWARD, Rosalind (1952-), British academic, writer and journalist. She has been Professor of Journalism at Roehampton University, a columnist for the *Guardian*, and a contributor to the *Daily Mail*, *Cosmopolitan*, *The Ecologist*, *New Statesman* and *Marxism Today*. She was a director of Greenpeace UK from 2005 to 2012.
Diana: The Portrait (2004)

COWLES, Virginia (*née* Harriet Virginia Spencer), OBE (1910 or 1912–83), was a noted American journalist and biographer. Born in Brattleboro, Vermont, she worked first on the gossip columns of Boston and New York newspapers, writing mainly about fashion, love and society, then went to Spain in 1936 as a war correspondent, covering the Spanish Civil War and the Second World War for British and American newspapers, and being awarded an OBE in 1947. She turned to writing histories and biographies after the war. Married to Aidan Crawley, MP (Labour, Buckingham, 1945-51, and Conservative, West Derbyshire, 1962-67), in 1983 she was killed in a road accident near Biarritz.
Edward VII and His Circle (1956) UK/*Gay Monarch: The Life and Pleasures of Edward VII* (1956) US; *The Kaiser* (1963); *The Romanovs* (1971); *The Last Tsar and Tsarina* (1977)

CRANKSHAW, Edward (1909-84), British historian and journalist, specialising mainly in Austrian, German and Russian history. Born in London, he began his writing career on *The Times*, then went to Vienna to teach English and learn German. Because of his linguistic abilities he was contacted by the Secret Intelligence Service in 1940 and served as a Signals Intelligence officer in the army during the Second World War. He joined *The Observer* in 1947 as its Soviet affairs correspondent and held the post until 1968. In addition to his own books, he also published an English translation of Hermann Kesten's *Spanish Fire: The Story of Ferdinand and Isabella* in 1937.

The Fall of the House of Habsburg (1963); *Maria Theresa* (1969); *The Habsburgs: A Dynasty* (1971)

CRAWFORD, Donald, London-based writer, barrister and national newspaper executive, and formerly publisher of the journal *Parliamentary Brief*. Becoming interested in imperial Russia, he collaborated with his wife Rosemary on a biography of the last Tsar and his wife, his second book being a sequel to the first.

Michael and Natasha: The Life and Love of the Last Tsar of Russia [with Rosemary Crawford] (1997); *The Last Tsar: Emperor Michael II* (2011)

CRAWFORD, Marion (1909-88), Scottish governess and writer. Raised in Dunfermline, she was appointed governess by the Duke and Duchess of York, later King George VI and Queen Elizabeth, to Princesses Elizabeth and Margaret. She remained in royal service until Princess Elizabeth married the Duke of Edinburgh. She was then persuaded to write articles about her life with the royal family for publication in *Woman's Own* in Britain and the *Ladies' Home Journal* in America, although she was not granted legal authorisation to do so as it would have reneged on an undertaking she had previously given as part of her condition of employment. The articles led to a book which sold well but resulted in her being ostracised by the royal family. Her new career as a regular columnist came

to an ignominious end when she wrote a piece in advance for *Woman's Own* describing the Queen at a Trooping the Colour ceremony and at Ascot races, both of which had been cancelled that year, and it was too late to halt publication.
The Little Princesses (1950)

CREIGHTON, Mandell (1843-1901), British historian and bishop, was born in Carlisle. He was a scholar of the Renaissance papacy, the first occupant of the Dixie Chair of Ecclesiastical History at the University of Cambridge, and the first Editor of the *English Historical Review* on its inception in 1886. He was also a Church of England cleric, serving successively as Vicar of Embleton, Northumberland, Bishop of Peterborough, and Bishop of London.
Queen Elizabeth (1896)

CRESSY, David, American historian. An authority on Tudor and early Stuart England, he was Professor of Humanities and History at Ohio State University.
Charles I and the People of England (2015)

CRESTON, Dormer (1881-1973) (*née* Dorothy Julia Baynes, later Dorothy Julia Colston-Baynes), British author, was the daughter of Sir Christopher William Baynes, Bt.
The Regent and his Daughter (1932); *The Youthful Queen Victoria* (1952)

CRIMP, Susan.
Caroline and Stephanie: The Lives of the Princesses of Monaco (1988)

CROFT, Christina, British author, born in Warwickshire, studied English and Divinity in Liverpool, also obtaining teaching and nursing qualifications. She began her writing career as a poet, then co-writing songs and musicals, then biographies and novels.

Alice, the Enigma: Queen Victoria's Daughter (2013); *Queen Victoria's Granddaughters, 1860-1918* (2013); *Dear Papa, Beloved Mama: Queen Victoria and Prince Albert as Parents* (2014); *Queen Victoria's grandsons (1859-1918)* (2015); *The Innocence of Kaiser Wilhelm II* (2015)

CRONIN, Vincent (Archibald Patrick), **FRSL** (1924-2011), British writer of biographies, histories and general non-fiction. Born in Tredegar, Monmouthshire, son of novelist A.J. Cronin, he served in the army during the Second World War, and studied at Harvard University, the Sorbonne, and Trinity College, Oxford.

Louis XIV (1964); *Napoleon* (1971) UK/*Napoleon Bonaparte: An Intimate Biography* (1972) US; *Louis and Antoinette* (1974); *Catherine, Empress of All the Russias* (1978)

CULLEN, Tom (Alden) (1913-2001), American biographer, born in Oklahoma City, studied Economics and Political Science at the University of California before becoming a journalist on the *United Progressive News*. He joined the US Army in 1942, and served during the Second World War in Europe and Africa as a military journalist. After being discharged as a technical sergeant in 1946, he worked on trade magazines, then freelanced in France, Germany and India, before arriving in Britain. When the American government confiscated his passport because of his Communist connections, he was allowed to stay in Britain on a visitor's passport on condition that he stayed out of trouble. His non-royal biographical subjects included Dr Crippen and Maundy Gregory.

The Empress Brown [Queen Victoria and John Brown] (1969)

CUNLIFFE-OWEN, Countess Marguerite (1855-1927), French biographer and historical novelist, was daughter of Count Jules du Planty de Sourdis. Having lost their fortunes in France, she and her husband Frederick settled in the United States in 1885 to make their careers as professional writers. After first becoming a syndicated newspaper columnist she wrote several biographies and studies of the courts of Europe, histories and novels. Some of the former included gossip and other contentious material and were published either anonymously or under the pseudonym La Marquise de Fontenoy, and she only admitted to their authorship on her deathbed.
The Martyrdom of an Empress (1899): *A Keystone of Empire, Francis Joseph of Austria* (1903); *Imperator et Rex: William II of Germany* (n.d.)

CURRY, Anne, British historian and specialist in 15th century history, particularly on the battle of Agincourt. Dean of the Faculty of Humanities, Southampton University, she was President of the Historical Association from 2008 to 2011, and lectured widely and broadcast on radio and TV.
Henry V: From Playboy Prince to Warrior King (2015)

CURTIS, Gila, *see* FALKUS, Gila

CUST, Sir Lionel Henry, KCVO, FSA (1859-1929), British art historian, courtier and museum director. He was born in London and studied at Trinity College, Cambridge. He joined the Department of Prints and Drawings, at the British Museum in 1884, where he compiled two catalogues of drawings, and contributed several entries to Bryan's *Dictionary of Painters and Engravers*. He was Director of the National Portrait Gallery from 1895 to 1909, and thereafter editor of the *Burlington Magazine* until 1919. On the accession of King Edward VII

in 1901 he was appointed a Gentleman Usher and Surveyor of Pictures in Ordinary to His Majesty, remaining in both posts until retirement in 1927.
King Edward and his Court (1930)

CUST, Richard (1954-), British historian, read History at Queen Mary College, and Bedford College, University of London. He became Professor in Modern History at University of Birmingham in 1978.
Charles I (2007); *Charles I and the Aristocracy* (2013)

D

DANGERFIELD, George (1904-86), British historian and biographer, born at Newbury, read English at Hertford College, Oxford, and then taught English in Prague and Hamburg. He moved to America in 1930 and worked in publishing, becoming Literary Editor of *Vanity Fair* from 1933 to 1935, during which time he discovered a fascination with and began writing on modern history. During the Second World War he served with the American army, becoming an American citizen in 1943. His biography of Edward VII was praised on its reissue thirty years later as being 'concerned with politics, not sex' (*The Times*, 29.12.1986).
Victoria's Heir: The Education of a Prince (1942)

D'AUVERGNE, Edmund (Basil Francis) (1876-1958), British author.
A Queen at Bay: The Story of Maria Christina and Don Carlos (1910); *John, King of England* (1934)

DAVIES, J.D. (John David) Griffith, OBE (1899-1953), British biographer and historian. He worked for some years for the City of Leeds Education Department, and later as Assistant Secretary of the Royal Society from 1937 to 1946.
King Henry IV (1935); *Henry V* (1935); *George the Third: A Record of a King's Reign* (1936); *A King in Toils* [George II] (1938)

DAVIES, Nicholas (1939-), British journalist and author (not to be confused with a contemporary *Guardian* journalist of the same name). He began his career with the *Birmingham Post and Mail*, then joined Mirror Group Newspapers in 1961 as foreign correspondent and investigative reporter, served as foreign editor of the *Daily Mirror* until 1991 and then turned to biographies on contemporary royalty.
Diana: A Princess and her Troubled Marriage (1992); *Queen Elizabeth II: A Woman Who is not Amused* (1994); *Elizabeth: Behind Palace Doors* (2000); *Diana: Secrets and Lies* (2003); *Diana: the Killing of a Princess* (2006)

DAVIS, Arthur N(ewton) (1879-?), Emperor William II's American dentist for fourteen years. At first he felt obliged by professional ethics to withhold his story from the world at large, until due consideration of the grave crisis facing the world and the persuasion of professional colleagues suggested he had a duty to do otherwise.
The Kaiser as I Know Him: My Fourteen Years with the Kaiser (1918)

DAVIS, John Paul.
The Gothic King - a Biography of Henry III (2013)

DAY, James Wentworth (1899-1983), British writer, journalist and broadcaster, born in Exning, Suffolk. After serving briefly in the First World War he worked for Express newspapers, *The Field, Country Life* and other sporting journals, and was successively Editor of *Illustrated Sporting and Dramatic News*, and the *Saturday Review*. During the Second World War he was a BBC correspondent in France, and stood for Parliament for Hornchurch as a Conservative in the 1950 and 1951 general elections. He wrote extensively on natural history and rural matters, particularly those relating to East Anglia where he spent most of his life. Unashamedly old-fashioned, he claimed in one of his books that he was 'an antediluvian, a reactionary, an out-of-date or, as I prefer it, a rural romanticist '.

King George V as a Sportsman (1935); *HRH Princess Marina, Duchess of Kent: The First Authentic Life Story* (1962); *The Queen Mother's Family Story* (1967)

DE BURGH, A. (Edward Morgan Alborough).
Elizabeth, Empress of Austria: A Memoir (1899)

DEHN, Lili (*née* Yulia Alexandrovna Smolskaia) (1888-1963), Russian biographer and friend of the last Tsarina. Born on Revovka, the family's Russian estate, she married Carl Alexander Akimovich von Dehn, a Russian naval officer on the imperial yacht, *Standart.* During the First World War she trained as a Red Cross nurse, tending to wounded soldiers in a military hospital. She was with the imperial family during the outbreak of the Russian revolution, and helped to nurse the imperial children and her distant cousin Anna Vyrubova, the Tsarina's companion, through an attack of measles. After the Tsar's abdication she and her family escaped from Russia, settling first in England and then in Poland. She wrote her memoir of the Tsarina partly to refute rumours about her and Rasputin, and stated that she blamed the revolution and downfall of the empire on Jewish agitators. After the death of her husband and the outbreak of the Second World War, she fled from Poland and went to settle in Venezuela, where her multilingual daughter Maria worked as an interpreter for the government. She died in Rome.
The Real Tsaritsa (1922)

DE LISLE, Leanda, British historian and biographer known for her studies of the Tudor and early Stuart period. She read Modern History at Oxford University, then

became a columnist for magazines and newspapers including the *Spectator*, *Country Life*, and the *Guardian*.
After Elizabeth: How James King of Scots Won the Crown of England in 1603 (2005); *The Sisters Who Would Be Queen: The Tragedy of Mary, Katherine and Lady Jane Grey* (2009); *Tudor: The Family Story* (2013)

DENNISON, Matthew, British author and journalist, has contributed to television documentaries and written on Roman history and biography.
The Last Princess: The Devoted Life of Queen Victoria's Youngest Daughter (2007); *Queen Victoria: A Life of Contradictions* (2013)

DENNY, Joanna (-2006), British historian and author specialising in the court of Henry VIII.
Katherine Howard: A Tudor Conspiracy (2005); *Anne Boleyn: A New Life of England's Tragic Queen* (2005)

DIMBLEBY, Jonathan (1944-), British writer, political commentator and radio and TV presenter born in Aylesbury, son of broadcaster Richard Dimbleby, and studied Philosophy at University College, London. His biography of the Prince of Wales was a companion to his controversial ITV documentary *Charles: The Private Man, The Public Face*.
The Prince of Wales: A Biography (1994)

DIMITROFF, Pashanko (1924-98), Anglo-Bulgarian author, spent much of his life in England where he died.
King of Mercy: A Biography of King Boris III of Bulgaria, 1894 to 1943 (1987)

DONALDSON, Frances (*née* Frances Lonsdale, later Lady Donaldson of Kingsbridge) (1907-94), was daughter of the playwright Frederick Lonsdale. While her husband John served with the Royal Engineers during the Second World

War, she ran the family farm, which resulted in her writing her first three books about agriculture. She later turned to biography, including lives of her father, Evelyn Waugh and P.G. Wodehouse, as well as those of royalty. Her study of Edward VIII was used as the basis for an ITV drama series starring Edward Fox, first shown in 1978.

Edward VIII (1974); *King George VI and Queen Elizabeth* (1977); *Edward VIII: The Road to Abdication* (1978)

DONALDSON, Gordon, CBE, FRHistS, DLitt, FBA (1913-93), Scottish historian. He was born in Edinburgh and read History at Edinburgh University, then worked as an archivist at the General Register Office for Scotland from 1938 to 1947. He then became a Lecturer in Scottish History at Edinburgh, becoming Professor in Scottish History and Palaeography in 1963, until retirement in 1979.

The First Trial of Mary Queen of Scots (1969); *Mary Queen of Scots* (1974)

DORAN, Dr John (1807–78), English editor and miscellaneous writer of Irish parentage, born in London. He travelled on the continent for some years as a young man, and studied Philosophy at the University of Marburg in Prussia. Returning to England he became a professional writer. From 1841 to 1852 he was literary editor of the *Church and State Gazette*, subsequently became a regular contributor to the *Athenæum*, editor in 1869, and later Editor of *Notes and Queries*. He wrote several works of biography and history, as well as editing Horace Walpole's *Journal of the Reign of George III*.

The Queens of the House of Hanover, 2 vols (1855); *Monarchs retired from Business*, 2 vols (1857); *Book of the Princes of Wales* (1860); *Memoir of Queen Adelaide* (1861)

DOUGLAS, David C., FBA (1898-1982), British historian, was born in London, and read Modern History at Keble College, Oxford. He was Professor of History at Bristol University from 1945 to 1963 and subsequently Emeritus Professor, and a recognised authority on the Norman age.
William the Conqueror (1964)

DUFF, David (1912-2008), journalist, biographer and novelist, served in the Royal Artillery during World War Two, and was later engaged on war work on the official histories of the war for the War Office and Cabinet Office.
Edward of Kent (1938); *Princess Louise, Duchess of Argyll* (1940); *The Duke of Cambridge* [with E.M. Duff]; *The Shy Princess: The Life of HRH Princess Beatrice, the Youngest Daughter and Constant Companion of Queen Victoria* (1958); *Mother of the Queen* (1965); *Hessian Tapestry: The Hesse Family and British Royalty* (1967); *Victoria in the Highlands: The Personal Journal of Her Majesty Queen Victoria* (1968); *Victoria Travels: Journeys of Queen Victoria between 1830 and 1900, with Extracts From her Journal* (1970); *Albert and Victoria* (1972); *Elizabeth of Glamis* (1973); *Whisper Louise: Edward VII and Mrs Cresswell* (1974); *Eugenie and Napoleon III* (1978); *Alexandra, Princess and Queen* (1980); *George and Elizabeth: A Royal Marriage* (1983); *Queen Mary* (1985)

DUFFY, Christopher, DPhil (1936-), British military historian, read History at Balliol College, Oxford, then taught Military History at Royal Military Academy, Sandhurst, and British General Staff College. He was Secretary-General of the British Commission for Military History and vice-president of the Military History Society of Ireland, and Research Professor at De Montfort University, Leicester from 1996 to 2001.
Frederick the Great: A Military Life (1985)

DUGGAN, J.N., BSc (1938-), British historian, born in Sheffield, went to live in Ireland at the age of twelve,

returned to Sheffield to train as a nurse and then studied at University College, Dublin. She has been involved, in an editorial capacity, in the reissue of several important works of Irish philosopher John Toland.
Sophie of Hanover: From Winter Princess to Heiress of Great Britain, 1630-1714 (2010)

DUNN, Susan, American author, Professor of Literature and the History of Ideas at Williams College and Senior Scholar and the Academy of Leadership at the University of Maryland. She is the author of several books on European and American history.
The Death of Louis XVI: Regicide and the French Political Imagination (1994)

E

EADE, Philip, British biographer, born in Shropshire, read History at Bristol University. He has been a criminal barrister, financial journalist, guidebook writer and taught English, and a former writer of obituaries for the *Daily Telegraph*.
Young Philip: His Turbulent Early Life (2012)

EARLE, Peter (1937-), British author, studied at University College, London, and London School of Economics, becoming a lecturer at the latter in 1964. He was a regular contributor to historical journals, and wrote several titles on English social and maritime history.
The Life and Times of Henry V (1972); *The Life and Times of James II* (1972)

EDWARDS, Anne (1927-), American author, born at Port Chester, New York, was a child performer on stage and radio. She began her writing career as a junior writer at MGM in 1944 and became a noted Hollywood screenwriter and television writer. Meanwhile she also studied at University of California and Southern Methodist University. She later wrote biographies of celebrities including Judy Garland, Barbra Streisand and Ronald Reagan, as well as fiction and children's books.
Matriarch: Queen Mary and the House of Windsor (1984)

EDWARDS, Arthur, *see* JOBSON, Robert

EDWARDS, Averyl (Averil Edith) (1896-1979), British author.
Frederick Louis, Prince of Wales, 1707-1751 (1947)

EDWARDS, Graham.
The Last Days of Charles I (1999)

EDWARDS, John, MA, DPhil (Oxon), British historian, was Modern Languages Faculty Research Fellow in Spanish, University of Oxford and wrote extensively on 16th century Spain.
Ferdinand and Isabella (2004); *Mary I: England's Catholic Queen* (2011)

EDWARDS, W.H. (William Hayden), German journalist. His study of Edward VII received an unfavourable (and anonymous) review in *The Times*, which called it 'a psychological fantasy', referring to the 'slipshod quality' of the author's mind, and suggesting that 'he lets his fancy roam at will without regard to the obstacle of fact'. (*The Times*, 25.9.1928). It provoked an indignant letter from Hayden, who described himself as a 'journalist of international experience' (*The Times*, 27.9.1938), leading to an equally testy letter from the reviewer two days later, declaring that his 'professional integrity' had been impugned.
The Tragedy of Edward VII: A Psychological Study (1928)

EILERS KOENIG, Marlene (1954-), American biographer, editor and academic librarian. She became fascinated by royalty at the age of twelve after coming across Queen Victoria's family tree, and undertook research for other writers, including David Duff (q.v.) and Hugo Vickers (q.v.). She founded *Royal Book News*, a subscription newsletter which became an online blog in 2011, and the blog *Royal Musings*. She has contributed to

Majesty magazine, *Royalty Digest*, *Eurohistory Journal* and *Berkswell's The Royal Year*, for which she covered British and foreign royal visits to America during the 1980s and 1990s. *Queen Victoria's Descendants* (1987); *A Romanov Diary: The Autobiography of H.I. & R.H. Grand Duchess George* (ed. with G. Nicholas Tantzos) (1990); *Queen Victoria's Descendants: A Companion Edition* (2004); *The Gleichens: the Unknown Royal Cousins* (2014)

EISENMENGER, Victor (1864-1932), Austrian physician and doctor, was a specialist in diseases of the larynx, and personal physician to Emperor Francis Joseph and his successive heirs Archduke Francis Ferdinand and Archduke Charles, destined to be the last Emperor of Austria-Hungary.   Eisenmenger's syndrome and the Eisenmenger complex were both named after him.
Archduke Francis Ferdinand (1931)

ELBORN, Geoffrey (1950-), British biographer and journalist, has contributed to the *Scottish Review of Books* and *Oxford Dictionary of National Biography*.
Princess Alexandra (1982)

ELLIOT, John (1918-97), British television producer and writer. Born in Castle Hill, he wrote several plays for BBC TV, as well as fiction and *Fall of Eagles*, the official book for the 13-part drama series of the same name first shown in 1974, which he created and for which he supplied several of the scripts.
Fall of Eagles (1974)

ELSBERRY, Terence, American biographer, was Editor of *Apartment Ideas Magazine*.   A fascination with Queen Marie of Roumania since reading her memoirs while still at school inspired him to write her biography.

Marie of Roumania: The Intimate Life of a Twentieth-Century Queen (1973)

EPTON, Nina Consuelo (1913-2010), British author, born in Hampstead, London, was educated in England and France, and graduated from the University of Paris. She became a radio producer, broadcaster and travel writer, and during the 1950s she was the producer of the BBC's French-Canadian department, with responsibility for BBC contributions to the Canadian Broadcasting Corporation's French-language newsreel, *Revue de l'actualité*. Between 1953 and 1969 she contributed to the BBC Home Service and Light Programme as a presenter, interviewer, and panellist. As an author she published biographies and fiction, though her most successful works were a trilogy of literary, historical and sociological books about the amorous relationships of the English, French and Spanish peoples.

Victoria and her Daughters (1971); *The Spanish Mousetrap Napoleon and the Court of Spain* (1973); *Josephine the Empress and her Children* (1975)

ERICKSON, Carolly (1943-), American author of biographies and fiction, read History at Universities of Washington and Columbia. She taught History at Barnard College and Brooklyn College, at San Fernando Valley State College and Mills College, before becoming a freelance writer, with particular interest in the Middle Ages and early modern Europe.

Bloody Mary: The Life of Mary Tudor (1978); *Josephine: A Life of the Empress* (1980); *Great Harry: The Extravagant Life of Henry VIII* (1980); *Royal Panoply: Brief Lives of the English Monarchs* (1980); *The First Elizabeth* (1983); *Mistress Anne: The Exceptional Life of Anne Boleyn* (1984); *Bonnie Prince Charlie* (1989); *To the Scaffold: The Life of Marie Antoinette* (1991); *Great Catherine: The Life of Catherine the Great, Empress of Russia*

(1994); *Her Little Majesty: The Life of Queen Victoria* (1997); *Alexandra: The Last Tsarina* (2001); *Lilibet: An Intimate Portrait Of Elizabeth II* (2004); (*Brief Lives of the English Monarchs* (2007)

ERLANGER, Philippe (1903-87), French author, born in Paris. He held various posts including that of Inspector General at the Ministry of Education and Director of the French Association for Artistic Action, and was partly responsible for launching the Cannes Film Festival in 1939. Although a prolific writer on French royalty, history and arts, only a few of his books were translated into English.
Margaret of Anjou (1970); *Louis XIV* (1972)

EYCK, Frank (Ulrich Franz Joseph) (1921-2004), Anglo-German historian and biographer, was born in Berlin and educated at College Francais, Berlin and, after coming to England at the age of fifteen, at St. Paul's School in London. He served in the British Army from 1940 to 1946, and was a member of an information control unit charged with establishing a democratic press in Germany. After demobilization he read Modern History at Worcester College, Oxford, and then joined the BBC in 1949, editing the weekly programme *Hier Spricht London* and then compiling news bulletins for transmissions abroad. He was a Research Fellow of St. Antony's College, Oxford, from 1956 to 1958 and Lecturer in Modern European History at Exeter University from 1959 to 1968, when he and his family moved to Canada and he became Professor of History at the University of Calgary.
The Prince Consort: A Political Biography (1959)

EYLERT, R.F. (Rulemann Friedrich) (1770-1852), German Bishop, was born at Hamm and studied theology at the University of Halle. He succeeded his father as

pastor of the reformed church in Hamm in 1794, and was later appointed chaplain to King Frederick William III.
Characteristic Traits and Domestic Life of King Frederick III, King of Prussia (1845)

F

FALKUS, Christopher (1940-95), British historian, read History at University College, London, then spent a year as a BBC trainee and worked for the children's partwork *Knowledge*. After moving to Australia, he became a Lecturer in Modern History at Queensland University, and also became a researcher, tennis and squash player, cricketer and an enthusiastic and knowledgeable naturalist. On returning to England in 1968 he joined the British Printing Corporation, where he edited historical partworks. In 1970 he joined Weidenfeld & Nicolson as Publisher of the Art and Illustrated list and became joint managing director with Alan Miles. He devised the 'Life and Times of the Kings and Queens of England' series with Book Club Associates and commissioned Antonia Fraser (q.v.) as editor, with both he and Gila Curtis (q.v.), later his wife, contributing titles to the series. In 1980 he went to work with Associated Book Publishers, where he became Chairman of the Methuen General Books Group, but returned to Weidenfeld after a brief unhappy experience of working with Robert Maxwell. He retired in 1992 due to ill-health to become a freelance writer and editor.
The Life and Times of Charles II (1972)

FALKUS, Gila, read History at Edinburgh University, and was part of the editorial team for Purnell's *History of the 20th Century*, and the partwork *History of the English-Speaking Peoples*, as well as a contributor to magazines and periodicals.

The Life and Times of Queen Anne (1972) [as Gila Curtis]; *The Life and Times of Edward IV* (1981)

FERRO, Marc (1924-), French historian and biographer, specializing in 20th century European and Russian history and the cinema. He was Director of Studies at *l'Ecole des hautes etudes en sciences sociales*, Paris, and presented several historical documentaries on TV.
Nicholas II: The Last of the Tsars (1991)

FISCHER, Henry W. (William) (1856-1932), German author, editor and probable ghost-writer of rather indiscreet, gossipy biographies and memoirs of early 20th century European royalty. He prefaced *Secret Memoirs* with a disclaimer at the front to say that the subject of the book 'is in no way, either directly or indirectly, interested in this publication'.
The Private Lives of William II and his Consort: A Secret History of the Court of Berlin: From the Papers and Diaries of Ursula, Countess von Eppinghoven, Lady-in-Waiting to Empress Augusta Victoria (1904); *Secret Memoirs: The Court of Royal Saxony, 1891-1902: The Story of Louise, Crown Princess* (1912); *Behind the Scenes with the Kaiser (1888-1922): The True Story of the Kaiser as he Lived, Loved, Played and Warred* (1922)

FISHER, Heather and Graham, British husband and wife team who were responsible for several popular contemporary biographies, especially in the early 1960s when, in Graham Fisher's words, 'there were not many authors writing about the royal family at that time because facts were so hard to come by and so the books sold very, very well' (*Royalty Digest*, March 1992). His interest and involvement in the subject began when he was a writer on the local press in Norfolk in 1952 and became 'the first person journalistically' to learn that George VI had died at Sandringham.

Elizabeth, Queen and Mother: The Story of Queen Elizabeth and the British Royal Family (1964) *Prince Charles: The Future King* (1966); *The Royal Family: A Personal Portrait* [with Ralphe M. White] (1969); *The Crown and the Ring: The Story of the Queen's Years of Marriage and Monarchy* (1972); *Bertie and Alix: Anatomy of a Royal Marriage* (1974); *The Queen's Life: And her Twenty-Five years of Monarchy* (1976); *Monarchy and the Royal Family: A Guide for Everyman* (1979); *Charles and Diana: Their Married Life* (1984); *Prince Andrew: Boy, Man and Prince* (1982); *Consort: The Life and Times of Prince Philip* (1980); *Charles: The Man and the Prince* (1984); *Monarch: A Biography of Elizabeth II* (1985); *The Queen's Travels* (1988); *Your Majesty: The Life and Reign of Elizabeth II* (1992)

FITZGERALD, Percy (Hetherington) (1834-1925), Irish author, a graduate of Trinity College, Dublin, initially pursued a legal career in Ireland, first as barrister and subsequently Crown Prosecutor on the north-eastern circuit in Ireland. He was encouraged to become a writer after successive meetings with Charles Dickens's biographer John Forster and then Dickens himself. He was a contributor to Household Words and dramatic critic for the *Observer* and *Whitehall Review*. Over the next seventy years he wrote over 200 books, including novels, histories and biographies. His two-volume life of King William IV was notable for containing not a single reference to his mistress Dorothea Jordan. As a sculptor he also produced statues of James Boswell and Dr Samuel Johnson, and a bust of Dickens.
Life of George IV (1881); *The Royal Dukes and Princesses of the Family of George III: A View of Court Life and Manners for Seventy Years, 1760-1830* (1882); *Life of William IV* (1884); *The Good Queen Charlotte* (1899)

FORBES, Archibald (1838-1900), British war correspondent and biographer, born in Morayshire, studied at Aberdeen University, and then enlisted in the Royal Dragoons. While in the army he began writing on military and historical subjects for the *Morning Star* and the *Cornhill Magazine.* Leaving the army in 1867, he started a weekly journal, the *London Scotsman.* In 1870 he was despatched to the siege of Metz as a war correspondent by the *Morning Advertiser*, entered Paris with the Prussians with whom he established cordial relations six months later, and narrowly avoided being drowned in a Parisian fountain as a German spy by a French mob. During the next few years he also reported for the paper from war zones in Spain, Serbia, Turkey, Afghanistan and Africa.

William of Germany: A Succinct Biography of William I, German Emperor and King of Prussia (1888); *The Life of Napoleon III* (1898)

FORBES, Grania (1950-), British biographer and curt correspondent with the Press Association.

My Darling Buffy: The Early Years of the Queen Mother (1997); *Elizabeth the Queen Mother: A Twentieth Century Life* (1999)

FORESTER, C.S. (Cecil Scott, real name Cecil Lewis Troughton Smith) (1899-1966), born in Cairo, was best known as a novelist and writer of sea stories, but also published several royal biographies during his early career.

Napoleon and his Court (1924); *Josephine, Napoleon's Empress* (1925); *Victor Emmanuel II and the Union of Italy* (1927); *Louis XIV, King of France and Navarre* (1928)

FOTHERGILL, Brian (1921-90), British biographer and historian, read History at King's College, London. He served with the Intelligence Corps from 1944 to 1947, then taught at various schools for the next ten years before becoming a full-time author and journalist.

The Cardinal King [Henry Stuart, Cardinal Duke of York, brother of 'Bonnie Prince Charlie'] (1958)

FOX, Julia, British author, historical researcher, and a former teacher, married to Tudor historian John Guy (q.v.).
Jane Boleyn: The Infamous Lady Rochford, (2007); *Sister Queens: Katherine of Aragon and Juana Queen of Castile* (2011)

FRANKLAND, (Anthony) Noble, CB, CBE, DFC, DPhil (1922-), British historian and biographer, attended Oxford, although his studies were interrupted by and resumed after the Second World War. During the war he served in the Royal Air Force from 1941 to 1945, as a navigator in RAF Bomber Command and was awarded the Distinguished Flying Cross in 1944. He left the RAF in 1945 with the rank of Flight Lieutenant. He worked at the Air Historical Branch of the Air Ministry from 1948 to 1951, and was an Official Military Historian to the Cabinet Office between 1951 and 1958. From 1960 to 1982 he was Director of the Imperial War Museum, and between 1971 and 1974 he was historical adviser to the Thames Television series, *The World at War*.
Nicholas II: Crown of Tragedy (1960); *Prince Henry, Duke of Gloucester* (1980); *Witness of a Century: the Life and Times of Prince Arthur, Duke of Connaught (1850–1942)* (1993)

FRASER, Lady Antonia, DBE (Antonia Margaret Caroline Pakenham) (1932-), British author, was the daughter of Frank and Elizabeth Pakenham, 7th Earl and Countess of Longford (q.v.). She was educated at Oxford and then went to work as an assistant at Weidenfeld & Nicholson, which later became her main publisher when she began writing. In addition to her own historical biographies and later fiction, she became editor of the company's 'Life and Times of' series on English and British monarchs. Her three daughters by her marriage to Sir Hugh Fraser, Conservative MP, all became writers and biographers in their own right. From 1988 to 1989, she was president of English PEN, the worldwide association of writers, and she chaired its Writers in Prison Committee.

Mary Queen of Scots (1969); *The Life and Times of King James VI and I* (1974); *The Lives of the Kings and Queens of England* (1975) ed; *King Charles II* (1979); *The Warrior Queens: Boadicea's Chariot* (1988); *The Six Wives of Henry VIII* (1996); *Marie Antoinette* (2001); *Love and Louis XIV: The Women in the Life of the Sun King* (2006)

FRASER, Flora, British biographer and novelist, daughter of Lady Antonia Fraser (q.v.), co-founded the Elizabeth Longford (q.v.) Prize and Grants for Historical Biography in memory of her grandmother.

The Unruly Queen: The Life Of Queen Caroline (1996), *Princesses: The Daughters of George III* (2004)

FREER, Martha Walker (married name Martha Walker Robinson) (1822–88), British writer who published works on French history under her maiden name, born in Leicester. She married the Rev. John Robinson, rector of Widmerpool, near Nottingham, in 1861.

Life of Marguerite d'Angoulême, Queen of Navarre, Duchesse d'Alençon, and De Berry, Sister of Francis I, 2 vols (1854); *The Life of Jeanne D'Albert, Queen of Navarre* (1855); *Elizabeth de Valois, Queen of Spain and the Court of Philip II*, 2 vols. (1857); *Henry III, King of France and Poland: his Court and Times*, 3 vols. (1858); *History of the Reign of Henry IV, King of France and Navarre*, Part I, 2 vols. (1860); Part II, 2 vols. (1861); Part III, 2 vols. (1863); *The Married Life of Anne of Austria, Queen of France, Mother of Louis XIV and Don Sebastian, King of Portugal*, 2 vols. (1864); *The Regency of Anne of Austria*, 2 vols. (1866)

FRIEDMAN, Dr Dennis (1924-2014), British psychiatrist and author, born in Stamford Hill, London, trained in Medicine at St Bartholomew's Hospital and Queens'

College, Cambridge. He set up in general practice in Edgware, then trained as a Psychiatrist, serving as Medical Director of the Stress clinics at the Devonshire Hospital in Marylebone from 1988 to 1991, and the Charter Clinic, Chelsea from 1991 to 1994, then as Consultant Psychiatrist at the Florence Nightingale and Cromwell Hospitals, with special responsibility for stress-related illness and its management. He wrote several books on psychology, a novel, and psychological studies of the royal family. In 1997 he criticised the Prince and Princess Wales for discussing their personal lives on TV on the grounds that it would cause 'catastrophic' damage to their eldest son, and in the *Daily Express* in 2001 he wrote that Queen Elizabeth II probably felt 'a sense of failure as a mother' as 'none of her children, certainly her sons, have been able to relate to women in a normal way – and she probably blames herself' (*Daily Telegraph*, 10.12.2014).

Inheritance: A Psychological History of the Royal Family [with Susan Hill] (1993); *Darling Georgie: The Enigma of King George V* (1999); *The Ladies of the Bedchamber: The Role of the Royal Mistress* (2003)

FULFORD, Sir Roger (Thomas Baldwin), **CVO** (1902-83), British biographer, editor and politician, was a journalist with *The Times* for some years, and a part-time lecturer in English at King's College, London, from 1937 to 1948. In the 1930s, he completed the editing of the standard edition of the diaries of Charles Greville. As a staunch member of the Liberal Party, he was a parliamentary candidate in three general elections, in 1929 at Woodbridge, in 1945 at Holderness, and in 1950 at Rochdale, and was Liberal Party President in 1964–65. He was assistant private secretary to Sir Archibald Sinclair, Liberal leader and Secretary of State for Air, from 1942 to 1945. His most lasting achievement as a royal biographer and editor came at the end of his career, when between

1964 and 1981 he edited five volumes of letters between Queen Victoria and Victoria, Princess Royal and German Crown Princess, covering the years 1858 to 1885. The series was completed with one more volume after his death by Agatha Ramm (q.v.).

Royal Dukes: The Father and Uncles of Queen Victoria (1933); *George the Fourth* (1935); *The Prince Consort* (1949); *Queen Victoria* (1951); *Hanover to Windsor* (1960); **Dearest Child: Letters between Queen Victoria and the Princess Royal, 1858-1861** (ed.) (1964); **Dearest Mama: Private Correspondence of Queen Victoria and the Crown Princess of Prussia, 1861-1864** (ed.) (1968); **Your Dear Letter: Private Correspondence of Queen Victoria and the Crown Princess of Prussia, 1865-1871** (ed.) (1971); **Darling Child: Private Correspondence of Queen Victoria and the Crown Princess of Prussia, 1871-1878** (ed.) (1976); **Beloved Mama: Private Correspondence of Queen Victoria and the German Crown Princess of Prussia, 1878-1885** (ed.) (1981)

G

GAIRDNER, James LL.D, CB (1828–1912), British historian, authority on 15th and 16th royal biography and history, entered the Public Record Office, London in 1846, and was Assistant Keeper of Public Records from 1859 to 1893. He also contributed to the *Encyclopedia Britannica*, *Dictionary of National Biography*, *Cambridge Modern History*, and *English Historical Review*.
History of the Life and Reign of Richard the Third (1878); *Henry the Seventh* (1889)

GAVIN, Catherine (Irvine), DLitt (1907-2000), Scottish author, born in Aberdeen, studied English and History at the University of Aberdeen. She contested a by-election in South Ayrshire in 1939 as an Unionist. During the Second World War she worked in France and the Netherlands as a war correspondent for Kemsley Newspapers. She moved to America after marrying John Ashcraft, an advertising executive, and continued publishing, mostly historical romances, into her eighties. Appearing on BBC Radio 3's *Desert Island Discs* in June 1978, she chose as her favourite book *The Letters of Queen Victoria*.
Edward the Seventh: A Biography (1941)

GAXOTTE, Pierre (1895-1982), French historian and biographer, born in Revigny-su-Ornain, Meuse. He was successively a history teacher at the Lycée Charlemagne and a columnist for *Le Figaro*.

Louis XV's Century, 1933; *Louis XV and His Times* (1934); *Frederick the Great* (1941); *The Age of Louis XI* (1970)

GELARDI, Julia P., MA (1962-), American biographer, obtained an MA in History at Simon Fraser University, British Columbia, then embarked on a writing career with the emphasis on European royalty. She has contributed to *Royalty Digest, Atlantis*, and *European Royal History Journal*.
Born to Rule: Five Reigning Consorts, Granddaughters of Queen Victoria (2005); In *Triumph's Wake: Royal Mothers, Tragic Daughters and the Price They Paid for Glory* (2008); *From Splendor to Revolution: The Romanov Women, 1847-1928* (2011)

GEORGE, Anita.
Memoirs of the Queens of Spain, From the Period of the Conquest of the Goths to the Accession of her Present Majesty Isabella II (1850)

GERNSHEIM, Helmut (1913-95) and Alison (*née* Eames) (-1969), Anglo-German historians of photography, collectors and photographers. Helmut was born in Munich, and studied Art History at the Ludwig Maximilan University, Munich, then took up photography in 1934 on the suggestion of his brother who thought it would be a more suitable profession. After graduating from the State School of Photography, Munich, he started working as a colour photographer. Working in Australia at the start of the Second World War, he was interned as a 'friendly enemy alien' for a year in New South Wales with other German nationals. He was given British citizenship in 1946 and thereafter lived and worked in London for almost the rest of his life. He and his wife Alison, whom he married in 1946, became avid collectors and historians of old photographs, jointly writing and publishing several articles and then books on the subject. According to an obituary, 'His influence on historians of the future generation cannot be overestimated' (*Independent*, 5.8.1995)

Queen Victoria: A Biography in Word and Picture (1959); *Edward VII and Queen Alexandra: A Biography in Word and Picture* (1962)

GILLEN, Mollie, BA, Hon.D.Litt, OA (*née* Mollie Woolnough) (1908-2009) was an Australian historian, researcher, writer and novelist, born in Sydney, New South Wales. Her parents died within a few months of each other when she was aged ten, her father being a doctor who succumbed in the influenza epidemic after tending his patients during the First World War, and she was brought up by her grandparents. She was educated at Sydney University and graduated in 1930, and moved to England where she married a Canadian stationed in England, and they lived in Canada after the Second World War. She began writing while editing government journals as a federal government information officer in Ottawa, and became associate editor and staff writer for the Canadian women's magazine Chatelaine, publishing several articles on social problems in the community. She was active on the executive of the University Women's Club of Ottawa, becoming as first vice-president. After publishing a mystery novel and several short stories in various publications including *The Sunday Evening Post*, she began writing and researching non-fiction. Her research led her to write and publish books, several on various Canadian and Australian topics. She later moved back to London, returning to Toronto at the end of her life.

The Prince and His Lady [Edward, Duke of Kent and Mme de St Laurent] (1970); *Royal Duke: Augustus Frederick, Duke of Sussex (1773-1843)* (1976)

GILLINGHAM, John, Emeritus Professor of Medieval History at London School of Economics and Medieval History at the London School of Economics and Political Science. He is renowned as an expert on the Angevin empire and 12th century history.

Richard the Lionheart (1978); *Richard Coeur de Lion: Kingship, Chivalry and War in the Twelfth Century* (1994); *Richard I* (1999); *William II: The Red King* (2015)

GODKIN, G.S. (Georgina Sarah).
Life of Victor Emmanuel II, First King of Italy (1879)

GOLDSTONE, Nancy (1957-), American biographer, born in Illinois, studied History at Cornell University and worked in banking before becoming a full-time writer. She has written fiction and on rare book collecting as well as medieval history.
Four Queens: The Provençal Sisters who Ruled Europe (2007); *The Lady Queen: The Notorious Reign of Joanna I, Queen of Naples, Jerusalem, and Sicily* (2010); *The Rival Queens: Catherine de' Medici, her daughter Marguerite de Valois, and the Betrayal That Ignited a Kingdom* (2015)

GORE, John (1885-1983), British biographer, was educated at Oxford, and in the First World War he served with the Bedfordshire Yeomanry. After the war he wrote for various publications including the *Daily Telegraph*, *Evening Standard*, and *The Sphere*. He wrote and published several privately-printed biographies, and was commissioned to write the official personal biography of George V, for which he was awarded the 1941 James Tait Black Memorial Prize for Biography (see p. 246).
King George V (1941)

GOULD LEE, Arthur, MC (1894-1975), born in Lincolnshire, served in Royal Flying Corps in First World War, awarded MC in 1917. In 1941, as a senior Air Force Officer in Greece, he was introduced to members of Greek royal family. When the country was occupied by the Nazis, he was one of the first officers to escape and was subsequently awarded the Order of King George I with

Crossed Swords. As Chief of the Air Section of the British Allied Control Commission to Roumania, he met King Michael and Queen Helen. His experiences made him an authority on Balkan monarchy, reflected in his subsequent books.

The Royal House of Greece (1948); *Crown Against Sickle: The story of King Michael of Roumania* (1950); *The Empress Frederick writes to Sophie* (ed). (1955); *Helen, Queen Mother of Roumania* (1956)

GRAHAM, Caroline, British biographer, was royal commentator and former Women's Editor at *The Sun*, and subsequently American correspondent for the *Mail on Sunday*.

Camilla: The King's Mistress (1994); *Camilla: Her True Story* (2001); *Camilla: The Love Story* (2005)

GRAHAM, Eleanor (1896-1984), British author and book editor, was born in Walthamstow. She worked for an aid mission in Czechoslovakia, then became a publishing editor at Heinemann and Methuen, and reviewer of children's books for the *Sunday Times*. She became editor of the newly-established Puffin Books, Penguin's children's books series, in 1941, remained in the post until retirement in 1961 and published two novels and an anthology of children's verse under the imprint.

The Making of a Queen: Victoria at Kensington Palace (1940)

GRAHAM, Stephen (1884-1975), British biographer, journalist, and travel writer, and writer of fiction. Born in Edinburgh, he left school at the age of fourteen, and went to work in London as a clerk in the law courts and the civil service. After a holiday in Russia and brief return to England, he moved to Russia where he travelled around much of the empire, supporting himself by writing books about his experiences and by teaching English in Moscow. He was commissioned by Lord Northcliffe to write reports

from Russia for *The Times*, which provided a basis for further books. Returning to Britain, he enlisted in the Scots Guards, and saw action on the Western Front. He also travelled in the United States after the war. Altogether he wrote over thirty books, also including novels.
Peter the Great: A Life of Peter I of Russia Called the Great (1929); *Ivan the Terrible of Russia* (1932); *A Life of Alexander II, Tsar of Russia* (1935)

GREEN, Alice Stopford (Mrs J.R.) (1848-1929), Irish historian and politician. She married the historian John Richard Green in 1877, and completed his last book, *The Conquest of England*, which he left unfinished on his death after years of ill-health in 1883. For years she was actively involved in humanitarian causes, including the Congo Reform Association, and in a call for the reprieve of Sir Roger Casement, executed as a spy in 1916. She was a Senator of the Irish Free State, and the author of several works of Irish historical subjects written from a strongly nationalist viewpoint.
Henry the Second (1903)

GREEN, David Brontë (1910-85), British historian.
Queen Anne (1970)

GREGG, (Gary) Edward (1945-2008), was formerly Emeritus Professor of History at the University of South Carolina.
Queen Anne (2001)

GREGG, Pauline (1909-2006), British historian, born in London. After working as a secretary at Longman, she studied at the London School of Economics. During the Second World War she worked at the Ministry of Supply. According to her granddaughter, she was a dashing hostess, but found housework dull. 'Instead, she would

cycle every day to the Bodleian library, where she continued her research on the 17th century.' (*Guardian*, 5.4.2006)
King Charles I (1981)

GREVE, Tim (1928-86), Norwegian historian, biographer, civil servant, diplomat and newspaper editor, born in Bergen, studied history at the University of Oslo. He was attached to Ministry of Foreign Affairs from 1951 to 1974, served as Norwegian delegate to NATO and the Organisation for Economic Co-Operation and Development (OECD), and was later secretary for the Minister for Foreign Affairs. He was two years at the Norwegian embassy in Bonn, and later served as Secretary for the Standing Committee on Foreign Affairs of the Norwegian Parliament. He then returned to the Ministry of Foreign Affairs, as assistant secretary from 1966 to 1967 and deputy under-secretary of state from 1967 to 1974. He was Director for the Norwegian Nobel Institute from 1974 to 1977 and Secretary for the Norwegian Nobel Committee. He was chief editor for the newspaper Verdens Gang from 1978 to 1986. He wrote several biographies and histories, including one on the explorer Fridtjof Nansen, his wife's grandfather, and on World War Two in Bergen.
Haakon VII of Norway: Founder of a New Monarchy (1983)

GREY, Sir Charles (1804-70), biographer, was born in Northumberland, served in the army for several years and rose to the rank of general. He was MP for Wycombe from 1832 to 1837, after which he was appointed Private Secretary to Prince Albert in 1849 until the latter's death and thereafter to Queen Victoria until his death. At her request, he compiled an account of her husband's youth and early life to the end of the first year of their marriage. It was initially intended for private circulation, but then

published in order to avoid the possibility of 'garbled pirate editions'. A slightly revised edition was published in 1967.
The Early Years of His Royal Highness The Prince Consort (1867)

GRIBBLE, Francis (Henry) (1862-1946), British biographer.
The Comedy of Catherine the Great (1912); *The Court of Christina of Sweden and the Later Adventures of the Queen in Exile* (1913); *The Tragedy of Isabella II* (1913); *The Life of the Emperor Francis Joseph* (1914)

GRISTWOOD, Sarah, British biographer, born in Kent, read English at St Anne's College, Oxford. She has contributed to *The Times*, the *Guardian*, *The Daily Telegraph*, *Cosmopolitan*, *Sight and Sound* and *The New Statesman*, and presented or worked on radio and TV documentaries as well as helping to provide live coverage on Elizabeth II's Diamond Jubilee and other royal events.
Arbella: England's Lost Queen (2002); *Elizabeth and Leicester: Power, Passion, Politics* (2007); *The Ring and the Crown* [with Tracy Borman, Alison Weir and Kate Williams] (2011); *Blood Sisters: The Women Behind the Wars of the Roses* (2012)

GROUEFF, Stephane (1922-2006), Bulgarian writer and journalist, born in Sofia. He was a Law student at Geneva University when the communists seized power in Bulgaria in 1944, His father, Chief of Cabinet of Boris III, was executed the following year. He lived in exile in Switzerland, France and America, became a reporter for *Paris-Match*, and was its New York Bureau chief from 1958 to 1978. He worked for Radio Free Europe, was a contributor to the Bulgarian Service of the BBC, and returned briefly to Bulgaria after the fall of the communist regime. Having become an American citizen, he spent his last years there and died in Southampton, New York.

Crown of Thorns: The Reign of King Boris III of Bulgaria, 1918-1943 (1987)

GUY, John (1949-), British biographer and historian. He was born in Warragul, Victoria, Australia, but moved to Britain at the age of three and read History at Clare College, Cambridge, under Tudor historian G.R. Elton. Later a Fellow of and lecturer at Clare College, he also held posts at Bristol and St Andrews Universities, as well as writing extensively on the Tudor period for adults and children.

My Heart is My Own: the Life of Mary, Queen of Scots (2004); *Henry VIII and his Six Wives* (2008); **Henry VIII: The Quest for Fame** (2014); *The Children of Henry VIII* (2015)

H

HADLOW, Janice (Vivienne), BA (1957-), British television executive and writer, born in Lewisham, London. She graduated in History from King's College, London in 1978, and became a Postgraduate History Researcher Royal Holloway College, University of London, from 1978 to 1981. Five years later she became a production trainee with the BBC. From 1987 to 1989 she was a Radio 4 producer, then moved to television, working in the BBC Music and Arts department between 1993 and 1995, when she became joint head of the History department. In 1999 she moved to Channel 4 where she became Head of History, Art and Religion, returning to the BBC as Controller of BBC Four after five years where she commissioned programmes on history, science and religion. In 2008 she became controller of BBC Two.
The Strangest Family: The Private Lives of George III, Queen Charlotte and the Hanoverians (2014)

HAILE, Martin (real name Marie Halle).
Queen Mary of Modena: Her Life and Letters (1905); *James Francis Edward, The Old Chevalier* (1907)

HAINES, Roy (Martin), FRHistS, DLitt, DPhil, FSA, BA, MA, MLitt, British historian, read History at Worcester College, Oxford. He taught at St Michael's Preparatory School, Otford, and later Westminster School. He was also Assistant Editor of the Victoria County History of Oxfordshire. Moving to Canada in 1966, he lectured at

Mount Allison University, New Brunswick, and at Dalhousie University, where he became Professor of Medieval History. He was Canada Council Killam Senior Research Scholar from 1978 to 1980, and for a while worked at the Vatican Archives. On retirement he returned to live in England.

King Edward II: Edward of Caernarfon, his life, his reign, and its aftermath, 1284–1330 (2003)

HALL, Coryne, British historian, broadcaster and consultant specialising in the Romanovs and British and European royalty, was born in Ealing, West London and developed a fascination for Imperial Russia in childhood when she learnt that her great-grandmother was born in St Petersburg, an almost exact contemporary of Nicholas II. She is a regular contributor to *Majesty* magazine, *European Royal History Journal*, *Royal Russia* and *Royalty Digest Quarterly*, and to the Eurohistory Grand Dukes and Grand Duchesses series. She acted as consultant on the Danish TV royal documentaries and has appeared on British radio and TV, including *Woman's Hour, BBC South Today*, the documentary *Russia's Lost Princesses*, live coverage of the wedding of the Prince of Wales and Camilla Parker-Bowles for Canadian television and co-hosting live coverage of the Duke and Duchess of Cambridge's wedding. She was the last person to have a private audience with Queen Elizabeth The Queen Mother, for her biography of Grand Duchess Xenia.

Little Mother of Russia. A Biography of the Empress Marie Feodorovna 1847-1928 (1999); *Once a Grand Duchess: Xenia, Sister of Nicholas II* [with John Van der Kiste] (2002); *Imperial Dancer: Mathilde Kschessinska and the Romanovs* (2005); *Hvidøre: A Royal Retreat.* (2012); *Apapa: King Christian IX of Denmark and his descendants* [with Arturo E Beéche] (2014); *Princesses on the Wards. Royal Women in Nursing Through Wars and Revolutions* (2014)

HAMILTON, Elizabeth (1928-).
William's Mary: A Biography of Mary II (1972); *Henrietta Maria* (1976)

HANBURY-WILLIAMS, Sir John, GCVO, KCB, CMG (1859-1946), British army officer and writer. He attended the Royal Military College, Sandhurst, was commissioned into the 43rd Light Infantry in 1878, and was aide-de-camp to Lieutenant General Sir E Hamley in Egypt in 1882, fought in the battle of Tel-El-Kebir, and was mentioned in despatches. He served in South Africa during the Second Boer War, was Military Secretary to the Secretary of State for War from 1900 to 1903, and was the Canadian Governor-General's Secretary and Military Secretary from 1904 to 1909. During the First World War he was head of the British military mission with the Russian Stavka, was in charge of the British Prisoners of War Department at The Hague and then Berne from 1917 to 1918, retiring from the army the following year. He became a fierce opponent of Bolshevism, and was a founding member of the Liberty League which was formed in the United Kingdom after the War with a view to combat the spread of this political creed. In 1934 he was called as a witness in Princess Irina Alexandrovna's successful libel suit against Metro-Goldwyn-Mayer Pictures Ltd after the release of the film *Rasputin, the Mad Monk*.
The Emperor Nicholas II as I Knew Him (1922)

HARDIE, Frank (Martin) (1911-89), British political historian. He studied Modern History at Christ Church, Oxford, and was President of the Union in February 1933 when it debated the motion 'That this House will in no circumstances fight for its King and Country', a motion later alleged to have encouraged Adolf Hitler in his belief that Britain would not go to war against Germany.

Thereafter he was dogged with the epithet 'King and Country Hardie' which he believed prevented him from securing a permanent university post or a winnable parliamentary seat, and made a career writing political history instead.

The Political Influence of Queen Victoria, 1861-1901 (1935)

HARDING, Bertita (*née* Bertita Carla Camille Leonarz) (1902-71), German-American biographer. Born at Nuremberg, she and her family moved to Mexico City when she was aged three. After they settled in Monterrey, she took piano lessons as a child, and her parents planned her a career as a concert pianist. She accordingly had some success in this field when she went to the United States, married in 1926 and became an American citizen. In 1930 she decided to give up music and turn to writing, publishing several books, becoming a studio scriptwriter at Hollywood and lecturing throughout America. She moved back to Mexico after the death of her first husband in 1953. Her last books were biographies of Richard Wagner and Clara Schumann. A second marriage ended in divorce within less than a year, and seven months after a third, she died of breast cancer.

Phantom Crown: The Story of Maximilian and Carlota of Mexico (1935); *Royal Purple: The Story of Alexander and Draga of Serbia* (1935); *Golden Fleece: The Story of Franz Joseph and Elizabeth of Austria* (1937); *Farewell Toinette: The Story of Marie Antoinette* (1938); *Imperial Twilight: The Story of Karl and Zita of Hungary* (1939)

HARDMAN, John, British author, until retirement lecturer in Modern History at the University of Edinburgh.

Louis XVI: The Silent King (1994)

HARDY, Alan (1932-), British author.

Queen Victoria was Amused (1976); *The Kings' Mistresses* (1980)

HARRISON, Michael (real name Maurice Desmond Rohan) (1907–1991), British author, born in Milton, Kent, and attended the University of London. He served with British Military Intelligence during the Second World War. The majority of his output consisted of fiction, including pastiches of Conan Doyle's Sherlock Holmes and Edgar Allan Poe's Auguste Dupin, although he also wrote biographies and history, generally associated with London. His sole royal book 'perhaps dwells a little too fondly on the lurid side of the Duke's career and appears to take seriously the ludicrous suggestion that he was actually Jack the Ripper. Those who believe that can believe anything.' (St Aubyn, *Queen Victoria*, 630-1)
Clarence [Albert Victor, son of Edward VII] (1972)

HASLIP, Joan (1912-94), born in London, was brought up in England and Florence, and in 1929 was appointed sub-editor of *The London Mercury*. After writing two novels she turned to biography, her career as a writer briefly interrupted during the Second World War when she worked in the Italian section of the BBC. Her non-royal subjects included Charles Stewart Parnell, Lucrezia Borgia and Lady Hester Stanhope. She later settled and died in Florence.
The Lonely Empress: a Biography of Elizabeth of Austria (1965); *Imperial Adventurer* (1971) UK / *The Crown of Mexico: Maximilian and his Empress Carlota* (1972) US; *Catherine the Great* (1977); *The Emperor and the Actress: The Love Story of Emperor Franz Josef and Katharina Schratt* (1982); *Marie Antoinette* (1989)

HASWELL, Jock (1919-), British biographer and author who wrote works on espionage and military intelligence.
James II (1972); *The Ardent Queen: Margaret of Anjou and the Lancastrian Heritage* (1976)

HATCH, Alden R. (1898-1975), American biographer. Born in New York City, he wrote several books on the Popes, American presidents and other celebrities.
HRH Prince Bernhard of the Netherlands (1962); *The Mountbattens* (1965)

HATTON, Ragnhild (*née* Ragnhild Marie Hanssen) (1913-95), Anglo-Norwegian historian and biographer, born at Bergen, qualified at Oslo University, married an Englishman and settled in London. Regarded as Britain's leading historian on 17th and 18th century Europe of her time, she was Professor in International History at the London School of Economics from 1968 to 1980.
Charles XII of Sweden (1968); *Louis XIV and his World* (1972); *Louis XIV and Absolutism* (ed.) (1976); *Louis XIV and Europe* (ed.) (1976); *George I, Elector and King* (1978)

HAWKSLEY, Lucinda, British author, art historian, lecturer in 19th-century art history, and travel writer. A great-great-great-granddaughter of Charles Dickens, she is a patron of the Charles Dickens Museum in London.
The Mystery of Princess Louise, Queen Victoria's Rebellious Daughter (2013)

HAY, Marie (*née* Agnes Blanche Marie Hay-Drummond, married name Agnes Blanche Marie Baron von Hindenburg) (1873-1938), British writer, born in Perthshire, was brought up partly at her family's ancestral home of Dupplin Castle, Perthshire, and Paris. Her husband, a diplomat, was nephew of Paul von Hindenburg, later President of Germany, and his employment took them to several European capitals in turn.
The Winter Queen: Being the Unhappy History of Elizabeth Stuart Electress Palatine, Queen of Bohemia (1910)

HEALD, Tim, MA (1944-), British writer, born in Dorchester, Dorset, read Modern History at Balliol College, Oxford. His books include biographies and mystery novels, and he has also contributed to *The Spectator, Daily Telegraph, The Times, The Sunday Times, Daily Express,* and *Punch.*
The Duke - a Portrait of Prince Philip (1991); *Princess Margaret - a Life Unravelled* (2007)

HEDLEY, Olwen, FRSL (1912-98), Britih author, a former writer with the *Windsor, Slough and Eton Express* 1932-1939, was a VAD in Windsor during the Second World War. From 1947 to 1964 she was Assistant Librarian at Windsor Castle and wrote extensively about royalty and Windsor. For some years she lived in accommodation in the castle.
Queen Charlotte (1975)

HERBERT, Basil (1899-?).
King Gustave of Sweden (1938)

HERTHELIUS, Antoinette Ramsay *see* ROSVALL, Ted

HIBBERT, Christopher, MC, FRSL (real name Arthur Raymond Hibbert) (1924-2008), was born in Enderby, Leicestershire, and read History at Oxford. He acquired a new first name on his first day in uniform with the London Irish Rifles in 1943 when the Regimental Sergeant-Major, thinking he looked even younger than his eighteen years, barked at him, 'What have we got here? Christopher f***ing Robin?' The name accordingly stuck. (*Guardian,* 27.1.2009) He served as an infantry officer in in Italy during World War II, reached the rank of Captain, and was wounded twice. From 1945 to 1959 he was a partner in a firm of land agents and auctioneers, and began his career as a historian and royal biographer shortly before retiring to write full-time. The *New Statesman* called him 'a pearl of biographers'.

The Court at Windsor (Longmans, 1964); *Charles I* (1968); *George IV, Prince of Wales, 1762-1811* (1972); *George IV, Regent and King, 1811-1830* (1973); *Edward VII: A Portrait* (1976); *The Virgin Queen: Elizabeth I, Genius of the Golden Age* (1991); *George III: A Personal History* (1998); *Queen Victoria: A Personal History* (2000)

HICKS, Michael, FRS (1948-), British historian, studied at Bristol University, and was Professor of Medieval History and Head of Department at Winchester until his retirement. He became Emeritus Professor in 2014.

False, Fleeting, Perjur'd Clarence (1980); *Richard III and his Rivals: Magnates and their Motives in the War of the Roses* (1991); *Warwick the Kingmaker* (1998); *Richard III* (2000); *Edward V* (2003); *Edward IV* (2004); *Anne Neville: Queen to Richard III* (2006); *The Family of Richard III* (2015)

HIGHAM, Charles (1931-2012), British biographer, poet, editor of anthologies and film/theatre historian, was born in London. Several of his biographical works made sensational claims about the lives of their subjects, his life of the Duchess of Windsor commenting on her alleged unusual sexual practices learnt in the brothels of Peking and her affairs with Joachim von Ribbentrop and Count Galeazzo Ciano.

The Duchess of Windsor: The Secret Life (1988); *Elizabeth and Philip: The Untold Story of the Queen of England and her Prince* (1991)

HIGHAM, F.M.G. (Florence May Greir) (1896-1980).
King James the Second (1934); *Charles I: A Study* (1979)

HILLIAM, David (1930-2012), British author, born in East Coker, near Yeovil, Somerset, attended Cambridge, Oxford and the Sorbonne, Paris. He taught English at schools and colleges in Woking, and finally Bournemouth where he was Head of the English Department and Deputy Headmaster. In retirement he wrote books on the monarchy, history, local history and Shakespeare, and worked as a chief examiner for Cambridge University.

Kings, Queens, Bones and Bastards: Who's Who in the English Monarchy from Egbert to Elizabeth II (1998)*; Monarchs, Murders and Mistresses: A Book of Royal Days* (2000)*; Crown, Orb and Sceptre: The True Stories of English Coronations* (2001)

HILTON, Lisa (1974-), British historian, biographer and novelist, read English at New College, Oxford, then studied History of Art in Florence and Paris. She has contributed to newspapers and journals including *Vogue, Elle, Literary Review, Evening Standard* and *Daily Telegraph.*

The Real Queen of France: Athenais and Louis XIV (2002); *Queens Consort: England's Medieval Queens* (2008); *Elizabeth: Renaissance Prince* (2014)

HOEY, Brian, British biographer, began his career in broadcasting as a presenter on BBC Wales TV News, and as a TV commentator at royal investitures, weddings and funerals.

Anne, The Princess Royal (1989); *Mountbatten: The Private Story* (1994); *Her Majesty: 50 Regal Years* (2001); *Prince William* (2003); *Snowdon: Public Figure, Private Man* (2005); *Life with the Queen* (2006); *Zara Phillips: A Revealing Portrait of a Royal World Champion* (2007); *Her Majesty: 60 Regal Years* (2012)

HOLDEN, Angus (William Eden), 3rd Baron Holden and 4th Baronet Holden (1898-1951), British biographer, succeeded to the barony on his father's death in 1937. He worked in the Diplomatic Service as honorary attaché in

Madrid from 1922, and in Berlin from 1925. He stood as Liberal candidate for Tottenham North in the 1929 general election. Joining the Labour Party in 1945, he was a Speaker and Deputy Chairman in the House of Lords and in 1950 became Under-Secretary of State for Commonwealth Relations. He was unmarried and the title became extinct on his death. As well as biographies, he also wrote and co-wrote several travel books.

Uncle Leopold: A Life of the First King of the Belgians (1936); *Four Generations of our Royal Family* (1936)

HOLDEN, Anthony (1947-), British author and journalist, began his career as a journalist on the regional press, then on the *Sunday Times*, *Observer*, and *The Times*, where he was assistant editor in 1981-2. As a broadcaster he presented a weekly BBC Radio 4 chat show, *In the Air* during the 1980s and a TV documentary, *Charles at Forty*. The author of biographies of Shakespeare, Tchaikovsky and Laurence Olivier, translations of classical literature and books on poker and true crime, and classical music reviews for *The Observer*, he was for a time best known as a somewhat critical writer on the contemporary British royal family.

Charles: Prince of Wales (1979) UK / *Prince Charles* (1979) US; *Their Royal Highnesses, The Prince and Princess of Wales* (1981); *A Week In The Life Of The Royal Family* (1983); *Great Royal Front Pages: A Scrapbook of Historic Royal Events from Queen Victoria to Baby Prince William* (1983); *Anthony Holden's Royal Quiz* (1983); *Of Presidents, Prime Ministers And Princes* (1984); *The Queen Mother* (1985); *Charles: A Biography* (1988) UK / *King Charles III* (1988) US; *The Queen Mother: A 90th Birthday Tribute* (1990); *A Princely Marriage: Charles & Diana, the First Ten Years* (1991); *H.M. Queen Elizabeth the Queen Mother In Private* (1993); *The Tarnished Crown* (1993); *Diana: Her Life and Legacy* (1997); *Charles at Fifty* (1998)

HOLLISTER, C. (Charles) Warren, FRHS, PhD (1930-97), American author and historian, born in Los Angeles and graduated from Harvard University in 1951, served in the US Air Force during the Korean War. A specialist in English medieval history, and spent his academic career at the University of California, Santa Barbara, where he helped to found the History department, and retired in 1994. His research into King Henry I was set back at a late stage by the loss of his manuscript and note cards and his entire research library in the Santa Barbara fire of 1990, and left incomplete at the time of his death but was subsequently finished by his doctoral student Amanda Clark Frost and published in 2001.
Henry I (2001)

HOLME, Thea (*née* Dorothea Johnston), (1904-80), British actress and author, began her career as an actress in the West End, on TV and radio drama. She turned to writing after she had retired from the stage.
Prinny's Daughter (1976); *Caroline* (1979)

HOLT, Edgar (1900-75), British journalist and historian, studied at Christ Church, Oxford. After a spell as news editor at the BBC, he was Deputy Editor of *The Listener* from 1935 to 1937, Chief Assistant Editor of the *Liverpool Daily Post* from 1937 to 1947, and Assistant Editor of the *Daily Despatch* from 1947 to 1955, then Information Officer for the Federation of British Industries. He wrote several books on European history and accounts of the Boer War and Carlist Wars in Spain.
Plon-Plon: The Life of Prince Napoleon, 1822-1891 (1973)

HOOKHAM, Mary Ann.
The Life and Times of Margaret of Anjou, Queen of England and France: And of her Father Rene 'The Good', King of Sicily, Naples and Jerusalem (1872)

HOPKINSON, M.R. (Marie Ruan, *née* Marie Ruan Du Bois) (1878-1949), British biographer.
Anne of England: The Biography of a Great Queen (1934)

HOPKIRK, Mary (*née* Frances Mary Elizabeth Dempster) (1902-80), British biographer and local historian.
Queen Adelaide (1946), *Queen over the Water: Mary Beatrice of Modena, Queen of James II* (1953)

HOUGH, Richard (1922-99), British biographer and naval historian, served with the Royal Air Force during the Second World War, then worked as a publisher with Bodley Head and as managing director of Hamish Hamilton. Turning later to naval history, he met and became a friend of Lord Mountbatten, which resulted in his writing several books on the royal family.
Louis and Victoria: The first Mountbattens (1974); *Mounttbatten: Hero of our Time* (1980); *Edwina, Countess Mountbatten of Burma* (1983); *Born Royal: The Lives and Loves of the Young Windsors* (1988); *Edward and Alexandra: Their Public and Private Lives* (1992); *Victoria and Albert* (1996)

HOURMOUZIOS, Stelio (1914-84), Greek biographer, born in Limassol and educated in London. His father Christodoulos Hourmouzios was Athens correspondent of *The Times*, and Press Attaché to the Greek Minister in London. During the Second World War he was a gunner in the British army. At various times he also served in the press department of the Greek Embassy in London, and as secretary to George II of the Hellenes both in exile and on his return to Athens after the restoration of the Greek monarchy, and he performed a similar role for the last two sovereigns, Paul and Constantine II. He also served as Director of the Greek Information Office in London, and regularly published letters in *The Times* on matters relating

to Greek affairs, especially on the issue of the Elgin marbles in the British Museum.
No Ordinary Crown: A Biography of King Paul of the Hellenes (1972)

HOWARTH, Patrick (1916-2004), British writer, born in Calcutta, where his father was manager of an insurance company, he had visited every continent by the time he was six. He read English at St John's, Oxford, was with the Special Operations Executive (SOE) during the Second World War, and afterwards became Press Attaché at the British Embassy in Warsaw. He was appointed public relations officer for the Royal National Lifeboat Institution (RNLI) in 1953.
George VI (1987)

HOWARTH, T.E.B. (Thomas Edward Brodie), MC (1914–1988), British historian and schoolmaster, born in Rutherglen, Lanarkshire, read History at Clare College, Cambridge. He taught at Canford School, Dorset, and at Winchester College. During the Second World War he was commissioned in the King's (Liverpool) Regiment, reaching the rank of Brigade Major, and in 1945 joined the personal staff of Field Marshal Bernard Montgomery. After a return to teaching at Winchester, he was appointed headmaster of King Edward's School, Birmingham, in 1948, going back to Winchester as second master four years later. He was appointed High Master of St Paul's School, London, in 1965, Senior Tutor of Magdalene College, Cambridge, in 1973, and Headmaster of Campion International School in Athens in 1982.
Citizen King: The Life of Louis Philippe, King of the French (1962)

HUBATSCH, (Karl) Walther (1915-84), German historian and biographer, born in Königsberg, fought with the German army during the Second World War. After the

war he lectured in universities at Göttingen, Bonn, and also England, America and Sweden.
Frederick the Great (1975)

HUDSON, Katherine.
A Royal Conflict: Sir John Conroy and the Young Queen Victoria (1994)

HUGHES, Lindsey (1949–2007), British historian and biographer, and expert on 17th and 18th century Russia. She became a lecturer at the School of Slavonic and East European Studies, University College, London, in 1987, a Reader in 1992, and Professor of Russian history five years later.
Sophia, Regent of Russia 1657–1704 (1990); *Peter the Great: A Biography* (2002); *The Romanovs: Ruling Russia, 1613-1917* (2008)

HUISH, Robert (1777-1850), British biographer, historian, translator and novelist, born at Nottingham. A prolific if not well respected writer, he was described by the *Quarterly Review* as 'an obscure and unscrupulous scribbler', whose books often exhibited strong anti-Tory prejudices.
Memoirs of Her Late Royal Highness Princess Charlotte Augusta (1818); *The Public and Private Life of George III* (1821); *An Authentic History of the Coronation of George IV* (1821); *Memoirs of Caroline, Queen of Great Britain*, 2 vols (1821); *Authentic Memoir of His Royal Highness Frederick, Duke of York and Albany* (1827); *Memoirs of George IV*, 2 vols (1830); *The History of the Life and Reign of William IV, the Reform Monarch of England* (1837)

HUME, Martin A.S. (real name Martin Andrew Sharp), MA (1847-1910), British author and historian. Born in London, he took the name Martin Andrew Sharp Hume as a condition of receiving a legacy from a Spanish-English relative with the family name. He was educated in Madrid and at Cambridge University, later becoming a lecturer in Spanish History and Literature at Pembroke College, Cambridge, then examiner in Spanish and Lecturer at the University of London, and examiner at the University of Birmingham.

Philip II of Spain (1897); The *Courtships of Queen Elizabeth* (1898); *The Love Affairs of Mary, Queen of Scots* (1903); *The Wives of Henry VIII, And The Parts they Played in History* (1905); *Queens of Old Spain* (1906); *The Court of Philip IV: Spain in in Decadence* (1928)

HUNTER, Richard, *see* MacALPINE, Ida

HURD, Douglas (1930-), British politician and author. As Conservative MP for Mid-Oxfordshire and then Witney between 1974 and 1997, he was successively Home Secretary, Foreign Secretary and Secretary of State for Northern Ireland, as well as writer of political thrillers and biographies of Robert Peel and Benjamin Disraeli.

Elizabeth II: The Steadfast (2015)

HUTCHINS, Chris (1941-), British writer and broadcaster, journalist, born in Torquay. He worked briefly with *New Musical Express*, then formed a PR company representing various rock groups and performers, and subsequently worked for the *Sunday Mirror*, *Daily Express* and *Today*.

Sarah's Story [with Peter Thompson] (1992); *Diana's Nightmare: The Family* [with Peter Thompson] (1993); *Diana on the Edge: Inside the Mind of the Princess of Wales* [with Dominic Midgley] (1996); *Harry: The People's Prince* (2013)

HUTCHINSON, Harold F. (1900-?), biographer and historian.

Edward II: The Pliant King (1971); *Richard II: The Hollow Crown* (1979)

HUTCHISON, Harold.
Henry V (1967)

HUTTO, Richard Jay, American historian, is a former attorney who served as White House Appointments Secretary to the Carter Family and was Chairman of the Georgia Council for the Arts. He was for ten years an elected member of the City Council of Macon, Georgia, and a Knight of Malta and a Knight of the Holy Sepulchre. He has acted as historical consultant on TV documentaries and is an international lecturer on historical topics.
Crowning Glory: American Wives of Princes and Dukes (2007)

HUTTON, Ronald (1953-), British historian and biographer with special interests in the study of Early Modern Britain, British folklore, and Paganism. Born in Ootacamund, India, after returning home to England with his family he read History at Pembroke College, Cambridge, and Magdalen College, Oxford, then became Reader in History and later Professor at the University of Bristol in 1981.
Charles II, King of England, Scotland and Ireland (1989)

HYDE, H (Harford) Montgomery (1907-89) was born in Belfast, a distant cousin of Henry James, was a barrister, politician, author and biographer. He read History at Queen's University, Belfast, and Law at Magdalen College, Oxford, and was called to the bar in 1934, working in London and on the North East circuit. From 1935 to 1939, he was librarian and private secretary to the Marquess of Londonderry, hired specifically to research the family papers and write its history. He joined the British Army Intelligence Corps in 1939 as an Assistant Censor, and was then commissioned in the intelligence corps (MI6), engaged in counter-espionage work in the United States. He also served as Military Liaison and Security Officer in Bermuda from 1940 to 1941 and Assistant Passport Control Officer in New York from 1941 to 1942. He was with British Army Staff, USA from 1942 to 1944, and seconded to the Allied Control Commission for Austria until 1945 as a legal officer. After the war he became assistant editor of the *Law Reports* until 1947. He was Unionist MP for Belfast North from 1950 to 1959, until deselected by his party in 1959 after arguing in favour of the decriminalisation of homosexuality. He wrote several biographies of legal and political figures and books on spying, with particular emphasis on Oscar Wilde, his immediate circle and trials.

The Empress Catherine and Princess Dashkov (1935); *Mexican Empire: The History of Maximilian and Carlota of Mexico* (1946)

I

IBANEZ, Vicente Blasco (1867-1928), Spanish journalist, novelist and politician, born in Valencia, and studied Law at university but never practised. A militant republican partisan in his youth, he founded a newspaper, *El Pueblo* (*The Town,* or *The People*), which aroused the wrath of the government and led to his appearing in court on several occasions on charges of sedition. Increasingly angry at the state of affairs in Spain, he moved to Paris at the start of the First World War and spent the rest of his life there. A prolific writer of fiction, he also published a book on King Alfonso which was less of a biography and more of a diatribe, calling him 'a schemer' and urging in the last chapter, 'let him be brought to trial when Spain has resumed her normal existence!'
Alfonso XIII Unmasked: The Military Terror in Spain (1925)

IMBERT-TERRY, H.M. (Sir Henry Machu Imbert-Terry) (1854-1938), British author and public servant. He was born of a French family, his father Henri Imbert de la Terriere anglicising the family name after they moved to England. His plans to study at Oxford were thwarted by ill-health, and in 1878 he joined the *Morning Post* as music critic. He was director of a provincial touring opera company, and wrote and published several songs. He was elected an Honorary Fellow of the Royal Society of Literature and became a Member of the Council of the Royal Society of Literature, elected Vice-President in 1922 and Treasurer in 1931. He stood unsuccessfully four times

for parliamentary seats in Devon and Somerset as a Conservative and Unionist, was created a Baronet in 1917, and after settling at Strete Ralegh, Devon, he was made a Deputy Lieutenant for the county. During the First World War, he was put in charge of organising the reception and welfare of Dominion troops on leave in England, and made Chairman of the Overseas Forces Reception Committee. In addition to his historical interests, he wrote and published several novels and books on English literature.
A Misjudged Monarch: Charles Stuart (1917); *A Constitutional King: George the First* (1927)

IREMONGER, Lucille (*née* Lucille d'Oyen Parks) (1919-89) was born in Jamaica where her mother's family had lived for several generations, originally as slave-owning planters. After she married Tom Iremonger, Conservative MP for Ilford North from 1954 to 1974, she combined a writing career with politics as a Conservative member of the London County Council for Lambeth from 1961 to 1965. As a writer she published articles in journals, books on exotic cookery and travel, psychological studies and fiction.
Love and the Princess [Sophia, daughter of King George III] (1958)

IVES, Eric (William), OBE, BA, PhD (1931-2012), British historian and biographer, noted for his work on the Tudor period. Born in Essex, he studied History and Philosophy at Queen Mary College, London. During national service, he was commissioned into the Education Branch of the Royal Air Force as a pilot officer, later promoted to Flying Officer and to Flight Lieutenant. He then worked as a research assistant with the History of Parliament Trust, then as a Fellow at the Shakespeare Institute, University of Birmingham. Following this he was a lecturer in Modern History at the University of Liverpool, then at University of

Birmingham, where he was Professor of English History, Head of the Modern History Department and Dean of the Faculty of Arts until retirement in 1997. His books and theories on the life of Anne Boleyn provoked some debate with historian Retha Warnicke (q.v.), whose subsequent books set out to challenge his findings.

Anne Boleyn (1986); *The Life and Death of Anne Boleyn* (2004); *Lady Jane Grey: A Tudor Mystery* (2009)

J

JACKMAN, S.W. (Sydney Wayne, 'Toby') PhD (1925-2011), American historian, born in Fullerton, Orange County, California. He read Physics at Washington University, and then History at Harvard, where he remained as a junior teaching fellow before moving to Bates College in Maine. Returning to Canada, where he had been partly brought up, he became Professor of History at Victoria University.

Romanov Relations: The Private Correspondence of Tsars Alexander I, Nicholas I and the Grand Dukes Constantine and Michael with Their Sister Queen Anna Pavlovna, 1817-1855 (1969), ed; *A Stranger in The Hague: The Letters of Queen Sophie of the Netherlands to Lady Malet, 1842-1877; The People's Princess: A Portrait of HRH Princess Mary, Duchess of Teck* (1984)

JAMES, Paul, British author and journalist, contributor to various magazines including *Royalty* and *This England*.

Anne: The Working Princess (1987); *Diana: One of the Family* (1988); *Margaret: A Woman of Conflict* (1990); *Princess Alexandra* (1992); *Prince Edward: A Life in the Spotlight* [Edward, Earl of Wessex]

JAMES, Sir Robert Rhodes, (1933-99), British MP and historian, born in India, was a second cousin of the ghost-story writer M.R. James. He studied at Worcester College, Oxford, and from 1955 to 1964 he worked in the Clerk's Department of the House of Commons. In 1968, he became Director of the Institute for the Study of

International Organisation at the University of Sussex, then in 1973 Principal Officer in the Executive Office of Kurt Waldheim, Secretary General of the United Nations. From 1976 to 1992 he was Conservative MP for Cambridge, and a Parliamentary Private Secretary at the Foreign Office. He wrote several biographies and histories, mostly political, and edited an eight-volume edition of Sir Winston Churchill's speeches.

Albert, Prince Consort: A Biography (1983); *A Spirit Undaunted: The Political Role of George VI* (1998)

JANETSCHEK, Ottokar (1884-1963), Austrian author, born at Heiligenkreuz, was a railway track inspector who also wrote novels and biographies.

Emperor Franz Joseph (1953)

JAY, Sir Antony (Rupert), **CBE, CVO** (1930-) British writer, broadcaster and director, read Classics and Comparative Philology at Magdalene College, Cambridge. After national service in the Royal Signals he joined BBC Television in 1955, helping to launch the current affairs programme *Tonight* of which he was Editor from 1962 to 1963, and becoming Head of Television Talk Features from 1963 to 1964. He then became a freelance writer and producer, was a partner in the Video Arts training film production company with John Cleese, and wrote the TV documentaries *Royal Family* and *Elizabeth R: A Life in the Year of the Queen*. He was co-writer with Jonathan Lynn of the BBC political situation comedy series *Yes, Minister* and *Yes, Prime Minister*.

Elizabeth R: The Role of the Monarchy Today (1992)

JENKS, Edward (1861-1939), British jurist and writer on law. He studied Law at King's College, Cambridge, was called to the bar in 1887 and held various academic posts at universities in Cambridge, Oxford, Manchester and Melbourne.

Edward Plantagenet (Edward I), The English Justinian: Or, The Making of the Common Law (1901)

JEPHSON, Patrick (1956-), British biographer, Royal Naval officer and former Private Secretary to Diana, Princess of Wales, who resigned shortly before the divorce in 1996. His book of his account of eight years of royal service, decision to publish was 'deeply deplored' in a joint statement by Queen Elizabeth II and the Prince of Wales.

Shadows of a Princess (2000)

JERROLD, Clare (*née* Clare Armstrong Bridgman) (1861-1936), British biographer, born at Paddington, London. Her husband Walter was also a biographer, newspaper editor and author of works on regional England.

Victoria the Good: True Stories of the Home Life of Queen-Empress, Wife and Mother (1901); *The Early Court of Queen Victoria* (1912); *The Married Life of Queen Victoria* (1913); *The Story of Dorothy Jordan* (1914); *Stories of the Kaiser and his Ancestors* (1915); *The Widowhood of Queen Victoria* (1916)

JOBSON, Robert (1964-), British biographer, born in Great Wakeling, Essex, dubbed the 'Godfather of Royal Reporting' by *Wall Street Journal*. He has reported on the royal family since 1991 as royal correspondent for the *Daily Express*, *The Sun* and *News of the World*, and been Royal Editor of *London Evening Standard*. He is a regular broadcaster on TV in Britain and America on royal events, and a contributor to *Forbes Magazine* in addition to writing several biographies about the family of Charles, Prince of Wales.

Diana: A Closely Guarded Secret [with Ken Wharfe] (2002); *William's Princess* (2006); *Harry's War: The True Story of the Soldier Prince* (2008); *William and Kate: The Love Story – A*

Celebration of the Wedding of the Century (2010); *The New Royal Family: Prince George, William and Kate, The Next Generation* (2013); *The Future Royal Family: William, Kate and the Modern Royals* [with Arthur Edwards] (2015)

JOHN, Katherine (-1984).
The Prince Imperial (1939)

JOHNSON, Paul (Bede) (1928-), born at Manchester, read History at Oxford, where one of his tutors was historian A.J.P. Taylor. He was successively a member of the King's Royal Rifle Corps and then the Royal Army Educational Corps. He became the Paris correspondent of the *New Statesman*, then its lead writer, deputy editor and editor from 1965 to 1970. Later his political views moved towards the right, and he was a columnist for the *Spectator* and the *Daily Mail*, as well as contributing book reviews and other material to the *Daily Telegraph*, *New York Times*, *Wall Street Journal* and other publications.
Elizabeth I: a Study in Power and Intellect (1974); *The Life and Times of Edward III* (1974)

JOHNSTONE, Hilda (1881-1961), British historian, studied History at the University of Manchester, and later lectured there and at King's College, London. She held the Chair of History at Royal Holloway College from 1922 to 1942. In retirement she worked as archivist to the Bishop of Chichester. She was the sister-in-law of T.F. Toft (q.v.).
Edward of Caernarvon 1284-1307 (1946)

JONAS, Klaus W., PhD, German biographer, studied Modern Languages and Literature at universities in German and Switzerland, was joint American curator of Thomas Mann Archive, Berlin, and Professor in Germanic Language and Literature, Pittsburgh.

The Life of Crown Prince William (1961)

JORDAAN, Bee (Beryl Constance) (1915-90), born in China, settled in South Africa where she worked as a librarian, then retired to Denmark.
Dearest Affie: Alfred, Duke of Edinburgh [with John Van der Kiste] (1984)

JORDAN, Ruth (*née* Ruth Cohen) (1921-94), was born in Haifa, Israel. After studying at Jerusalem, in 1946 she read French and Phonetics at University College, London. She then joined the Hebrew Section of the BBC World Service as a broadcaster and programme organiser, and later turned to journalism, research and writing biographies.
Sophie Dorothea [Consort of George I] (1971); *Princess Margaret and her Family* (1974)

JUDD, Denis, FRHistS (1938-), born in Northamptonshire, read Modern History at Oxford and London University. He became Head of History, and then Professor Emeritus of Imperial and Commonwealth History, at the London Metropolitan University, and subsequently Professor to New York University at their London Campus. He wrote books on 19th and 20th century British and British Empire history, and contributed articles and reviews to newspapers and journals including *BBC History Magazine* for which he writes and reviews. He has reviewed extensively in academic journals *History, The Journal of Contemporary British History, South Asia* and the *Journal of Imperial and Commonwealth History*, and the national press, including *Times Literary Supplement, Guardian, New Statesman, Literary Review, Sunday Telegraph, Financial Times, Independent and Daily Telegraph*. He has contributed articles and features to various publications including the *International Herald Tribune* and the part-works *A History of the English-Speaking Peoples* and *The British Empire*, and to *History*

Today, The Mail on Sunday, BBC History Magazine, Sunday Telegraph, New Statesman, New Society, Financial Times. He wrote documentaries for **BBC** Radio, and was a regular presenter, consultant and major interviewee for radio and television programmes.

The House of Windsor (1973); *The Life and Times of George V* (1973); *Edward VII: A Pictorial Biography* (1975); *Eclipse of Kings: European Monarchies in the Twentieth Century* (1976); *Prince Philip: A Biography* (1980); *George VI, 1895-1952* (1982)

JUDTMANN, Fritz (1899-1968), Austrian architect, stage designer and author. His book on the tragedy of Crown Prince Rudolf was based on family papers in the possession of the grandson of Count Eduard Taaffe, a leading government minister at the time.

Mayerling: The Facts Behind the Legend (1971)

JULLIAN, Philippe (1920-77), French author and painter, was born in Bordeaux. He was best known as an artist, but also wrote biographies, studies of art and fiction.

Edward and the Edwardians (1967)

JUNOR, Penny (Penelope Jane) (1949-), British author, journalist and TV presenter, born in Leatherhead, Surrey, read History at St Andrews University. Daughter of *Sunday Express* Editor John Junor, as a journalist she worked on the *Evening Standard* and wrote a column for *Private Eye*. As a TV presenter she fronted the consumer programme *4 What It's Worth* from 1982 to 1984, and *The Travel Show* for nine years.

Diana, Princess of Wales (1982); *Charles, Prince of Wales* (1987 and 1998); *Charles and Diana: Portrait of a Marriage* (1991); *The Firm: The Troubled Life of the House of Windsor* (2005); *Prince William: The Man Who Will Be King; Prince Harry: Brother, Soldier, Son* (2014)

K

KEATES, Jonathan, FRSL (1946-), British writer, born in Paris. He read History at Magdalen College, Oxford, and taught English at the City of London School from 1974 to 2013, retiring to concentrate on his work as Chairman of the Venice in Peril Fund. He has written several biographies and books on travel.
William III and Mary II: Partners in Revolution (2015)

KEAY, Douglas.
Elizabeth II: Portrait of a Monarch (1991)

KELLY, Amy (1877-1962), American teacher and biographer. She was born in Port Clinton, Ohio, graduated from Oberlin College, was Professor of English at Lake Erie and Wellesley College, and Headmistress at Bryn Mawr School, Baltimore, retiring from teaching in 1943. Throughout her working career she spent much of her spare time researching 12th century documents, and travelling throughout Europe and the Holy Lands each summer, then devoted the next seven years to writing and rewriting her book, an immediate bestseller.
Eleanor of Aquitaine and the Four Kings (1952)

KENDALL, Paul Murray (1911-73), American biographer, historian, playwright, novelist and poet, born in Philadelphia. He studied at University of Virginia, and in 1959 became a Professor of English at Ohio University, where his teaching was concerned mostly with Renaissance writing and Shakespeare. His sympathetic biography of Richard III, which he wrote after being awarded a Ford Foundation Fellowship, was highly acclaimed on publication and remains one of the most well-regarded biographies of the King.

Richard III (1955); *Warwick the Kingmaker* (1957); *Louis XI: The Universal Spider* (1971)

KERR, Mark Edward Frederic, CB, CVO (1864-1944), British officer and writer. He joined the Royal Navy in 1877, served in the Naval Brigade in Egypt and the Sudan, then became Naval Attaché in Italy, Austria, Turkey and Greece. In 1913 he was appointed head of the British Naval Mission to Greece, then became Commander-in-Chief of the Royal Hellenic Navy, a post that enabled him to resolve King Constantine to remain neutral during the First World War. Having learned to fly in 1914, he was the first British flag officer to become a pilot. He was Commander-in-Chief of the British Adriatic Squadron from 1916 to 1917, became involved in helping to create the Royal Air Force during the last stages of the war in Britain and was Deputy Chief of the Air Staff at the Air Ministry. He retired from the RAF in 1918 to become a writer, publishing poetry, books on naval matters, and a biography of Nelson.

Prince Louis of Battenberg: Admiral of the Fleet (1934)

KING, Edmund, MA, PhD (Cantab), FSA, took his bachelor and doctoral degrees at the University of Cambridge. A specialist in English medieval history, particularly on the reign of Stephen, he joined the History department at Sheffield in 1966 and was later Emeritus Professor. He has held visiting fellowships at the Huntington Library, USA, and at All Souls College, Oxford, and taught also at the universities of Connecticut and Michigan in the USA.

The Anarchy of King Stephen's Reign (ed.) (1994); *King Stephen* (2010)

KING, Greg, American biographer, historian and journalist. He has contributed to various journals including *Atlantis*, *Majesty* magazine, *Royalty Digest Quarterly*, and *Imperial Russian Journal*.

The Last Empress: The Life and Times of Alexandra Feodorovna, Tsarina of Russia (1995); *The Mad King: A Biography of Ludwig II of Bavaria* (1997); *The Fate of the Romanovs* [with Penny Wilson] (2003); *Twilight of Splendor: The Court of Queen Victoria During Her Diamond Jubilee Year* (2007); *The Court of the Last Tsar: Pomp, Power and Pageantry in the Reign of Nicholas II* (2008); *The Resurrection of the Romanovs: Anastasia, Anna Anderson, and the World's Greatest Royal Mystery* [with Penny Wilson] (2010); *Wallis: The Uncommon Life of the Duchess of Windsor* (2011); *The Assassination of the Archduke: Sarajevo 1914 and the Murder that Changed the World* [with Sue Woolmans] (2013)

KINGSFORD, Charles Lethbridge (1862-1926), historian and authority on the 15th century, was born at Ludlow. He studied Classics and Modern History at St John's, Oxford, and was a member of the editorial staff of the *Dictionary of National Biography*, contributing over four hundred articles, as well as several to the *Encyclopaedia Britannica*. He was an examiner and then assistant secretary in the Education Department from 1890 to 1912. During the First World War he was a special constable in London, and private secretary at the Ministry of Pensions from 1917 to 1918. In addition to several books, he was also a contributor to the *Camden Miscellany*, *English Historical Review*, and *Cambridge Medieval History*.

Henry V: The Typical Medieval Hero (1923)

KISHLANSKY, Mark, PhD, MA (1948-2015), American historian and biographer, was born in Brooklyn, New York. He studied at the State University of New York, and taught at the University of Chicago, then became a Professor at Harvard University and was Associate Dean of the Harvard Faculty of Arts and Sciences. He was editor of the *Journal of British Studies* from 1984 to 1991, and Editor-in-Chief of *History Compass* from 2003 to 2009.
Charles I: An Abbreviated Life (2014)

KLAUSEN, Inger-Lise, *see* ROSVALL, Ted

KNAPTON, Ernest John (1902-81), American historian, read History at University of British Columbia, Oxford and Harvard Universities. He was a Professor at Wheaton College, Massachusetts, from 1931 to 1969, and Professor Emeritus from 1969 to 1989, and regarded as the major Napoleonic scholar in America.
Empress Josephine (1964)

KNIGHT, Roger, naval historian, museum curator and historian, has worked in curatorial and research roles at the National Maritime Museum and the Greenwich Maritime Institute, University of Greenwich. He was also a Senior Research Fellow at the Institute of Historical Research, University of London.
William IV: A King at Sea (2015)

KOCH, Adolf.
Prince Alexander of Battenberg: Reminiscences of his Reign in Bulgaria (1887)

KOLLANDER, Patricia (1959-), American historian and biographer, became a member of the faculty at Florida Atlantic University in 1991, and served as Department Chair from 2007 to 2013. Her research, writing and

teaching interests included modern Germany, modern Russia, World War II, and the history of European women. She was the author of several books and a regular contributor *German History, European Review of History, Yearbook of German-American Studies* and *The Historian*.
Frederick III: Germany's Liberal Emperor (1995)

KORNEVA, Galine, *see* BEECHE, Arturo E.

KROLL, Maria.
Letters from Liselotte, Elizabeth Charlotte, Princess Palatine and Duchess of Orléans (ed.) (1970); *Sophie, Electress of Hanover: A Personal Portrait* (1973)

KURENBERG, Joachim (real name Eduard Joachim von Reichel) (1892-1954), narrator and playwright, but was mainly through biographical novels known to important personalities of the 19th and 20th centuries. He studied art history at the universities of Koenigsberg, Berlin, Zurich and Heidelberg. During the First World War he was an attaché in Constantinople Opel, Rome and Vienna. He worked as a dramatist and was a freelance writer since 1930. Since he refused to write articles in praise of National Socialism, journals were forbidden to publish his material, and in 1935 he settled in Switzerland. Because of his well-known dislike of the Nazi regime, on a visit to Italy during the Second World War, he was arrested and imprisoned in Landsberg from 1943 to 1945. After being released he spent the rest of his life in Hamburg.
The Kaiser: A Life of Wilhelm II, last Emperor of Germany (1954)

KURTZ, Harold (-1972), German biographer and historian, came from a Stuttgart family, and settled in England in 1933 after Hitler's rise to power. During the Second World War he worked in the German section of the BBC, and became a British subject after the war. He contributed regular book reviews to *The Times* until shortly before his death.

The Empress Eugenie, 1826-1920 (1965); *The Second Reich: Kaiser Wilhelm and his Germany* (1970)

L

LACEY, Robert (1944-), British historian and biographer and commentator on TV for royal events, began as a journalist on the *Illustrated London News* and later *Sunday Times*. His second wife Lady Jane Rayne, daughter of the 8th Marquess of Londonderry, was maid of honour at Elizabeth II's Coronation.

The Life and Times of Henry VIII (1972); *Majesty: Elizabeth II and the House of Windsor* (1977); *Princess* [Diana, Princess of Wales] (1982); *God Bless Her! Queen Elizabeth, the Queen Mother* (1987); *Grace* [Grace Kelly, Princess of Monaco] (1994); *The Queen Mother's Century* (1999); *Royal: Her Majesty Queen Elizabeth II* (2002) UK/*Monarch, Life and Reign of Elizabeth II* (2002) US; *A Brief Life of the Queen* [Elizabeth II] (2012)

LAMONT-BROWN, Raymond, historian and lecturer in Departments of Continuing Education, Universities of London and St Andrews.

Edward VII's last loves: Alice Keppel & Agnes Keyser (1998); *John Brown, Queen Victoria's Highland servant* (2000); *Royal Poxes and Potions: The Lives of the Royal Physicians, Surgeons and Apothecaries* (2001)

LANE, Peter.

The Queen Mother (1979); *Prince Philip* (1980); *Princess Michael of Kent* (1986); *Prince Charles: A Study in Development* (1988)

LANGDON-DAVIES, John, *see* NADA, John

LEE, Sir Sidney (real name Solomon Lazarus Lee) (1859-1926), British biographer and critic, born in London, read Modern History at Balliol College, Oxford. He was also Professor of English Literature and Language at East London College from 1913 to 1924. In 1883 he became Assistant Editor of the *Dictionary of National Biography*, joint Editor in 1890, and next year succeeded Leslie Stephen as Editor. He wrote about 800 articles, mostly on Elizabethan authors and statesmen, and his sister became a fellow contributor. His article on Queen Victoria was published in the third supplementary volume of the *Dictionary* in October 1901, and substantially rewritten for publication when published as a separate volume the following year. In 1912 a further supplementary volume of the *Dictionary* included his article on King Edward VII, which was laced with critical comments on its subject, his intellectual shortcomings, and suggesting among other things that he possessed 'no conception of any readjustment of the balance of European power'. As a result of the controversy he was invited to study official papers in the Royal Archives, Windsor, and when he admitted he had not done the King full justice, he was invited to write the official biography. The task took him over ten years. According to Virginia Cowles (q.v.), 'the book is a mine of detail and information, but the King remains lifeless…a curiously contradictory and lethargic work.' (*Edward VII and his Circle*, 364) He only lived long enough to see the publication of the first volume of his biography, covering the King's life as Prince of Wales, but died the following year. He had drafted several chapters and planned the composition of the second volume which was completed by his assistant, Mr S.F. Markham.

Queen Victoria: A Biography (1902); *King Edward VII, A Biography, Vol. 1, From Birth to Accession* (1925); *King Edward VII, A Biography, Vol. 2, The Reign* (1927)

LEGGE, Edward (-1927), British author. He was initially a war correspondent for the Irish Times during the Franco-Prussian war, then studied law at Middle Temple, and was called to the Bar in 1875. He also worked on the staff of the *Morning Post* and *Whitehall Review*, and was editor of *Life*. He wrote several titles on the royal family, his books on Edward VII being partly a defence against Sidney Lee's (q.v.) critical account in the *Dictionary of National Biography*. According to an obituary, he died in London 'at an advanced age' (*The Times*, 22.4.1927).

The Empress Eugénie, 1870-1910: Her Majesty's Life Since "The Terrible Year" Together with the Statement of her Case, The Emperor's Own Story Of Sedan, An Account of his Exile and Last Days (1910); *King Edward in his True Colours* (1912); *More about King Edward* (1913); *The Public and Private Life of Kaiser William II* (1915); *King Edward, the Kaiser and the War* (1917); *King George V and the Royal Family* (1918); *Our Prince: Sailor, Soldier, and Empire Ambassador* (1921)

LESLIE, Anita (1914-85), Anglo-Irish biographer and writer, was a first cousin once removed of Sir Winston Churchill.

Mrs Fitzherbert: A Life (1960)

LEVER, Evelyne, French historian and writer. She was a research engineer at CNRS (*Centre national de la recherche scientifique*, The French National Centre for Scientific Research (CNRS), prior to writing French 18th-century history. Several of her books, including studies of Louis XVI and Louis XVIII, have yet to be published in English.

Marie Antoinette: The Last Queen of France (2001)

LICENCE, Amy, British biographer with a special interest in women's lives in the medieval and early modern period, the Bloomsbury Group and Post-Impressionism, and writer of literary fiction. She has contributed to the *Guardian*,

Times Literary Supplement, *New Statesman*, *BBC History Magazine*, *The English Review*, and *The London Magazine*, and has appeared on BBC radio and TV in *The Real White Queen and her Rivals* documentary.

Anne Neville: Richard III's Tragic Queen (2013); *In Bed With the Tudors: The Sex Lives of a Dynasty from Elizabeth of York to Elizabeth I* (2013); *The Six Wives and many Mistresses of Henry VIII: The Women's Stories* (2014); *Cicely Neville: Mother of Kings* (2014); *Richard III: The Road to Leicester* (2014); *Elizabeth of York: The Forgotten Tudor Queen* (2014); *Edward IV and Elizabeth Woodville: A True Romance* (2015); *25 Royal Babies that Changed the World: A History, 1066 to the Present* (2015)

LICHTERVELDE, Comte Louis de (1889-1959), Belgian historian and politician, was chief of staff to Charles Broqueville, Belgian Prime Minister during the First World War, and cabinet secretary.
Leopold of the Belgians (1929)

LIEVEN, Dominic (1952-), an authority on Russian history, read History at Christ College, Cambridge, and was a Kennedy Scholar at Harvard University.
Nicholas II (1993)

LINCOLN, W. Bruce, PhD (1938-2000), American historian and biographer, born in Suffield, Connecticut. He read History at College of William and Mary, taught at Memphis State University from 1966 to 1967 and at Northern Illinois University from 1967 to 1999, and wrote extensively on Russian history.
Nicholas I, Emperor and Autocrat of all the Russias (1978); *The Romanovs: Autocrats of All the Russias* (1981)

LINDSAY, Philip (1906–1958), Australian biographer, educated at Brisbane, came from Australia to England in the 1930s. The majority of his books were novels but he also wrote biographies, and worked in the film industry as a screenplay writer for and technical adviser on historical pictures.

King Richard III: A Chronicle (1933); *King Henry V* (1934); *Crowned King of England: The Coronation of King George VI in History and Tradition* (1937); *Kings of Merry England from Edward the Confessor 1042-1066 to Richard the Third 1483-1485* (1936)

LINKLATER, Eric, CBE (1899-1974), Scottish writer, was born at Dounby, Orkney. His study of Medicine at Aberdeen University was briefly interrupted by service with the army during the First World War, but after resuming the subject changed to reading English instead. He then became assistant to the Professor of English at Aberdeen, and some years later Rector. Thereafter he became a prolific author, writing novels, non-fiction, plays, autobiographies and books for children, and travelled widely throughout the world. He was Assistant Editor with *The Times of India* in Bombay from 1925 to 1927, and stood as a Scottish Nationalist candidate in a by-election at East Fife in 1933 in which he came last. He was an officer in the Territorial Army, and a Major in the Royal Engineers from 1939 to 1941, commanding the Orkney fortress, then spent the rest of the Second World War with the Directorate of Public Relations at the War Office.

Ben Jonson and King James: Biography and Portrait (1923); *Mary Queen of Scots* (1934); *The Prince in the Heather* [Bonnie Prince Charlie] (1965)

LISTOWEL, Judith (Judith de Marffy-Mantuano, later Judith Hare, Countess of Listowel) (1903-2003), was born in Kaposvar, Hungary, and was the first woman political editorial writer in Hungary. During World War Two she was a civilian lecturer to the forces, then became publisher

of the weekly *East Europe and Soviet Russia*. She wrote several works of fiction and non-fiction.
A Habsburg Tragedy: Crown Prince Rudolf (1978)

LOACH, Jennifer (1945-95), born at Darlington, read History at St Hilda's College, Oxford, became a Research Fellow and Lecturer of Somerville College, and in 1974 a Tutorial Fellow of Somerville and a University Lecturer. For several years she also held a Lecturership at Corpus Christ College. She wrote extensively on the Tudor period, and at the time of her early death she was writing a biography of Edward VI, completed by George Bernard.
Edward VI (1999)

LOADES, David, FSA (1934-), British historian and biographer specialising in the Tudor era. After military service in the Royal Air Force from 1953 to 1955, he read History at Cambridge University, taught at the universities of St Andrews and Durham, and from 1980 until 1996 he taught at the University of Wales, where he later became Emeritus Professor. He was Honorary Research Professor at the University of Sheffield from 1996 until 2008. From 1993 until 2004 he acted as Literary Director of the John Foxe Project at the British Academy, and later Honorary Member of the History Faculty at the University of Oxford.
The Reign of Mary Tudor (1979); *Mary Tudor: A Life* (1989); *The Politics of Marriage: Henry VIII and his Queens* (1994); *Elizabeth I* (2003); *Elizabeth I: The Golden Reign of Gloriana* (2003); *Intrigue and Treason: The Tudor Court 1547–1558* (2004); *Mary Tudor: The Tragical History of the First Queen of England* (2006); *Henry VIII: Court, Church and Conflict* (2007); *The Princes of Wales* (2008); *The Fighting Tudors* (2009); *The Tudor Queens of England* (2009); *Henry VIII: King and Court* (2009); *Henry VIII* (2011); *The Boleyns* (2011); *The Tudors: History of a Dynasty* (2012); *Mary Rose: Tudor Princess, Queen of*

France. The Extraordinary Life of Henry VIII's Sister (2012); *Catherine Howard: The Adulterous Wife of Henry VIII* (2012); *Jane Seymour: Henry VIII's Favourite Wife* (2013)

LOCKRIDGE, Norman.
Lese Majesty: The Private Lives of the Duke and Duchess of Windsor (1952)

LOLIEE, Frederic (1856-1915), French biographer and journalist, known especially for his works of literary criticism.
The Life of an Empress (Eugenie de Montijo) (1908)

LONGFORD, Elizabeth (*née* Elizabeth Harman, later Countess of Longford) (1906-2002), a great-niece of Joseph Chamberlain and first cousin once removed of Neville Chamberlain, was an undergraduate at Oxford. She married Frank Pakenham, later 7th Earl of Longford, in 1931, and their eight children included Antonia Fraser (q.v.). After an unsuccessful attempt to stand for Parliament as a Labour candidate, she allegedly became a writer because she was so frequently telephoned by journalists for advice on parenthood that Lord Beaverbrook asked her to write a column in the *Sunday Express* in the 1950s. Her husband advised her to devote her talents to history and biography. Her biography of Queen Victoria was awarded the James Tait Black Memorial Prize for Biography (see p. 246), and for some years was regarded as the standard life; in the words of fellow biographer Giles St Aubyn (q.v.), Lady Longford was 'the envy and despair of those who venture to follow her' (*Royalty Digest*, November 1991).
Victoria R.I. (1964) UK/*Queen Victoria: Born to Succeed* (1964) US; *The Royal House of Windsor* (1974); *Elizabeth R: A Biography* (1983); *The Oxford Book of Royal Anecdotes* (1986); *Darling Loosy: Letters to Princess Louise 1856-1939* (ed.) (1991);

Royal Throne: The Future of the Monarchy (1993); *Queen Victoria* (1999)

LONGUEVILLE, Thomas (1844-1922), British biographer, born in Shropshire, and educated at Christ Church, Oxford. He served as a cornet in the Shropshire Yeomanry from 1865 to 1868, and later served as a Justice of the Peace in the county. He also wrote fiction and contributed to the *Saturday Review* and other periodicals.
The Adventures of King James II of England (1904)

LONYAY, Count Carl, Hungarian biographer, nephew of Elemér Edmund Lónyay, Count and Prince of Nagy-Lónya and Vásáros-Namény, who married Princess Stephanie of Belgium, the widow of Crown Prince Rudolf of Austria-Hungary and died in 1946, the year after her. Count Carl inherited his titles and also the family papers, which he used as a basis for his book, which is however regarded as lacking in objectivity in view of his evident antipathy towards the Habsburg dynasty.
Rudolf: The Tragedy of Mayerling (1950)

LOTH, David (Goldsmith) (1899-1988), American author, born in Illinois. He wrote several biographies, including lives of the Brownings and Woodrow Wilson, and extensively on sexual behaviour and erotica.
Royal Charles, Ruler and Rake (1931); *Philip II of Spain* (1932)

LUCAS, Reginald (Jaffray) (1865-1916), British politician and author. After studying at Trinity College, Cambridge, he joined the army, serving with the 3rd Battalion of the Hampshire Regiment. After retiring with the rank of Captain, he was Private Secretary to two Unionist Chief Whips at Westminster, then served as Conservative MP for Portsmouth from 1900 to 1906. After standing down he turned to writing, contributing to various journals as well as publishing non-fiction and novels. Having suffered for some time from a painful disease, he committed suicide by shooting himself.

George II and his Ministers (1910)

LUDWIG, Emil (real name Emil Cohn) (1861-1948), German biographer and playwright, born in Breslau, whose subjects included Goethe, Napoleon, Bismarck and Abraham Lincoln. His work on ex-Emperor William II, which was extremely hostile to his mother the Empress Frederick, was largely responsible for persuading Sir Frederick Ponsonby (q.v.) to edit and publish *Letters of the Empress Frederick*. After the latter's appearance, Ludwig admitted that had it been published earlier, he would have made substantial changes in his own work. In 1932 he took Swiss citizenship and spent the rest of his life in America and Switzerland.

Kaiser Wilhelm II (1926)

M

MacALPINE, Ida (*née* Wertheimer) (1899-1974), and her son Richard Alfred HUNTER (1923-81), German psychiatrists. As a young woman she worked in Berlin as a physician and medical officer. In 1933 the family moved to England, where they had family ties. She devoted the rest of her life to the science and art of psychological medicine. After they had collaborated on a history of English psychiatry, they became fascinated by the illness of King George III. Their researches concluded that he was not mad but suffered from a neurological disorder that might have been porphyria.
George III and the Mad-Business (1969)

MacDONNELL, John de Courcy (1869-1915), British biographer, served on the western front in the Gordon Highlanders and was killed in action during the First World War, probably in Belgium.
King Leopold II: His Rule in Belgium and the Congo (1905); *The Life of His Majesty Albert, King of the Belgians* (1915)

MacDONOGH, Giles (1955-), British historian and journalist. He read Modern History at Balliol college, Oxford, and carried out historical research at the *Ecole pratique des hautes etudes* in Paris. He worked as a journalist at the Financial Times from 1988 to 2003, covering mainly food and drink. He has published books on German history, gastronomy and wine.

Frederick the Great (1999); *The Last Kaiser: William the Impetuous* (2000)

MACKENZIE, Sir Morell (1837-92), British physician and pioneer of laryngology. Born at Leytonstone, Essex, he helped to found the London Hospital for Diseases of the Throat in 1863, and within a few years he was recognized as one of the leading laryngologists throughout Europe. In 1887 he was summoned to attend the German Crown Prince Frederick William, who was suffering from suspected cancer of the larynx, and his treatment brought him into conflict with the German physicians. After the Crown Prince's accession as Emperor Frederick III and death three months later, quarrels between Mackenzie and his German colleagues escalated. After they had published their accounts of the illness, he responded with his own, which brought him censure from the Royal College of Surgeons. His own practice and health never recovered from the episode and he died four years later.
The Fatal Illness of Frederick the Noble (1888)

MADOL, Hans Roger (real name Gerhard Salomon) (1903-56), poet and biographer, born in Berlin of a Jewish family. He left Nazi Germany in the early 1930s and settled in London for the rest of his life.
Ferdinand of Bulgaria (1930); *The Shadow King: The Life of Louis XVII of France and the Fortunes of the Naundorff-Bourbon Family* (1930); *Christian IX* (1939); *The Private Life of Queen Alexandra* (1940)

MAGNUS, Philip (Sir Philip Montefiore Magnus-Allcroft, 2nd Baronet) (1906-88), was the grandson of Conservative politician Sir Philip Magnus, 1st Baronet, to whose title he succeeded in 1933. In the Second World War he was a Captain in the Royal Artillery and Army Intelligence Corps, where he rose to the rank of Major. After the war

he wrote biographies of Edmund Burke, W.E. Gladstone and Lord Kitchener. His last, on King Edward VII, on which the ATV drama series of the same title starring Timothy West first shown in 1975 was partly based, remains his best-known work.
King Edward the Seventh (1964)

MAHAFFY, Robert Pentland (1871-1943), Irish political journalist, barrister and judge. Born in Ireland, he studied at King's College, Cambridge, and from 1896 to 1914 he was one of the editors of the Calendar of State Papers. He was called to the Bar in 1901. During the First World War he served with the Devonshire Regiment and the Egyptian Army. In 1919 he became Judge of the Blue Nile and Kordofen Provinces, and later legal adviser to the Rhineland Commission, and to the Governor of Malta.
Francis Joseph I, His Life and Times: An Essay in Politics (1915)

MANDACHE, Diana, Roumanian historian and biographer and specialist in Roumanian royalty, and organiser of several royalty-themed exhibitions in the country.
Americans and Queen Marie of Romania, ed. (1998); *Later Chapters of My Life: The Lost Memoir of Queen Marie of Romania* (2004); *Marie of Romania. Images of a Queen* (2007); *Dearest Missy: The Correspondence Between Marie, Grand Duchess of Russia, Duchess of Edinburgh and of Saxe-Coburg and Gotha and her Daughter, Marie, Crown Princess of Romania* (ed.) (2011)

MANGOLD, Tom (Thomas Cornelius) (1934-), British broadcaster, journalist and author. Born in Hanburg, he came to Britain as a child, did National Service with the Royal Artillery, then became a freelance reporter specialising in intelligence and travel. He worked for the SundayMirror and then the Daily Express, then joined

BBC TV News as a war correspondent, then on current affairs programmes.
The File on the Tsar: The Fate of the Romanovs [with Anthony Summers (q.v.)] (1976)

MANSEL, Philip (1951-), British historian, born in London. He read Modern History and Modern Languages at Balliol College, Oxford. An authority on the later French monarchy, he has contributed reviews and articles to *History Today*, *English Historical Review*, *International Herald Tribune*, *Daily Telegraph* and other publications, and has appeared on various radio and TV documentaries.
Louis XVIII (1981)

MAREK, George R. (Richard) (1902-87), Austrian-born American music executive and author, mainly of biographies of classical composers, his main interests being musical rather than historical. He was born in Vienna and studied at university there until emigrating to the United States in 1920, becoming an American citizen in 1925. After a career in advertising, he worked at RCA Victor Records, as Manager of Artist & Repertory, then Vice-President and General Manager, until retirement in 1972, and wrote the liner notes to several classical releases. He was also Music Editor of *Good Housekeeping*, a contributor to *Harper's Bazaar*, and a co-founder of the *Reader's Digest* Record Club.
The Eagles Die: Franz Joseph, Elizabeth, and Their Austria (1975)

MARKHAM, Sir Clements (Robert), KCB, FRS (1830–1916), British geographer, explorer, and writer, was Secretary of the Royal Geographical Society between 1863 and 1888, and subsequently the Society's President 1893-1905. He was mainly responsible for organising the National Antarctic Expedition of 1901–04. After his retirement from the RGS presidency, he led an active life

as a writer and traveller, with books on travel, history and biography. In his biography of Richard III he called him one of the best Kings England has ever had, stating that his evil reputation was entirely due to 'the accumulated garbage and filth of centuries of calumny.'
Richard III: His Life and Character (1906)

MARKHAM, Felix (Maurice Hippisley) (1908-92), British historian, born at Brighton, studied at Oxford and was Fellow and History Tutor at Hertford College Oxford from 1931 to 1973.
Napoleon (1963)

MARLOW, Joyce (1929-), British actress and historian, born in Manchester, trained as an actress and had a long career appearing on the stage and in various television drama series, including *Z Cars* and *Emergency Ward 10*. After retiring from acting she turned to writing, specialising in historical works, biographies and novels. She was a leading member of the Writers' Action Group which campaigned for the introduction of Public Lending Right in 1979, and was a co-founder of the Copyright Licensing Agency. Of her status as the author of a title in the 'Life and Times of' series on British monarchs, she later said on her website: 'It was another flat fee, no royalties deal, but the series was so popular its authors were invited to a party to meet readers who'd won a competition. Each author was handed an envelope containing a cheque, a nice surprise but it prompted the cynical to conclude Weidenfelds must have made a fortune from the series.'
The Life and Times of George I (1973)

MARPLES, Morris (1901-76), British author. In addition to royal biographies, he also published books on university slang, countryside walks and football.

Princes in the Making: A Study of Royal Education (1965); *Six Royal Sisters: Daughters of George III* (1969); *Poor Fred and the Butcher: Sons of George II* (1970); *Wicked Uncles in Love* [Sons of King George III] (1972)

MARR, Andrew (1959-), British broadcaster and journalist, born in Glasgow, read English at Trinity Hall, Cambridge. Joining *The Scotsman* in 1981, he later joined the staff of *The Independent* and *The Economist*, returning to *The Independent* where he became Political Editor in 1992 and Editor in 1996, leaving two years later to become a columnist for the *Daily Express* and *The Observer*. He later turned increasingly to TV journalism, becoming Political Editor at the BBC and presenter of a weekly current affairs programme on Sunday mornings, in addition to writing and presenting several documentary series on modern British history.
The Diamond Queen: Elizabeth II and her People (2011)

MARSHALL, Dorothy (1900-94), author of biographies and histories of the 18th and 19th centuries, read History at Cambridge, was a member of the History Department, University of South Wales and Monmouthshire, and later a Reader in History at the University of Wales.
The Life and Times of Victoria (1972)

MARSHALL, Rosalind K., writer and historian, has written widely on the sixteenth and seventeenth centuries, specialising in women's history. She is a research associate of the *Oxford Dictionary of National Biography*.
Henrietta Maria: The Intrepid Queen (1990); *The Winter Queen: The Life of Elizabeth of Bohemia, 1596-1662* (1998); *Scottish Queens, 1034-1714* (2003); *Mary, Queen of Scots: Truth or Lies* (2010); *Mary, Queen of Scots: 'In My End is My Beginning'* (2013)

MARTIN, Sir Theodore, KCB KCVO (1816-1909), Scottish poet, biographer, and translator, practised as a solicitor in Edinburgh 1840-45, then went to London where he became head of the firm of Martin and Leslie, parliamentary agents. In his spare time he wrote poetry and translated the work of Dante, Horace and Catullus. He was commissioned by Queen Victoria to write the official biography of the Prince Consort, and granted access to his private papers. As the Queen wrote to her eldest daughter the German Crown Princess (16.6.1874), 'he has written the whole – and really in a masterly style – for no one writes better'. When he was asked some years later to write a memoir of her favourite Highland servant John Brown shortly after his death in 1883, he tactfully declined on the grounds of his wife's ill-health. He was appointed Lord Rector of St. Andrews in 1881.

Life of the Prince Consort, 5 vols (1874-80); *Queen Victoria as I Knew Her* (1908)

MASON, Emma.
William II: Rufus, the Red King (2005)

MASSIE, Robert (Robert Kinloch Massie III) (1929-), American historian and biographer, born in Lexington, Kentucky, worked as a journalist for *Newsweek* and the *Saturday Evening Post*. He became interested in the Romanovs after discovering that his son Robert had haemophilia, and this led to his first book, *Nicholas and Alexandra*, on which a feature film was largely based four years later. He subsequently wrote several volumes of biography and history, one of which, *Peter the Great*, won the Pulitzer Prize for Biography in 1981.

Nicholas and Alexandra (1967); *Peter the Great: His Life and World* (1981); *Dreadnought: Britain, Germany, and the Coming of the Great War* (1992); *The Romanovs: The Final Chapter* (1995); *Catherine the Great: Portrait of a Woman* (2011)

MASSON, Georgina (1912-80), biographer and travel writer.
Frederick II of Hohenstaufen: A Life (1957); *Queen Christina* (1968)

MATHEW, David (James) (1902-75), British historian, born at Lyme Regis, Dorset, was a midshipman in the Royal Navy at the end of the First World War. He read Modern History at Balliol College, Oxford, and then went to Beda College, Rome. He was ordained in 1929, and became Chaplain to the Roman Catholic community at the University of London, and was appointed Auxiliary Bishop of Westminster in 1938. Having served London during the Second World War and the blitz, he then spent eight years in Africa, as apostolic visitor to Ethiopia, apostolic delegate to the British colonies in Africa, and with helping the Vatican to prepare for the appointment of native African bishops. After returning to England he was appointed Bishop-in-Ordinary to the British armed forces. He retired in 1963 to write history.
The Age of Charles I (1951); *King James I* (1967); *Lady Jane Grey* (1972)

MAURER, Helen E., biographer. According to a review, her biography of the Lancastrian Queen is 'an avowedly revisionist and feminist study', calling for a fresh analysis of the history of the Wars of the Roses, which has been told almost entirely from a male point of view' (*Speculum*, April 2005).
Margaret of Anjou: Queenship and Power in Late Medieval England (2004)

MAUROIS, André (real name Emile Salomon Wilhelm Herzog) (1885-1967), French author, was born at Elbeuf. He joined the French army during the First World War,

serving as an interpreter and later a liaison officer with the British army. During the Second World War he was appointed French Official Observer attached to the British General Headquarters, accompanied the British Army to Belgium, was sent on a brief mission to London, then served in the French army and the Free French Forces. His pseudonym became his legal name in 1947. He was a prolific writer of novels, biographies, histories, children's books and science fiction.
King Edward and his Times (1933)

MAYER, Catherine (1960-), American-born author and journalist, who moved to Britain as a child with her family, and studied at Manchester University. She began her career at *The Economist*, was Foreign Correspondent at Focus, and was President of the Foreign Press Association in London from 2003 to 2005. She worked for *Time* from 2004 to 2015, successively as Europe editor, London bureau chief, and Senior Editor. In 2013 she was granted an interview with the heir to the throne in 2013, resulting in the publication of her biography of him. When it was published she said, 'I used to think the monarchy was a sideshow and I didn't take the Royals seriously. Now I've seen the work they do, I would describe myself as a republican who has reluctantly come to believe in the monarchy.' (*Independent*, 3.2.2015) According to a statement from Clarence House, the Prince of Wales's London residence, the biography was unauthorised and the author did not have exclusive access to the Prince or his staff.
Charles: The Heart of a King (2015) UK/*Born To Be King* (2015) US

MAYLUNAS, Andrei, Russian author and historian and specialist on pre-Soviet Russia, and MIRONENKO,

Sergei, Russian historian and Director of the State Archives of the Russian Federation.
A Lifelong Passion: Nicholas and Alexandra: Their Own Story (ed.) (1996)

MAYR-OFEN, Ferdinand (real name Otto Zarek), (1898-1958), German biographer, journalist, critic, playwright and director, born in Berlin. After studying Law at Munich University, he decided to pursue a career in writing and the theatre. Being Jewish and homosexual he left Berlin in 1933 for Hungary, working in Bucharest until 1938 as a correspondent for the *Basler National-Zeitung*. Then settling in England for some years where he joined the army in 1940. After the Second World War, he worked as a senior translator in the German Division of the BBC until 1948. He returned to Berlin in 1954 to work for the press and radio, contributing to Jewish magazines and organising volunteer cultural events for the Berlin Jewish community. All his writings except for his Ludwig II biography were published under his own name.
Ludwig II of Bavaria: The Tragedy of an Idealist (1937)

McGEOCH, Sir Ian, KCB, DSO, DSC (1914-2007), British naval officer and writer, was born in Helensburgh, Dumbartonshire. He commanded the submarine HMS *Splendid* during the Second World War, and during active service lost the sight of his right eye. After the war he commanded various submarine squadrons, and was Director of Undersurface Warfare in the Admiralty for two years. He was promoted to Vice-Admiral in 1967, and appointed Flag Officer Submarines and Flag Officer Scotland and Northern Ireland.
The Princely Sailor: Mountbatten of Burma (1996)

McGRIGOR, Mary, British biographer and local historian, born in London but brought up in Stirlingshire,

with a love of history and literature inspired particularly by the works of Robert Louis Stevenson.
The Other Tudor Princess: Margaret Douglas, Henry VIII's Niece (2015)

McINTOSH, Christopher (1943-), British biographer and historian. He studied Philosophy, Politics, Economics and History at Oxford University and German at London University.
The Swan King: Ludwig II of Bavaria (1982)

McINTOSH, David, *see* BEECHE, Arturo E.

McKINLAY, Brian (1933-), author of books on Australian history and politics, including one on the visits of Alfred, Duke of Edinburgh.
The First Royal Tour, 1867-1868 (1970)

McLEOD, Kirsty, British author, was a publisher's editor before becoming a full-time writer, and contributed to the *Daily Telegraph* and *Yorkshire Post*.
Battle Royal: Edward VIII and George VI, Brother Against Brother (1999)

McNALTY, Sir A.S. (Arthur Salisbury), KCB, MRCS, FRCP, FRCS (1880-1969), British Chief Medical Officer from 1935 to 1941 and author of medical case histories.
Henry VIII, A Difficult Patient (1952)

MEADE, Marion (1934-), American biographer and novelist, was born in Pittsburgh. She studied Journalism at Northwestern University, became a reporting assistant on the New York Post, then a freelancer writing for the *New York Times*, *The Nation*, and *McCall's*. She wrote several biographies, her other subjects including Dorothy Parker, Buster Keaton and Woody Allen.

Eleanor of Aquitaine: A Biography (1978)

MELVILLE, Lewis (Lewis Saul Benjamin) (1864-1932), British biographer, born in London. He was also briefly an actor, wrote extensively on actors and stage history, was an authority on William Makepeace Thackeray and edited some of his work, and a contributor to *Dictionary of National Biography*. His last-mentioned book includes a section on Anne Hyde, Duchess of York alongside various aristocratic figures.
The First Gentleman of Europe [George IV], 2 vols (1905); *Farmer George*, 2 vols (1907); *The First George, in Hanover and England*, 2 vols (1908); *An Injured Queen: Caroline of Brunswick*, 2 vols (1912); *The Windsor Beauties: Ladies of the Court of Charles II* (1928)

MICHAEL of Kent, Princess Marie Christine Anna Agnes Hedwig Ida (*née* Marie von Reibnitz) (1945-), married Prince Michael of Kent in 1978. Her first book was the subject of legal action after Daphne Bennett (q.v.) sued her for plagiarism and was awarded undisclosed damages.
Crowned in a Far Country: Portraits of Eight Royal Brides (1986); *Cupid and the King: Five Royal Paramours* (1991); *The Serpent and The Moon: Two Rivals for the Love of a Renaissance King* [Henry II of France, Diane de Poitiers, and Catherine de Medici] (2004)

MICHAEL of Greece and Denmark, Prince (1939-), born in Rome, son of Prince Christopher of Greece and Denmark (q.v.). He has written several biographies, works of history and fiction, and has contributed to *Architectural Digest*.
Louis XIV: The Other Side of the Sun (1984); *The Royal House of Greece* (1986); *The Royal Hellenic Dynasty* (2007)

MICHAEL, Maurice (1909-78), biographer. He and his wife Pamela published several translations and retelling of fairy stories.
Haakon, King of Norway (1958)

MIDDLEMAS, (Robert) Keith (1935-2013), British historian, was a clerk in the House of Commons, and subsequently Emeritus Professor of History at the University of Sussex. As an author he specialised in 20th century British political, social and economic history and biography.
The Life and Times of Edward VII (1972); *The Life and Times of George VI* (1974)

MIJATOVICH, Chedomille (Čedomilj Mijatović) (1842-1932) was a Serbian politician, economist, historian, writer and diplomat. He served several terms as Minister of Finance, and as Minister of Foreign Affairs in Serbia, and as Ambassador to Great Britain as well as more briefly to Roumania and to the Ottoman Empire. His last term of office to the Court of St James coincided with the coup in Belgrade in 1903 which led to the murder of King Peter and Queen Draga, as a result of which he resigned his post, and Britain broke off diplomatic relations with Serbia. He spent the rest of his life in London and wrote several books, mostly history and fiction, and contributed to two editions of the *Encyclopaedia Britannica*. According to a *Times* correspondent, he was 'generally regarded by his fellow-countrymen as the most learned man in Serbia.'
A Royal Tragedy. Being the Story of the Assassination of King Alexander and Queen Draga of Servia (1906)

MILLER, Ilana, American biographer and historian, was born in Santa Monica, California. Adjunct Professor of History at Pepperdine University, Malibu, CA, Editor of and contributor to *European Royal History Journal*. She has also contributed to *The Grand Dukes* (2010), and published historical fiction.

The Four Graces: Queen Victoria's Hessian Granddaughters (2011); *Royal Gatherings, Vol. 1: 1914-1939* [with Arturo Beéche] (2015); *Royal Gatherings, Vol. 2: 1914-1939* [with Arturo Beeche] (2015)

MILLER, John, was a Research Fellow at Gonville and Caius College, Cambridge, and a Lecturer at Queen Mary's College, specialising in the late Stuart era. He contributed to various journals, including *English Historical Review* and *Historical Journal*.

The Life and Times of William and Mary (1974); *James II: A Study in Kingship* (1989)

MINET, Paul (Piers Brissault), FSA (1937-2012), British antiquarian book dealer and journalist. He founded the *Antiquarian Book Monthly Review* in 1974 and wrote two books about the book trade, and for some years was President and Treasurer of the Antiquarian Booksellers' Association. As one of the major British dealers in new and secondhand books on European royalty, Piccadilly Rare Books, in 1991 he launched *Royalty Digest*, which he edited and to which he regularly contributed until its closure in 2005, to be succeeded by *Royalty Digest Quarterly*, edited by Ted Rosvall (q.v.). He also organised the annual Royalty Digest weekends at Ticehurst, East Sussex, and launched a catalogue of reprints of old and hard-to-find royal biographies and memoirs.

Royalty Digest (ed.) (monthly), 1991-2005

MIRONENKO, Sergei, *see* MAYLUNAS, Andrei

MITFORD, Nancy (*née* Nancy Freeman-Mitford, later Nancy Rodd), CBE (1904-73), British novelist, biographer and journalist. One of the daughters of the Hon. David

Freeman-Mitford, later 2nd Baron Redesdale, elder sister of Diana Mosley (q.v.), and daughter-in-law of Sir Rennell Rodd (q.v.), she is best remembered for her novels about upper-class life in England and France. Moving from London to Paris in 1946, she spent the rest of her life in France, where she established a reputation for herself as a writer of popular historical biographies towards the end of her career.

The Sun King (1966); *Frederick the Great* (1970)

MOFFAT, Mary Maxwell.
Queen Louisa of Prussia (1906)

MOODY, Marcia, British journalist and former Features Editor, then Royal Correspondent with *OK! Magazine*.
Kate: The Biography (2013); *Harry: A Biography* (2014)

MORAND, Paul (1888-1976), French novelist, biographer and writer on travel. Born in Paris, he joined the diplomatic corps, working in London, Rome, Berne and Bucharest, before becoming a full-time writer.
The Captive Princess: Sophia Dorothea of Celle (1968)

MORRAH, Dermot (1896–1974), British journalist and author, was born in Ryde, Isle of Wight and read History at New College, Oxford. During the First World War he joined the Royal Engineers, and served in Palestine and Egypt, being wounded at Gaza. On demobilization he returned to Oxford, obtained first-class honours in modern history, and was elected to a prize fellowship at All Souls College. In 1922 he entered the civil service. He also joined the *Daily Mail*, worked as an assistant to G. E. Buckle while writing his history of *The Times*, and in 1932 became a full member of *The Times* staff. After the Second World War he began writing studies of contemporary members of the royal family. In 1961 he retired from *The*

Times and joined the *Daily Telegraph* as a leader writer. He continued contributing to various magazines including *West Indian Cultural Circular*, *Farmers' Weekly*, and the *Policewoman's Gazette*.

Princess Elizabeth (1947); *The Royal Family in Africa* (1947); *Princess Elizabeth, Duchess of Edinburgh* (1950); *Most Excellent Majesty* (1955); *The Work of The Queen* (1958): *The Queen's Visit: Elizabeth II and India and Pakistan* (1961); *To Be a King: A Privileged Account of the Early Life and Education of HRH The Prince of Wales* (1968)

MORRIS, Marc (1973-), historian and broadcaster, specialising in the Middle Ages. He was presenter of *Castle*, a TV series for Channel 4 in 2003, wrote the accompanying book, and has written for *History Today*, *BBC History Magazine* and *Heritage Today*.

A Great and Terrible King: Edward I and the Forging of Britain (2009); *King John: Treachery, Tyranny and the Road to Magna Carta* (2015)

MORROW, Ann, British biographer, is a former Court Correspondent for the *Daily Telegraph* and regular contributor to newspapers and magazines.

The Queen [Elizabeth II] (1983); *The Queen Mother* (1985); *Princess* [Diana, Princess of Wales] (1991); *Without Equal, Her Majesty Queen Elizabeth, The Queen Mother* (2000); *Cousins Divided: George V and Nicholas II* (2006)

MORTIMER, Dr Ian, MA, PhD, DLitt (1967-), British historian and biographer, was born in Petts Wood, near Orpington, Kent, and read History at the University of Exeter and Archive Studies at University College London. Between 1991 and 2003 he worked for various archive and historical research organisations, including the Royal Commission on Historical Manuscripts, the Universities of Exeter and Reading, and the Devon Record Office, and has been a member of the Lord Chancellor's Forum on Historical Manuscripts and Academic Research. He has written several biographical and social history titles dealing with medieval and Tudor England.

The Perfect King: The Life of Edward III, Father of the English Nation (2006); *The Fears of Henry IV: The Life of England's Self-Made King* (2007)

MORTIMER, Penelope (*née* Penelope Ruth Fletcher) (1918-99), British journalist, biographer, and novelist, born in Rhyl, North Wales. She attended University College, London, but left after only one year. She became a freelance journalist, writing for *The New Yorker* and the *Daily Mail* as Ann Temple, and later film critic for *The Observer* as well as a writer of screenplays. She was commissioned by Macmillan to write a biography of Queen Elizabeth the Queen Mother, but they rejected it and it was published by Viking. Her former agent Giles Gordon called it 'the most astute biography of a royal since Lytton Strachey was at work. Penelope had approached her subject as somebody in the public eye, whose career might as well be recorded as if she were a normal human being.' She was married to John Mortimer from 1947 to 1971. She also published fiction and two volumes of autobiography.

Queen Elizabeth: A Portrait of the Queen Mother (1986)

MORTON, Andrew (1953-), British journalist and biographer, read History at University of Sussex, and then joined the *Daily Star*, replacing their royal correspondent James Whitaker. He subsequently worked in a similar capacity on *News of the World*, the *Daily Express* and the *Daily Mail*, until 1987, when he left to concentrate on writing mainly unauthorised celebrity biographies. His controversial book on Diana, Princess of Wales, was written with her cooperation, and in his words, 'it transformed my reputation and finances'.

Diana, her True Story (1992); *17 Carnations: The Windsors, the Nazis, and the Cover-up* (2015)

MOSLEY, Diana (*née* Freeman-Mitford, then Mrs Bryan Walter Guinness, then The Hon Lady Mosley) (1910-2003), British author, was the third of the Mitford (q.v.) sisters, daughters of David Bertram Ogilvy Freeman-Mitford, 2nd Baron Redesdale. Born in Belgravia, she grew up in the country estate of Batsford Park, then at the family home, Asthall Manor, Oxfordshire, and later at Swinbrook House, a home her father had built in the village of Swinbrook. She was married first to Bryan Walter Guinness, and secondly to Sir Oswald Mosley, leader of the British Union of Fascists. Her involvement with Fascism led to three years' internment in Holloway during the Second World War, when she was described as 'the most hated woman in England' (*Guardian*, 14.8.2003). After being released she moved to Paris, where she became editor of *The European*, and contributed articles and book reviews to various journals and papers, including *Books & Bookmen* and the *Evening Standard*. She wrote and published her memoirs and a royal biography which was described by one reviewer as 'a curiously unworldly book' (*London Review of Books*, 16.10.1980).
The Duchess of Windsor (1980)

MOWAT, R.B. (Robert Balmain) (1883-1941), historian, was born at Edinburgh, and studied Literature and Modern History at Edinburgh University and Balliol College, Oxford. He taught as an assistant master at Eton College from 1906 to 1907, when he was elected a fellow of Corpus Christi College, Oxford, where he was successively Assistant Tutor in History, Dean, and Vice-President. During the First World War he served in the naval intelligence department, then in the war cabinet secretariat, and as an aide to General Jan Smuts at the

Paris peace conference in 1919. He was Visiting Professor of Modern History at the University of Wisconsin from 1925 to 1926, and then Professor of Modern History at the University of Bristol from 1928 until his death. His earlier books had focused on medieval history, but later he also wrote on Europe from the 18th century onwards. A prolific author, he published over fifty books. After the outbreak of the Second World War he lectured extensively in America, and was killed while flying home from the States in an accident at Auchenhone, Argyll.

Henry V (1919)

MUNZ, Sigmund, PhD (1859-1934), Austrian journalist, born at Leipnik, Moravia, and studied at the universities of Vienna and Tübingen. He contributed regularly to the *Neue Freie Presse*, particularly on foreign politics and Italy.

King Edward VII at Marienbad: Political and Social Life at the Bohemian Spas (1934)

MURPHY, Charles J.V. (1904-87), American biographer and journalist, was born in Newton, Massachusetts. He joined the staff of The Associated Press, Manhattan, in 1925, then worked for the United Press, *The New York Evening Post* and *The New York World* before becoming a freelance writer in 1930. Later he joined the staff of *Fortune*, and was a reporter for *Life*. He was a friend of the Duke and Duchess of Windsor (q.v.), and is believed to have ghost-written or largely written his *A King's Story*.

The Windsor Story [with J. Bryan III] (1979)

N

NADA, John (real name John Eric Langdon-Davies), MBE (1897–1971), British author and journalist. Born in Eshowe, Zululand, later South Africa, he came to England at the age of six. He lived successively in the United States and then in Spain for some years and became a war correspondent during the Spanish Civil and Russo-Finnish wars. Returning to Britain, during the Second World War he was a military instructor for the Home Guard. He was a prolific author of over forty books, largely on historical and military subjects, mostly published under his own name. In the 1960s he created the Jackdaw series of history educational aids for schoolchildren.
Carlos the Bewitched: The Last Spanish Habsburg, 1661-1700 (1962) UK / *Carlos: The King Who Would Not Die* (1962) US

NEALE, Sir John Ernest, FBA (1890-1975), English historian and specialist in Elizabethan history. He was trained by the political historian A.F. Pollard. Appointed to the chair of Modern History at the University of Manchester, he succeeded Pollard as Astor Professor of English History at University College, London in 1927, where he remained until 1956 when he became Professor Emeritus.
Queen Elizabeth (1934); *Elizabeth I and her Parliaments* (1953)

NELSON, Walter Henry.
The Soldier Kings: The House of Hohenzollern (1971)

NICHOLL, Katie (1977-), British journalist and biographer. She has been the royal correspondent for *Mail on Sunday*, a contributing editor to *Vanity Fair* and royal correspondent on TV in Britain, America and Australia. *William and Harry: Behind the Place Walls* (2010); *The Making of a Royal Romance* (Prince William and Catherine Middleton) (2011); *Kate the Future Queen* (2013)

NICOLSON, Sir Harold (George), KCVO, CMG (1886–1968), diplomatist and politician, born at Tehran, third son of Arthur Nicolson, 1st Baron Carnock, was educated at Balliol College, Oxford. In 1909 he joined the Diplomatic Service, serving at Madrid and then Constantinople. During the First World War, he joined the Foreign Office where he was promoted Second Secretary, and in August 1914 he was responsible for handing Britain's revised declaration of war to the German ambassador in London. He was among the staff at the Paris Peace Conference in 1919, and promoted to First Secretary in 1920. In 1925, he was posted to Tehran as *Chargé d'Affaires*. He was National Labour MP for Leicester West from 1935 to 1945, became Parliamentary Secretary and official Censor at the Ministry of Information in 1940. From 1941 to 1946 he was on the BBC Board of Governors. Since the 1920s he had published books on current affairs, history, biographies and fiction, and after losing his parliamentary seat in 1945 he devoted himself to writing, including book reviews for *The Observer*, and a weekly column in *The Spectator*. In 1948 he was asked by Sir Alan Lascelles, Private Secretary to George VI, to write the official biography of George V, concentrating on the political aspects as opposed to the personal life by John Gore (q.v.). He initially doubted his fitness for the task, particularly as he despised the late King's twin devotions to shooting and philately, but he was persuaded, largely by Queen Mary's belief in him as the man for the job. The task took him

three years, and shortly after publication he was knighted and granted honorary fellowship of Balliol in 1953. He was however shocked to received a demand from the Inland Revenue for £6,000 (Rose, *Kings, Queens & Courtiers*, 1985, 224-6). He was married to fellow writer Victoria Sackville-West; one of their sons, Nigel, was a Conservative MP and co-founder of publishers Weidenfeld & Nicolson.
George V: His Life and Reign (1952)

NOEL, Gerard, FRSL (1926-) was formerly editor of *Catholic Herald*, before turning to royal biography.
*Princess Alice, Queen Victoria's Forgotten Daug*hter (1974); *Ena, Spain's English Queen* (1984)

NORGATE, Kate (1853-1935), British historian. born in St Pancras, London, became the protégée of the historian John Richard Green, who encouraged her in her work on the Angevins. Her first book, a two-volume study of England under the Angevin Kings, was followed by three biographies. She was also a contributor to the *Dictionary of National Biography*. Regarded as one of the first women to achieve academic success in this sphere, she was credited as having coined the name Angevin Empire to describe the domains of the medieval monarchs. She was elected an Honorary Fellow of Somerville College, Oxford, in 1929. According to an obituary, she was the 'most learned woman historian of the pre-academic period' (*The Times*, 6.5.1935).
John Lackland (1902); *The Minority of Henry the Third* (1912); *Richard the Lion Heart* (1924)

NORTON, Elizabeth (1986-), British historian, specialising in the Queens of England and the Tudor period. She studied Archaeology and Anthropology at New Hall, Cambridge, and European Archaeology at Hertford College, Oxford. She has appeared regularly on radio and

TV, and contributed to journals including *New Statesman*, *Britain* and *Your Family Tree* magazines. In addition to her writing career she has also practised as a solicitor.

She Wolves, The Notorious Queens of England (2008); *Anne Boleyn, Henry VIII's Obsession* (2008); *Jane Seymour, Henry VIII's True Love* (2009); *Anne of Cleves, Henry VIII's Discarded Bride* (2009); *Catherine Parr* (2010); *Margaret Beaufort, Mother of the Tudor Dynasty* (2010); *Anne Boleyn, In Her Own Words and the Words of Those Who Knew Her* (2011); *England's Queens: The Biography* (2011), *Bessie Blount* (2011), *The Boleyn Women* (2013)

O

OCCLESHAW, Michael, British historian.
The Romanov Conspiracies: The Romanovs and the House of Windsor (1993)

ODDIE, E.M. (Elinor Mary O'Donoghue) (1898-?), biographer and novelist.
Marie-Louise, Empress of France (1931); *Napoleon II, King of Rome* (1932)

OLDENBOURG, Zoe (1916-2002), Russian-born French historian and novelist. She was born in Petrograd, but left Russia with her family in 1925 and settled in Paris. She studied at the Sorbonne, and was encouraged by her journalist father to become a writer of historical fiction and non-fiction, mostly set in or based around the Middle Ages.
Catherine the Great (1965)

OLLARD, Richard (Lawrence) (1923-2007), British historian and biographer, born in Yorkshire. During the Second World War he served in the Riyal Navy, then studied at New College, Oxford. He taught History at the Royal Naval College, Greenwich, from 1948 to 1959. He joined Collins Publishing as a Senior Editor in 1960 until retirement in 1983, and pursued a parallel career as a writer of books on the 17th century.
The Escape of Charles II (1966)

OMAN, Carola, CBE (1897-1978), English historical novelist, biographer, poet and children's writer. She was born in Oxford, daughter of military historian Sir Charles Oman, and initially worked as a probationary VAD nurse in Oxford, Dorset, London and France before becoming a full-time writer.
Henrietta Maria (1936); *The Winter Queen: Elizabeth of Bohemia* (1938)

ORMROD, Mark, FRS, British historian, was Professor in the Department of History and Academic Co-ordinator for the Arts and Humanities at the University of York. A Fellow of the Society of Antiquaries, he has served as a Trustee and Councillor of various organisations including the Richard III and Yorkist History Trust, the Pipe Roll Society and the Royal Historical Society. He was a former general editor of York Medieval Press, a member of the editorial board of the *Yorkshire Archaeological Journal* and a co-editor of *Fourteenth-Century England*.
Edward III (2011)

P

PACKARD, Jerrold M(ichael), BA (1943-), American biographer, born in Orange, California, served in the US Airforce from 1961 to 1965 and attained the rank of sergeant, then studied at Portland State University. He became a health administrator, and then a dealer in rare books before turning to writing history and biography in 1980.

Farewell in Splendour: The Death of Queen Victoria and her Age (1995); *Victoria's Daughters* (1998)

PADOVER, Saul (Kussiel), BA (1905-81), historian, biographer and political scientist. Born in Vienna, he came to the United States with his parents in 1920, and attended Wayne State University and Yale University. He accepted research positions at the University of Chicago in 1932 and the University of California. From 1938 to 1944, he worked in the United States Department of the Interior, leaving to become a political analyst based in London for the Federal Communications Commission. He also worked as an intelligence officer for the Office of Strategic Services, a forerunner of the Central Intelligence Agency, and for the United States Army from 1944 to 1946. He was editorial writer from 1946 to1948 for the New York City newspaper *PM*. In 1949 he joined the graduate faculty of The New School, university in New York City, where he remained until his death. In addition to European royal history he also published books on Thomas

Jefferson and Karl Marx, and on 20th century European and American politics.

The Life and Death of Louis XVI (1939); *The Revolutionary Emperor: Joseph II of Austria* (1967)

PAIN (*née* Taylor), (Florence) Nesta (Kathleen) (1905–95), broadcaster and author, was born in Liverpool. She was educated at West Heath School, Liverpool, and at Liverpool University, where she took a first-class honours degree in classics and then went to Somerville College, Oxford, to study for a doctorate in comparative philology. She became closely involved with the Liverpool Playhouse and wrote two plays. In 1942 she went to London, joined the BBC and began writing and producing programmes for the external services and domestic audiences. In 1947 she was given a permanent staff contract at the BBC and for the next twelve years played a major role in the features department, writing, producing, and directing an enormous range of talks, features, and plays for radio. In 1956 she was seconded to the television service where she wrote, produced, or directed several programmes. After resigning from her post as producer and taking a part-time post as scriptwriter–producer, she combined her BBC work with writing books.

George III at Home (1975); *The Empress Matilda, Uncrowned Queen of England* (1978)

PAKULA, Hannah (*née* Hannah Cohn Boorstin) (1933-), American biographer, attended Wellesley College, the Sorbonne and Southern Methodist University. As well as writing biography, she was a book reviewer for the *Los Angeles Times* and the *Dallas Morning Post*. Her husband was the film director Alan J. Pakula.

The Last Romantic: A Biography of Queen Marie of Roumania (1984); *An Uncommon Woman: The Empress Frederick* (1996)

PALEOLOGUE, Maurice (1859-1944), French diplomat and author, was born in Paris, the son of a Wallachian Roumanian revolutionary who had fled to France after the revolution of 1848. After graduating in Law, he obtained a position at the French Foreign Ministry in 1880, and became Embassy Secretary at successively Tangier, Peking and Italy. As Minister Plenipotentiary he represented France inn Bulgaria from 1907 to 1912, and Russia from 1914 to 1917. After the First World War he was General Secretary of the Foreign Ministry in the French cabinet. He wrote several histories of Russia and biographies of Russian and French royalty, as well as novels and essays, after the First World War. He was elected a member of the Academie Française in 1928.

The Tragic Romance of Alexander II of Russia (1926); *The Tragic Empress: Intimate Conversations with the Empress Eugenie 1901-1911* (1928); *The Enigmatic Czar: The Life of Alexander I of Russia* (1938)

PALMER, Alan, FRSL (1926-), British historian, was head of history at Highgate School, London, before becoming a full-time historian and biographer. He collaborated with his wife Veronica on several titles.

Napoleon in Russia (1967); *The Life and Times of George IV* (1972); *Frederick The Great* (1974); *Alexander I: Tsar of War and Peace* (1974); *The Kaiser: Warlord of the Second Reich* (1978); *Bernadotte: Napoleon's Marshal, Sweden's King* (1990); *Twilight of the Habsburgs: The Life and Times of Emperor Francis Joseph* (1994); *Napoleon & Marie Louise: the Emperor's second wife* (2001)

PALMER, Dean, British biographer and TV journalist. He has worked in television as a producer and executive producer for the BBC, Channel 4, ITV, Sony Pictures and NBC-Universal.

The Queen and Mrs Thatcher: An Inconvenient Relationship (2015)

PARDOE, Julia (1806-62), English poet, novelist, historian and traveller. Born at Beverley, Yorkshire, she travelled regularly to the middle east and was renowned for her books on travel as well as her royal and historical biographies.
Louis the Fourteenth, and the Court of France in the Seventeenth Century (1886); *The Court and Reign of Francis the First, King of France*, 2 vols. (1887); *The Life of Marie de Médicis, Queen of France* (1890) - Dates of publication, from the British Library Catalogue, are presumably revised editions, having appeared several years after her death

PARKER, Geoffrey, BA, MA, PhD, LittD (1943-), British historian, born in Nottingham, and read History at Cambridge University. He has taught at the universities of St Andrews, Illinois, Yale and Ohio State.
Philip II (1978); *The Grand Strategy of Philip II* (2000); *Imprudent King: A New Life of Philip II* (2014)

PARKER, John, British biographer, journalist, and editor, has written widely on, military history and investigative works.
Prince Philip: A Critical Biography (1990); *The Queen: The New Biography* (1991)

PARRY, Sir Edward (Abbott) (1863-1943), British judge and author, born in London. He studied at the Middle Temple and was called to the Bar in 1885, becoming Judge of Manchester County Court from 1894 to 1911 (during which he was shot at and seriously wounded in Court on one occasion when he had to cancel the certificate of a bailiff who attempted instant revenge), and then Judge of Lambeth County Court. He was appointed to sit on a Pensions Appeal Tribunal in 1917, dealing with appeals against governmental decisions on military pensions. He

wrote on law, history, medicine, and a volume of memoirs, as well as plays and fiction.
Queen Caroline (1930)

PAULI, Hertha E. (Ernestine) (1906-73), Austrian actress, author and journalist, was born in Vienna. From around 1972 to 1933 she worked as an actress in Germany, then turned to writing and working with a literary agency. The family went to Switzerland via France and during the Second World War they moved to America, where she spent the rest of her life.
The Secret of Sarajevo: The Story of Franz Ferdinand and Sophie (1966)

PEARSON, Hesketh, MC (1887-1964), British writer, actor and theatre director, regarded as the leading British biographer of his time, in terms of commercial success. He was born in Hawford, Claines, Worcestershire. During the First World War he served with the Army Service Corps in Mesopotamia and came close to death from diseases on three occasions, attributing his survival to a practice of reciting long passages of Shakespeare while he was critically ill. He returned to the stage after the war, alternating acting with his career as a prolific author.
Charles II: His Life and Likeness (1960)

PEARSON, John (1930-), British biographer and novelist, born in Epsom, read History at Peterhouse College, Cambridge. He worked for *The Economist*, BBC TV, and the *Sunday Times*, where he was assistant to Ian Fleming and later wrote the first biography of him. He has also written books on the Sitwell family and the Kray twins.
Edward the Rake (1975)

PENN, Thomas, Ph.D., British biographer, studied Medieval History at Clare College, Cambridge, became editorial director at Penguin Books, and has contributed to the *Guardian, Daily Telegraph,* and *London Review of Books. Winter King: The Dawn of Tudor England* (2011)

PERRY, Maria, British historian and actress, read English at Somerville College, Oxford.
The Word of a Prince: Life of Elizabeth I from Contemporary Documents (1990); *Sisters to the King: The Tumultuous Lives of Henry VII's Sisters, Margaret of Scotland and Mary of France* (1998)

PETRIE, Sir Charles Alexander, 3rd Baronet, CBE (1895-1977), **British** historian, was born in Liverpool and educated at Oxford. His first work of major interest was an essay in counterfactual history, *If: A Jacobite Fantasy* (*The Weekly Westminster*, 30.1.1926), speculating on the possible course of events had Bonnie Prince Charlie won the battle of Culloden and brought about a restoration in the house of Stuart lasting until the 20th century and beyond. In 1927 he succeeded to the family baronetcy. He was literary editor for the *New English Review*, and co-editor of its shortlived successor, *English Review Magazine*, later becoming editor of the *Household Brigade*, and contributed to the *Illustrated London News and Catholic Herald.*
The Stuart Pretenders: A History of the Jacobite Movement, 1688-1807 (1933); The Letters Speeches and Proclamations of King Charles I (1935); *The Four Georges: A Revaluation of the Period from 1714 to 1830* (1935); *The Stuarts* (1937); *Louis XIV* (1938); *The Duke of Berwick and His Son; Some Unpublished Letters and Papers* (1951); *The Marshal Duke of Berwick; The Picture of an Age,* (1953); *The Spanish Royal House* (1958); *King Alfonso XIII and His Age* (1963); *Philip II of Spain* (1963); *Don John of Austria* (1967); *The Letters of King Charles I* (1968); *King Charles III of Spain: An Enlightened Despot* (1971); *King Charles, Prince Rupert, and the Civil War: from Original Letters* (1974)

PETROPOULOS, Jonathan (1961-), American historian and Professor of European History at Claremont McKenna College, Claremont, California. Regarded as an expert on the fate of art looted during the Second World War, he was Research Director for the Presidential Advisory Commission on Holocaust Assets from 1986 to 2000, and has served as an expert witness in several legal cases concerning Nazi-looted assets.
Royals and the Reich (2006)

PHILLIPS, Seymour, British biographer, has been Emeritus Professor of Medieval History, University College, Dublin, and a member of the Royal Irish Academy.
Edward II (2011)

PIMLOTT, Ben (Benjamin John) FBA, PhD (1945–2004), British political writer, studied Philosophy, Politics and Economics at Oxford University, and became a lecturer in Politics at Newcastle University in 1970. As a Labour candidate he contested seats at Arundel and then Cleveland and Whitby in 1974 and 1979. He was Political Editor of the *New Statesman* from 1987 to 1988, when he became Professor of Contemporary History at Birkbeck, and later Warden of Goldsmiths, University of London, a post he held at the time of his death from leukaemia. He was best remembered for his lives of Hugh Dalton and Harold Wilson and his last book, a biography of Elizabeth II. In view of his socialist background it was a choice of subject that surprised many of those who knew him, and according to a colleague he was 'mortified that he might be mocked by his friends'.
The Queen: A Biography of Elizabeth II (1996)

PLOWDEN, Alison (Margaret Chichele) (1931–2007), British historian and biographer, born at Quetta, India.

Between 1963 and 1988 she worked for the BBC as a script editor, produced the script for a TV series *Mistress of Hardwick*, about Bess of Hardwick, which won her a Writers' Guild Award for the best educational television series, and several radio and television plays. She later recalled: 'A secretary writing scripts was a little like a performing monkey at the BBC - there was a sort of "Fancy, what a clever little girl" attitude' (*Daily Telegraph*, 29.8.2007) In 1970 she left the BBC to concentrate on writing historical biographies, mostly of monarchs and consorts from the Tudor and Stuart eras.

Young Elizabeth (1971); *Danger to Elizabeth* (1973); *The House of Tudor* (1976); *Marriage with My Kingdom: The Courtships of Queen Elizabeth I* (1977); *Tudor Women - Queens and Commoners* (1979); *Elizabeth Regina* (1980); *Young Victoria* (1983); *Two Queens in One Isle: The Deadly Relationship of Elizabeth I and Mary Queen of Scots* (1984); *Lady Jane Grey: Nine Days Queen* (1985); *Caroline and Charlotte* (1989); *The Stuart Princesses* (1996); *Women All on Fire: Women of the English Civil War* (1998); *Henrietta Maria: Charles I's Indomitable Queen* (2001); *In a Free Republic* (2006); *The Winter Queen* [Elizabeth Stuart, wife of Frederick V, Elector Palatine and King of Bohemia] (2008)

PLUMB, Sir J.H. (John, or Jack, Harold), FBA (1911-2001), British historian and biographer, born in Leicester, read History at Christ's College, Cambridge. During the Second World War he worked in the codebreaking department of the Foreign Office, Bletchley Park. He became a Fellow and Tutor of Christ's College and later lectured in History, was appointed Reader in Modern History at Cambridge University in 1962, Professor of Modern English History in 1966, and Master of Christ's College from 1978 to 1982. He was an advisory editor for history for Penguin Books, and published several books on 18th century subjects, and was involved in *Royal Heritage*, the

BBC series about the royal collections made for and screened to coincide with Queen Elizabeth II's Silver Jubilee, as well as co-writing the accompanying book with Sir Huw Wheldon.
The First Four Georges (1956)

PLUMPTRE, George (1956-), British author of books on gardening and biographer, was a gardening correspondent of *The Times*, has also been consultant editor and then director of business development, Sotheby's, and director in charge of business development at Bonhams, and chief executive of the National Gardens Scheme.
Edward VII (1997)

POCOCK, Tom (Thomas Allcot Guy) (1925-2007), English biographer, war correspondent, journalist and naval historian, joined the Royal Navy in 1943, and was a naval 'minder' to war correspondents covering the Battle of Normandy. He worked for four years with the Hulton Press current affairs magazine group, and was one of the first journalists to see the Bergen-Belsen concentration camp. Later he was successively a feature-writer and Naval Correspondent with the *Daily Mail*, Naval Correspondent of *The Times*, foreign correspondent and special writer for the *Daily Express*, and feature writer, Defence Correspondent, War Correspondent and Travel Editor on the Evening Standard. He wrote about twenty books, including biographies of Admiral Nelson, and Alan Moorehead.
Sailor *King: The Life of William IV* (1991)

POLLARD, Albert Frederick (1869–1948), British historian specializing in the Tudor period. He was born in Ryde, Isle of Wight, and read Modern History at Jesus College, Oxford. He was Assistant Editor of and a contributor of about 500 entries to *Dictionary of National*

Biography, then became Professor of Constitutional History at University College, London, from 1903 to 1931. He was a member of the Royal Commission on Historical Manuscripts, a founder of the Historical Association, Editor of *History* from 1916 to 1922, and of the *Bulletin of the Institute of Historical Research* from 1923 to 1939.

The Reign of Henry VII, From Contemporary Sources (1913); *Henry VIII* (1930)

POLLOCK, Kassandra and Sabrina, *see* BEECHE, Arturo E.

POLNAY, Peter de (1906-84), born in Budapest, the son of a minister of Admiral Horthy, travelled widely around the world. First and foremost a novelist, he was in France when the Second World War broke out, and in another book he left a vivid account of Paris under German occupation. He died in Paris.

A Queen of Spain: Isabel II (1962)

PONSONBY, Arthur, later Lord Ponsonby of Shulbrede (1871-1946), British author and politician. The third son of Sir Henry Ponsonby, Queen Victoria's Private Secretary, and younger brother of Sir Frederick (q.v.), he studied at Balliol College, Oxford, then worked in the diplomatic service and at the Foreign Office. He was elected Liberal MP for Stirling Burghs in 1908, and after joining the Labour Party, MP for Sheffield Brightside from 1922 to 1930, when he became Chancellor of the Duchy of Lancaster and Leader of the Opposition in the House of Lords, until resigning after disagreements with the party. In addition to a short life of Queen Victoria, he also wrote the official life of his father, which was awarded the James Tait Black Memorial Prize for Biography in 1942 (see p. 246), and which in the view of Sir Philip Magnus (q.v.), provided probably 'the best sketch of the personality of the

Sovereign whose example King Edward did his utmost to follow' (*King Edward the Seventh*, xv).
Queen Victoria (1933)

PONSONBY, D.A. (Doris Almon) (1907-93), British biographer, also wrote under the names Doris Rybot and Sarah Tempest.
The Lost Duchess: The Story of the Prince Consort's Mother (1958)

PONSONBY, Sir Frederick (Edward Grey), GCB, GCVO, PC, 1st Baron Sysonby (1867-1935), British courtier and author, was the second son of Sir Henry Ponsonby, Private Secretary to Queen Victoria. He served in the Grenadier Guards during the Boer War, in which he was wounded, and the First World War. At court he was Equerry-in-Ordinary to Queen Victoria from 1894 to 1901, and Assistant Keeper of the Privy Purse and Assistant Private Secretary to the Queen from 1897 until her death and to Edward VII throughout his reign, appointed Keeper of the Privy Purse to George V from 1914 to 1935, and Lieutenant-Governor of Windsor Castle from 1928. As godson of the Crown Princess of Prussia, later the Empress Frederick, when he accompanied Edward VII on the latter's final visit to the dying Empress in 1901 she asked him to take a large collection of her letters to Queen Victoria to England as she did not wish Emperor William II to have charge of them. His decision to publish a selection in 1928 proved controversial and met with a mixed reaction from members of the royal family. He was raised to the peerage as Baron Sysonby, of Wonersh in the County of Surrey, a few months before his death. His memoirs, published posthumously, was described by Philip Magnus (q.v.), as an 'indiscreet volume of memoirs' which 'provide a vivid sketch of the personality of Edward VII' (*King Edward the Seventh*, xv).

Letters of the Empress Frederick (ed.) (1928); *Sidelights on Queen Victoria* (1930); *Recollections of Three Reigns* (1951), ed. Colin Welch

POPE-HENNESSY, (Richard) James (Arthur), CRVO (1916-74), British biographer, born in London, was an editorial assistant for Catholic publishers Sheed & Ward. During the Second World War he was a member of the British army staff at Washington. He was literary editor of *The Spectator* between 1947 and 1949, before becoming a full-time writer of royal and literary biographies and works on travel. His official life of Queen Mary, according to Kenneth Rose (q.v.) 'remains the masterpiece of royal biographies: lively yet respectful, impeccable scholarship dowered with Proustian insight, as much a smiling intimate portrait as an evocation of a vanished age'. (Rose, *Kings, Queens and Courtiers*, 244) He was murdered in his London flat by a group of young drinking companions, having heard him boast of a large advance for a recently-commissioned biography of Noel Coward and assumed that he kept the money in his house. His brother James, an art historian, was successively Director of the Victoria and Albert Museum and British Museum. Selections from his letters and entries from his 'intermittent diary', the title taken from a letter of his written in 1964, were edited and published seven years after his death.
Queen Mary (1959); *Queen Victoria at Windsor and Balmoral* (ed.) (1959); *A Lonely Business: A Self-Portrait of James Pope-Hennessy*, ed. Peter Quennell (1981)

PORTER, Ivor (Forsyth), CMG, OBE (1913-2012), British ambassador and author, brought up in the Lake District. After studying at Leeds University, he was sent to Bucharest on an academic post with the British Council, was transferred to the Legation, and recruited by SOE (Special Operations Executive) as part of a three-man

mission parachuted into Roumania in December 1943 to instigate resistance against the Nazis. The SOE agents were captured and held as prisoners of war until King Michael carried out an anti-German *coup d'état* in 1944. Porter stayed in the country during the King's attempts to hold out against Soviet domination. He joined the Foreign Office in 1946, serving in London, Washington DC, Cyprus and India, and served on the Arms Control Committee in Geneva. He was made Commander of the Romanian order of 'Meritul Cultural' in 2005.
Michael of Romania: The King and the Country (2005)

PORTER, Linda (1947-), born in Exeter, but moved to the London area and studied History at University of York. She later became a university lecturer in New York.
The First Queen of England: The Myth of 'Bloody Mary' (2008); *Katherine the Queen: The Remarkable Life of Katherine Parr* (2010); *Tudors Versus Stewarts: The Fatal Inheritance of Mary, Queen of Scots* (2014)

PORTER, (John) McKenzie, MC, FRSA (1911-2006), British author and journalist. Beginning his career as a film critic and feature writer in Fleet Street, he erved with the army during World War Two in the Italian campaign and was wounded at Cassino. Promoted to Major, after the war he worked with British Intelligence in Rome, Athens and Vienna, then becoming Paris correspondent with Kemsley Newspapers from 1946 to 1948. Emigrating to Canada, he was a columnist and arts critic at *The Telegram and Toronto Sun* from 1962 to 1990.
Overture to Victoria: A Biography of Edward, Duke of Kent (1961)

POSCHINGER, Heinrich Joseph Karl Ludwig von (1845-1911), German writer and historian. He studied philosophy and law at university in Munich and held various government posts in Bavaria and then Berlin, where he came into contact with Chancellor Otto von Bismarck, and published several volumes of his documents, letters and interviews, as well as writing several papers on him. He retired from the civil service and he and his wife Margaretha (Margaretha Maria Victoria Freiin von Landau, 1861-1911), born at Breslau, Silesia, both settled in La Bollène, Nice, where he founded the German newspaper *Riviera-Tageblatt*. A three-volume biography of Emperor Frederick III was published in German between 1898 and 1900 and a one-volume edition in English edited by Sidney Whitman followed in 1901. It is credited on the title page to Margaretha, and a review of the German edition in *The Times* credits husband and wife with authorship, suggesting it was a joint effort. Both died a few weeks apart in La Bollène, France. His obituary observed that once he came into contact with Bismarck, 'he soon set himself the task of accumulating everything that there was to accumulate about the great Chancellor. He has far outdistanced all competitors in his chosen sphere, and up to the time of his death was still deluging the German newspapers with anecdotes and Bismarckian records of every sort and kind. His countless and now for the most part unreadable volumes defy criticism.' (*The Times* 11.8.1911)

Life of the Emperor Frederick, ed. Sidney Whitman (1901); *Diaries of the Emperor Frederick during the Campaigns of 1866 and 1870-71, as well as his Journeys to the east and to Spain,* ed. (1902)

POTTS, D.M. (David Malcolm), M.A., Ph.D., & W.T. W. (William Taylor Windle), M.A., Ph.D., and D.Sc., British academic scientists. D.M.P. was a Fellow of Sidney Sussex College, Cambridge, and first Medical Director of the International Planned Parenthood Federation, London. He held the Bixby Chair in Population and Family Planning at the University of California, Berkeley.

W.T.W.P. studied Animal Physiology at Cambridge, was lecturer at universities of Aberdeen, Birmingham and Washington, and editor of the Journal of Comparative Psychology B. As brothers they shared 'a long-established interest in the light that human genes can throw on human behavior and history'.

Queen Victoria's Gene: Haemophilia and the Royal Family (1995)

POUND, Reginald (1894-1991), was Literary Editor of the *Daily Express*, and later Features Editor of the *Daily Mail*. During the Second World War he worked with the Ministry of Information, was a member of the BBC Radio Newsreel team, and from 1942 he was Editor of *The Strand* magazine. From 1952 onwards he was the author of several biographies, including those of Arnold Bennett and Sir Alfred Munnings.

Queen Victoria (1970); *Albert, a Biography of the Prince Consort* (1973)

POURTALES, Count Guy de (1882-1941), French biographer and novelist, served with the British Expeditionary Force during the First World War.

Ludwig II of Bavaria: The Man of Illusion (1928)

POWER, Alan, author of a book claiming Diana, Princess of Wales was murdered by MI6 and the SAS. Shortly after its publication, he claimed that his life was in danger and that he was being followed by men working for the security services.

The Princess Diana Conspiracy (2013)

POWICKE, Sir F.M. (Frederick Maurice) (1879-1963), born at Alnwick, read History at University of Manchester and Balliol College, Oxford, returning to Manchester as a lecturer. He was appointed Professor of Medieval History at Manchester in 1919, becoming Head of Department in

1925 until his retirement in 1947. He was a contributor to the Cambridge Medieval History.
King Henry III and the Lord Edward: The Community of the Realm in the Thirteenth Century, 2 vols. (1947)

PRESCOTT, H.F.M. (Hilda Frances Margaret), MA, DLitt, FRSL (1896-1972), British biographer and novelist, read History at Lady Margaret Hall, Oxford University. Her biography of Mary Tudor, reprinted under that title in 1953, was awarded the James Tait Black Memorial Prize for Biography (see p.246) in 1940.
Spanish Tudor (1940)

PRESTON, Paul, CBE (1946-), British historian and biographer, born in Liverpool, is a specialist in the modern Spanish era. From 1991 he taught at the London School of Economics as Príncipe de Asturias Professor of Contemporary Spanish Studies and Director of the Cañada Blanch Centre for Contemporary Spanish Studies.
Juan Carlos: A People's King (2004) UK/*Juan Carlos: Steering Spain from Dictatorship to Democracy* (2004) (US)

PRESTWICH, Michael, OBE (1943-), British historian and biographer, an authority on medieval England, read History at Magdalen College, Oxford. He lectured for a year at Christ Church, then St Andrews University for ten years, then to Durham where he was a Reader, then Professor, Head of the Department and Pro-Vice-Chancellor, retiring in 2008.
War, Politics and Finance under Edward I (1972); *The Three Edwards: War and State in England, 1272-1377* (1980); *Edward I* (1988)

PYE, Michael (1946-), British historian and biographer, studied History at Oxford, joined the staff of *The Scotsman* and then the *Sunday Times* for which he was chief financial reporter. He also wrote and presented documentaries for the BBC and Scottish TV. He later went to live and work in New York before moving to and settling in southern Europe.

The King Over The Water: The Windsors in the Bahamas, 1940-45 (1981)

Q

QUENNELL, Sir Peter (Courtney), CBE (1905-93), British biographer, social and literary historian, editor and poet. He was born at Bickley, Kent, and studied at Balliol College, Oxford. He was Editor of the *Cornhill Magazine* from 1944 to 1951, after which he was founder Editor of *History Today* from 1951 to 1979, and edited a volume of writings by James Pope-Hennessy (q.v.), published several years after the latter's death.
Caroline of England (1939)

QUINTRELL, Brian.
Charles I, 1625-1640 (1993)

R

RADZINSKY, Edvard Stanislavovich (1936-), Russian biographer, historian and playwright, born in Moscow. He has written over forty non-fiction books, including biographies of Stalin and Rasputin.
The Last Tsar: The Life and Death of Nicholas II (1992); *Alexander II: The Last Great Tsar* (2006)

RADZIWILL, Catherine, (*née* Countess Ekaterina Adamovna Rzewuska) (1858-1941), Polish-Lithuanian biographer, who married Prince Wilhelm Radziwill when she was fifteen, and moved to Berlin. She wrote several rather gossipy titles about the courts of Europe, and was believed to have written a controversial book about Emperor William II under the name of Count Paul Vassili.
The Intimate Life of the Last Tsarina (1928); *Nicholas II: The Last of the Tsars* (1931); *The Taint of the Romanovs* (1931); *The Empress Frederick* (1934)

RAMM, Agatha (1914-2004), Anglo-German historian, was born in Berlin to an English father and a German mother of Huguenot descent. She and her mother moved to England after the outbreak of the First World War. She was Tutor in Modern History, Somerville College, Oxford, from 1952 to 1981, wrote extensively on modern European history, and edited a volume of correspondence between W.E. Gladstone and Lord Granville. Her last book was the final volume in the series of correspondence between

Queen Victoria and her eldest daughter, begun by Sir Roger Fulford (q.v.)
Beloved and Darling Child: Last Letters between Queen Victoria and her Eldest Daughter 1886-1901 (ed.) (1990)

RAPPAPORT, Helen (*née* Ware) (1947-), British actress and author, was born in Bromley, Kent. As an actress she appeared in several television series including *Crown Court, Love Hurts,* and *The Bill.* In the 1990s she went into writing and publishing, becoming a copy editor for Blackwell and Oxford University Press, and contributing to historical and biographical reference works. She became a full-time writer in 1998, with particular interests in Russian and Victorian history. In addition to writing biographies, she also appeared in royal biographical documentaries, and was historical consultant on a BBC2 documentary about the Romanov sisters, *Russia's Lost Princesses.* She also broadcast on Victorian and Russian history for BBC radio, and appeared in several episodes of a Radio 4 series *The Art of Monarchy.*

Queen Victoria: A Biographical Companion (2003); *Ekaterinburg: The Last Days of the Romanovs* (2009) UK / *The Last Days of the Romanovs: Tragedy at Ekaterinburg* (2010) US; *Magnificent Obsession: Victoria, Albert and the Death that Changed the Monarchy* (2012); *Four Sisters* (2014) UK / *The Romanov Sisters* (2014) US

RAPPOPORT, Angelo S. (Solomon) (1871-1950), Russian biographer and historian, born in the Ukraine, studied at universities in Basle and Paris. He was sent in 1899 by the Alliance Israelite Universelle, Paris, to investigate and report on the conditions of the Falashas or Jewish population in the region. After settling in London early in the 20th century he became a Lecturer in Modern Languages and Literature at Birkbeck University. He went to live in Paris after the First World War.

The Curse of the Romanovs: A Study of the Lives and the Reigns of Two Tsars, Paul I and Alexander I of Russia, 1754-1825 (1907); *Royal Lovers and Mistresses: The Romance of Crowned and Uncrowned Kings and Queens of Europe* (1908); *Leopold the Second, King of the Belgians* (1910)

REDLICH, Joseph (1869-1936), Austrian statesman and historian, born in Bohemia, studied Law and History at the University of Vienna, and then became Professor of Constitutional Law there in 1906. He was German Liberal representative in the imperial Reichsrat of Austria-Hungary from 1907 to 1918, and in June 1917 was asked to head a reform cabinet in order to try and establish a constitutional democracy within the empire as a precondition for a peace settlement. Although it came to nothing, he remained in Vienna after the end of the empire, writing studies of recent history. He refused further participation in political affairs except for a short term as finance minister in 1931.
Emperor Francis Joseph of Austria: A Biography (1929)

REES, Neil, British author and computational linguist. His book was based upon interviews with people who knew the King and Queen of the Albanians.
A Royal Exile: King Zog and Queen Geraldine, Including Their Wartime Exile in the Thames Valley and Chilterns (2010)

REINERS, Ludwig (1896-1957), German biographer and historian, born in Ratibor. After fighting in the First World War he studied Law and Economics at university. For a while he worked in banking and was the author of several economic textbooks before becoming a historian. He was working on a three-volume biography, of which only two volumes were completed and published, at the time of his death.
Frederick the Great (1960)

RENIER, G.J. (Gustaaf Johannes Petrus) (1892-1962), Dutch biographer, journalist and translator. Born in Flushing, Holland, he studied History at Ghent University. Settling in England soon after the outbreak of the First World War, he resumed his studies at University College, London, where he became Reader in Dutch History from 1936 to 1957.

The Ill-fated Princess: The Life of Charlotte, Daughter of the Prince Regent (1932); William of Orange (1932)

RENNELL, Tony, British journalist and author, was a regular contributor to British newspapers and former associate editor of *The Sunday Times.*

Last Days of Glory: The Death of Queen Victoria (2000)

RICHARDSON, Joanna (Leah), FRSL (1925-2008), British biographer, historian, translator, and literary critic, was born in London. She read French at St Anne's College, Oxford, then worked for a short time as a research assistant to the illustrations editor of *Chambers's Encyclopaedia* and as a correspondent and book critic for the *New English Weekly*. Although she had graduated with a Third, she went on to do post-graduate research at Oxford. She published several biographies of 19th century British and French royalty, British and French poets, including Keats, Tennyson, Edward Fitzgerald and Edward Lear, and Théophile Gautier. A life of the latter's daughter Judith in 1986 made her the first non-French winner of the Prix Goncourt, one of the highest literary awards in France. She also was a prolific journalist and critic for *The Times*, the *Times Literary Supplement, The Listener, History Today* and several French literary journals. She also worked for the BBC, translating plays from the French and recording features for radio.

The Disastrous Marriage: A Study of George IV and Caroline of Brunswick (1960); *My Dearest Uncle: A Life of Leopold, First King of the Belgians* (1961); *George IV: A Portrait* (1966); *Princess Mathilde* [cousin of Napoleon III] (1968); *Louis XIV* (1973); *Victoria and Albert: A Study of a Marriage* (1977); *Portrait of a Bonaparte: The Life and Times of Joseph-Napoleon Primoli, 1851-1927* (1987)

RICHARDSON, Walter C. (Cecil) (1902-83)
Mary Tudor, The White Queen (1970)

RIDDELL, Mary, British journalist and biographer, studied Modern Languages at Nottingham University. She was formerly Deputy Editor of *Today*, Women's Assistant and Assistant Editor of the *Daily Mirror*, a columnist for *The Observer*, and contributor to the *Daily Mail* and *New Statesman*, before becoming Assistant Editor of the *Daily Telegraph*.
The Duchess of Kent: The Troubled Life of Katherine Worsley (1999)

RIDGWAY, Claire (*née* Brassington) (1971-), British biographer, and specialist in the Tudor era. A former teacher, she formerly ran a company History Tours of Britain, set up a Tudor history website, www.TheAnneBoleynFiles.com, and claims to be 'on a crusade to debunk the myths surrounding Anne Boleyn and educate the world about the REAL Anne Boleyn'.
The Anne Boleyn Collection (2012); *The Fall of Anne Boleyn: A Countdown* (2013); *The Anne Boleyn Collection II* (2013); *George Boleyn: Tudor Poet, Courtier and Diplomat* (2014)

RIDLEY, Jane (1953-), English historian, biographer, author and broadcaster, born in Northumberland, was eldest daughter of Nicholas Ridley, Conservative MP for Cirencester and Tewkesbury, 1959-92, and government

minister, and was also great-great-granddaughter of novelist Edward Bulwer-Lytton. She read History at St Hugh's College, Oxford, and was a research student at Nuffield College. In 1979 she was appointed Lecturer in history at the University of Buckingham, promoted to Senior Lecturer in 1994, to Reader in 2002, to Senior Tutor responsible for student discipline the next year, and to Professor in 2007. She was in charge of the university's Master of Arts course in biography after establishing it in 1996. Her career as a writer began with an edition of the letters of Edwin Lutyens, her great-grandfather, which she edited jointly withy her mother Clayre Percy. She later wrote the biography of Lutyens and of Disraeli, and has contributed to the *Oxford Dictionary of National Biography*.
Bertie: A Life of Edward VII (2012) UK / *The Heir Apparent: A Life of Edward VII, the Playboy Prince* (2012) US; *Victoria: Queen, Matriarch, Empress* (2014)

RIDLEY, Jasper (Godwin) (1920–2004), born in West Hoathly, Sussex, was educated at Magdalen College, Oxford, and the Sorbonne. He trained and practised as a barrister before becoming a writer. During World War Two he was a conscientious objector, and claimed he was violently abused while in a detention camp. He served on St Pancras Borough Council from 1945 to 1949, and stood as a Labour candidate for Winchester in the 1955 general election. He was awarded the 1970 James Tait Black Memorial Prize for his biography of Lord Palmerston.
Napoleon III and Eugénie (1979); *Life and Times of Mary Tudor* (1973); *Henry VIII: The Politics of Tyranny* (1984); *The Love Letters of Henry VIII* (1988) ed; *Elizabeth I: the Shrewdness of Virtue* (1988); *Maximilian & Juarez* (1992); *The Houses of Hanover and Saxe-Coburg-Gotha: A Royal History of England* [with John Clarke] (2000)

ROBB, Nesca A. (Adeline), DPhil (1915-76), British historian and biographer, born in Ulster and studied at Oxford.
William of Orange: A Personal Portrait, Vol 1, 1650-1673 (1962); *William of Orange: A Personal Portrait*, Vol 2, 1674-1702 (1966)

ROBERTS, Andrew, FRSA, FRSL (1963-), British historian and journalist, was born in London. Best-known as a military and political historian and biographer, he has also contributed to the Spectator and Daily Telegraph, and has been a Visiting Professor at the Department of War Studies, King's College, London.
Letters to Vicky: The Correspondence between Queen Victoria and her Daughter Victoria, Empress of Germany, 1858-1901 (ed.) (2011); *Napoleon: A Life* (2014)

ROBERTS, Dorothea.
Two Royal Lives: Gleanings from Berlin and from the Lives of Their Imperial Highnesses the Crown Prince and Princess of Germany (1887)

ROBY, Kinley (1929-), American author, writer of mostly mystery fiction, but also of studies of Arnold Bennett and Joyce Cary.
The King, the Press and the People: A Study of King Edward VII (1975)

RODD, Sir (James) Rennell, 1st Baron Rennell, GCB, GCMG, GCVO, PC (1858-1941), British diplomat and author. He studied at Balliol College, Oxford, where he was a contemporary and friend of Oscar Wilde and helped him to obtain publication, though their relationship did not outlast Wilde's controversial behaviour and conviction. Rodd joined the Diplomatic Service in 1883 and served at the British embassies in Berlin, where he became a close friend of Crown Prince and Princess Frederick William, later briefly Emperor and Empress, then in Rome, Athens and Paris. He was made Minister Plenipotentiary to Sweden in 1904, and played a major role in the dissolution of the Union between Sweden and Norway the following year, and was awarded the Grand Cross of the Order of the Polar Star by King Oscar II. He was Ambassador to Italy from 1909 to 1919, and was heavily involved in securing Italian support for the Entente during the First World War. He left the diplomatic service in 1919, and was British delegate to the League of Nations from 1921 to 1923. Entering politics, he was Unionist Member of Parliament for St Marylebone from 1928 to 1932. As a writer, he published books on ancient Greece and Rome, poetry, and memoirs. His short biography of Frederick III was written at the request of the Empress Frederick, with royalties being donated to the Throat Hospital, London. He was the father-in-law of Nancy Mitford (q.v.).

Frederick, Crown Prince and Emperor: A Biographical Sketch Dedicated to his Memory (1888)

RÖHL, John C.G. (Charles Gerald) (1938-), Anglo-German historian, was born in London to a German father and an English mother. He accompanied his parents back to Germany and then Hungary after the outbreak of the Second World War and lived briefly in the care of the Red Cross in an international children's home in Adelboden, Switzerland. He was reunited with his mother and sisters in Manchester in December 1946, completed his education in England, and then served in the Royal Air Force on the German-Dutch border near Aachen. After researching the history of Imperial Germany after Bismarck's fall from power, he was appointed to a Lectureship in History in the School of European Studies at the University of Sussex, Brighton in 1964, and in 1979 Professor of European History. Between 1982 and 1985 he served as Dean of the

School of European Studies. He also taught Modern European History at the University of Hamburg and at the University of Freiburg. After *Germany without Bismarck* (1967), he edited the political correspondence of Prince Philipp zu Eulenburg-Hertefeld, in three volumes under the auspices of the Historical Commission of the Bavarian Academy of Sciences. In 1996 in collaboration with Martin Warren and David Hunt, he exhumed the remains of the Kaiser's sister Charlotte Hereditary Princess of Saxe-Meiningen in Thuringia and her daughter Princess Feodora of Reuss in Poland. The analysis of their DNA showed that both women had suffered from a form of *porphyria variegata*, so demonstrating the validity of the theory that this illness had been the probable cause of George III's 'madness'.

Kaiser Wilhelm II: New Interpretations: The Corfu Papers (1982); *The Kaiser and His Court: Wilhelm II and the Government of Germany*, (1994); *Purple Secret: Genes, 'Madness' and the Royal Houses of Europe* [with Martin Warren and David Hunt] (1998); *Young Wilhelm: The Kaiser's Early Life, 1859-1888*, (1998); *Wilhelm II: The Kaiser's Personal Monarchy, 1888-1900* (2004); *Wilhelm II: Into the Abyss of War and Exile, 1900-1941* (2014); *Kaiser Wilhelm II 1859-1941: A Concise Life* (2014)

ROSE, Kenneth, CBE, FRSL (1924-2014), British historian and biographer, went to study History at Oxford, left to fight in the Second World War, then returned to complete his degree. He taught history at Eton, and in 1952 he joined the Peterborough column of *The Daily Telegraph*. In 1961 he began his long spell as diarist on the newly-formed *Sunday Telegraph*. 'Albany at Large', the social diary he wrote over four decades, dealt mainly with the doings and sayings of royalty and nobility, senior politicians, diplomats and academics. His biography of King George, his most successful title, won three awards,

the Wolfson Award for history, and the Whitbread and Yorkshire Post awards for biography.
King George V (1983); *Kings, Queens and Courtiers* (1985)

ROSS, Charles (Derek) (1924-86), British historian, was reader and then Professor of Medieval History at Bristol University, and specialist in 15th century history and royalty. Six days after he cancelled his wedding because of problems with a divorce, his fiancée stabbed him to death and was jailed for manslaughter.
Edward IV (1974); *Richard III* (1981)

ROSS, Josephine (1950-), British historian and biographer, read English at London University and then worked for *Vogue*, resulting in the publication of several illustrated books associated with the magazine. She was the wife of biographer James Chambers (q.v.).
The Tudors (1979); *The Winter Queen: The Story of Elizabeth Stuart* (1979); *The Men Who Would Be King: Suitors to Queen Elizabeth I* (2005)

ROSVALL, Ted (1952-), Swedish author and publisher, is a church musician by profession, and genealogist who was President of the Federation of Swedish Genealogical Societies from 2000 to 2008. He launched his imprint Rosvall Royal Books in 1985, and relaunched *Royalty Digest*, a monthly edited by Paul Minet (q.v.) which had ceased publication in 2005, as *Royalty Digest Quarterly* the following year. Since 2008 he has also been the host of the Swedish version of *Who do you think you are?*, a TV series on genealogy.
The Bernadotte Descendants, (1992); *Astrid (1905-1935) –* (Queen of Belgium) [with Antoinette Ramsay Herthelius] (2005); *Ingrid 1910-2000* (Queen Ingrid of Denmark) [with Randi Buchwaldt] (2010); *Marie (1865-1909) - A French*

Princess in Denmark [with Inger-Lise Klausen] (2012); *Axel &*
Margaretha - A Royal Couple [with Randi Buchwaldt] (2013)

ROTH-NICHOLLS, Karen (*née* Karen Nicholls) (1938-),
British-born translator, was born in Hayes, Kent of Anglo-
Viennese parentage. She spent her teenage years in
Denmark, where she completed her education and became
proficient in Danish, moving to Switzerland and acquiring
Swiss nationality on marriage. She has undertaken
extensive historical translation work. She has undertaken
extensive translation work for other biographers, including
Coryne Hall (q.v.) and Ted Rosvall (q.v.).
25 Chapters of my Life: Grand Duchess Olga Alexandrovna (2009),
(ed.) (with Paul Kulikovsky, Sue Woolmans)

ROWELL, George (-2001), British theatre historian, was
an authority on Victorian stage history. He lectured in
Drama at Bristol, which in 1947 became the first British
university to offer it as a degree subject. Over a writing
career of forty years he published several works on drama.
His contribution to royal biography discusses almost every
theatre performance ever seen by Queen Victoria.
Queen Victoria Goes to the Theatre (1978)

S

SAALER, Mary, biographer.
Anne of Cleves, Fourth Wife of Henry VIII (1997); *Edward II, 1307-1327* (1997)

St AUBYN, Hon Giles (Rowan), FRSL, (1925-2015), son of 3rd Baron St Levan of St Michaels Mount, served in World War Two and gained the rank of Ordinary Seaman in 1944 in the service of the Royal Navy Volunteer Reserve. He graduated from Oxford with an MA, and joined the staff at Eton in 1947, becoming a Housemaster in 1959 and Head of History in 1961, retiring in 1985. On the subject of official royal biographies, he once said that 'Being an official biographer is a great advantage as it gives you more access and more facilities. As with any biographer, there is a conflict between putting something in that isn't known but might be wounding to others and the desire to tell the truth' (*Daily Mail*, 13.9.2009).
The Royal George, 1819-1904: The life of HRH Prince George, Duke of Cambridge (1963); *William of Gloucester: Pioneer Prince* (1977); *Edward VII: Prince and King* (1979); *The Year of Three Kings, 1483* (1983); *Queen Victoria: A Portrait* (1991)

SALWAY, Lance (1940-), British author, born in Brighton, biographer and author of children's fiction and studies of children's literature.
Queen Victoria's Grandchildren (1991)

SALZMAN, L.F. (Louis Francis), CBE (1878-1971), British economic and local historian and biographer who specialised in the medieval period, was born in Brighton, and educated at Pembroke College, Oxford. He was excused military service in the First World War because of ill-health, and initially taught as a career. He became the Honorary Editor of the Sussex Archaeological Society in 1909, and was President from 1954 to 1956. He was General Editor of the Victoria County History from 1934 to 1949.

Henry II (1914); *Edward I* (1968)

SARA, M.E.

The Rt Hon the Earl of Athlone (1941); *The Life and Times of HRH Princess Beatrice* (1945)

SARAH, Duchess of York, *née* Sarah Margaret Ferguson (1959-), was formerly married to Andrew, Duke of York, second son of Queen Elizabeth II. She has written extensively for adults and children, and collaborated on two royal biographies. Under her maiden name, she co-produced and was largely responsible for the idea of the 2009 feature film *The Young Victoria*.

Victoria and Albert: A Family Life at Osborne House [with Benita Stoney] (1991); *Travels with Queen Victoria* [with Benita Stoney] (1993)

SAUL, Nigel (1952-), British historian, a former Head of Department of History at Royal Holloway, University of London, was acknowledged one of the leading experts in medieval English history.

Richard II (1997); *The Three Richards: Richard I, Richard II and Richard III* (2005)

SAUNDERS, Edith. Her biography gives a detailed account of the state visit of Victoria and Albert to Paris in 1855.
A Distant Summer (1946)

SCARISBRICK, John Joseph ('Jack'), MBE, FRHistS (1928-), British historian, aught at Warwick University. He and his wife Nuala founded the pro-life charity LIFE in 1970, in response to the Abortion Act of 1967.
Henry VIII (1968)

SCHEELE, Godfrey and Margaret (*née* Margaret Smith), British historians, were former Assistant Keepers in the Department of Printed Books, British Museum, and collaborated on an exhibition for the centenary of the Prince Consort's death in 1961. Godfrey also published a history of the Weimar Republic.
The Prince Consort :Man of Many Facets (1977)

SCHOFIELD, Cora L (Louisa).
Edward IV (1923)

SEBBA, Anne, biographer, lecturer, journalist and former Reuters foreign correspondent. She formerly worked for the BBC World Services in the Arabic Department, has contributed to biographical dictionaries, published short stories and introductions to reprints of classic novels as well as biographies of Laura Ashley and Enid Bagnold, and has presented documentaries on BBC radio.
That Woman: The Life of Wallis Simpson, Duchess of Windsor (2011)

SENCOURT, Robert (Esmonde), MA, B.Litt (1890-1969), British biographer and historian, born in New Zealand, read English at St John's College, Oxford. He was Vice-

Dean of the Faculty of Arts and Professor of English Literature at the University of Egypt from 1933 to 1936.
The Life of the Empress Eugenie (1931); *Spain's Uncertain Crown: The Story of the Spanish Sovereigns, 1808-1931* (1932) *Napoleon III: The Modern Emperor* (1933); *King Alfonso: A Biography* (1942); *The Reign of Edward VIII* (1964)

SENIOR, Michael, author of local history, plays, poetry and mythology.
The Life and Times of Richard II (1981)

SEWARD, Desmond (1935-), British author, born in Paris, was educated at Cambridge, and specialised in British and French history of the Middle Ages.
The First Bourbon [Henry IV of France] (1971); *Prince of the Renaissance* (1973); *The Bourbon Kings of France* (1976); *Eleanor of Aquitaine* (1978); *Marie Antoinette* (1981); *Richard III: England's Black Legend* (1983); *Napoleon's Family* (1986); *Henry V (Henry V as Warlord;* 1987); *Eugénie* (2004); *The Last White Rose: Dynasty, Rebellion and Treason – The Secret Wars against the Tudors* (2010); *The Demon's Brood: A History of the Plantagenet Dynasty* (2014); *Eleanor of Aquitaine: The Mother Queen of the Middle Ages* (2014)

SEWARD, Ingrid (1948-), British journalist, magazine editor and author, worked in public relations for the Playboy Empire and in Naim Atallah's theatrical agency. In 1983 she became Editor-in-Chief of *Majesty* magazine, founded three years earlier. She has also published several books on contemporary British royalty and contributed to publications worldwide, as well as working for radio and TV, in particular as commentator for ABC network's *Good Morning America*. She was married to Ross Benson (q.v.).
Sarah Duchess of York (1989); *Royal Children of the 20th Century* (1993); *Prince Edward: A Biography* (1995); *Diana: An Intimate Portrait* (1998); *The Last Great Edwardian Lady: The Life and*

Style of Queen Elizabeth the Queen Mother (1999); *The Queen and Di* (2000); *William and Harry: The People's Princes* (2008)

SHAWCROSS, William (Hartley Hume), CVO (1946-), British biographer and historian, attended University College, Oxford, and St Martin's Art School. He has worked as a regular journalist on the *Sunday Times* and also contributed to *The Spectator, Time, Newsweek, International Herald Tribune* and other publications, and has served on the councils of the Disasters Emergency Committee and the BBC World Service Advisory Council. He wrote the BBC TV series *Monarchy* in 1995, and his BBC TV series and book *Queen and Country* celebrated the Golden Jubilee. He was commissioned by Queen Elizabeth II in 2003 to write the official biography of the Queen Mother. His other books include biographes of the Shah of Iran and Rupert Murdoch. He was formerly married to Marina Warner (q.v.).
Queen and Country (2002); *Allies* (2004); *Queen Elizabeth The Queen Mother: The Official Biography* (2009); *Counting One's Blessings: The Selected Letters of Queen Elizabeth the Queen Mother* (2012)

SIMON, Edith (1917–2003), British author, historian, artist and sculptor. Born in Berlin, her parents moved to Britain when she was fourteen, and she spent most of her working life in Edinburgh. She published several fiction and non-fiction titles as well as being a prolific artist.
The Making of Frederick the Great (1963)

SIMONS, Eric N.
The Reign of Edward IV (1966); *Henry VII: The First Tudor King* (1968)

SINCLAIR, Andrew, FRSL (1935-) is a British novelist, historian, biographer, critic and film director, and was a

Founding Member of Churchill College, Cambridge. His non-royal biographies include Dylan Thomas, Jack London, Francis Bacon and Che Guevara. He directed a film version of Thomas's *Under Milk Wood*.
The Other Victoria: The Princess Royal and The Great Game of Europe (1981); *Death by Fame: A Life of Elisabeth, Empress of Austria* (1998)

SITWELL, Dame Edith (Louisa), DBE (1887-1964), British biographer, poet and critic, was the eldest child of Sir George Sitwell, 4th Baronet, of Renishaw Hall, and elder brother of Sir Osbert (q.v.). She regarded herself primarily as a poet, saying that she only wrote prose for money.
Victoria of England (1936); *Fanfare for Elizabeth* (1946); *The Queens and the Hive* (1962)

SITWELL, Sir (Francis) Osbert (Sacheverell) (1892-1969), British writer, was the brother of Dame Edith Sitwell (q.v.) and became 5th Baronet in 1943. At the time of the Edward VIII abdication crisis he wrote a poem, *Rat Week*, in defence of the King, yet in spite of this he later became a friend of Queen Elizabeth. His sole contribution to royal biography, a collection of essays published posthumously, was described by US book review journal *Kirkus* as a 'maundering tour through the drawing rooms of the pedigreed class'.
Queen Mary and Others (1974)

SKIDMORE, Chris (Christopher James), FRHistS, FSA, MP (1981-), British politician and author, born at Longwell Green, Gloucestershire, read Modern History at Christ Church, Oxford. He was elected Conservative MP for Kingswood in 2010.
Edward VI: The Lost King of England (2007)

SMITH, E.A. (Ernest Anthony), MA, Litt.D. (Cantab). F.R. Hist.S. (1924-98), British historian, born in Grimethorpe, Yorkshire, won an open scholarship to Emmanuel College in 1942, though service in the Royal Air Force intervened and he did not take up his place until October 1947. He moved to Reading in 1949 to take a Diploma in Education, subsequently becoming Assistant Lecturer from 1951 to 1954, Lecturer from 1954 to 1964, Senior Lecturer from 1964 to 1976, and Reader from 1976 to 1990. While he was there he met Arthur Aspinall, Professor of History at Reading, who appointed him to an assistant lectureship in 1951 and made him his research assistant. Working for both Aspinall and Sir Lewis Namier as a research assistant on the History of Parliament, he was credited with Aspinall as joint editor of *English Historical Documents 1783-1832* (1959). He turned to writing in retirement, specialising in histories and biographies relating to the Hanoverian era. Shortly before his death he had begun a biography of William IV, and was planning to write one of George III.

A Queen on Trial [Caroline, Consort of George IV] (1993); *George IV* (1998)

SMITH, G. (George) Barnett (1841-1909), British author and journalist, born at Ovenden, Yorkshire, and worked on the editorial staff of the *Globe*, and of the *Echo*. He wrote extensively on history, literary and political biography, and was a contributor to the *Encyclopaedia Britannica* and *Dictionary of National Biography*, as well as *The Times* and the *Edinburgh Review, Fortnightly Review* and *Cornhill Magazine*. He wrote and published three volumes of verse under the name Guy Roslyn. Ill-health and lung trouble forced him to leave London in 1889 for Bournemouth, where he spent the rest of his life as a semi-invalid.

William I and the German Empire (1887); *Life of Her Majesty Queen Victoria* (1887); *Life of Queen Victoria, 1819-1901* (1901)

SMITH, Gene, American biographer and historian, wrote extensively on modern American history and its leading figures.

Maximilian and Carlota: A Tale of Romance and Tragedy (1973) US/*Maximilian and Carlota: The Habsburg Tragedy in Mexico* (1974) UK

SMITH, Lacey Baldwin, FRSL (1922-2013), historian and author specialising in 16th century England. He was born in Princeton, New Jersey, and taught History at Princeton University.

A Tudor Tragedy: The Life and Times of Catherine Howard (1961); *Henry VIII: The Mask of Royalty* (1973); *Elizabeth Tudor: Portrait of a Queen* (1976); *Anne Boleyn: The Queen of Controversy* (2013)

SMITH, Sean (1955-), British celebrity biographer. He has also written lives of Tom Jones, Kylie Minogue and J.K. Rowling.

Kate (2011)

SNELL, Kate, British author and filmmaker. She was a reporter on *Woman's Hour*, *Panorama*, and other BBC radio and TV programmes. Her biography of Princess Diana was the basis for a feature film of the same title in 2013.

Diana: Her Last Love (2000)

SOMERSET, Anne (Lady Anne Somerset) (1955-) read History at King's College, and began her professional career as a research assistant to several historians. The majority of her histories and biographies have concentrated on the Tudor and Stuart eras.

The Life and Times of King William IV (1980); *Elizabeth I* (1991); *Queen Anne: The Politics of Passion* (2012)

SPADA, James (1950-), American biographer, born in New York City.
Grace, the Secret Life of a Princess: An Intimate Biography of Grace Kelly (1988)

SPECK, William Arthur (1938-), British historian, specialising in 17th and 18th century British and American history. Educated at Queens College, Oxford, he later became Emeritus Professor of History, University of Leeds, and Special Professor in School of English Studies, University of Nottingham.
The Butcher: The Duke of Cumberland and the Suppression of the '45 (1981); *James II* (2002)

SPIELMAN, John P., BA, MA, PhD (1931-2009), American historian, and expert in Habsburg history. He was born at Anaconda, Montana, and read History at the University of Wisconsin. He was a Professor at Haverford College for over thirty years.
Leopold I of Austria (1977)

STAKHOVSKY, Leonid I, Russian historian.
Alexander I of Russia: The Man who Defeated Napoleon (1949)

STANHOPE, Gilbert.
A Mystic on the Prussian Throne: Frederick William II (1912)

STARKEY, David (Robert), CBE, FSA, FRHistS (1945-) studied Tudor history at Cambridge University, then became a Lecturer in History at the London School of Economics from 1968 to 1998. By this time he had become well-known as a radio and television personality, appearing on programmes such as *Question Time*, and contributing regularly to the BBC Radio 4 debate programme *The Moral Maze* from 1992 onwards, on which his airing of often outspoken opinions led to him being dubbed 'the rudest man in Britain'. He also became well known for his historical documentaries, several dealing with the 16th century, as well as Monarchy, a chronicle of the history of English Kings and Queens from the Anglo-Saxon age. He was once quoted as saying that the Tudor dynasty was 'a most glorious and wonderful soap opera. It makes the House of Windsor look like a dolls house tea party.'

The Reign of Henry VIII: Personalities and Politics (1986); *Rivals in Power: the Lives and Letters of the Great Tudor Dynasties* (1990); *Henry VIII: A European Court in England* (1991); *The Inventory of Henry VIII: The Transcript*, Vol 1 (1998) [with Philip Ward and Alistair Hawkyard]; *Elizabeth: Apprenticeship* (2000) UK/*Elizabeth: The struggle for the throne* (2000) US; *The Inventory of Henry VIII: Essays and Illustrations*, Vol 2 (2002) [with Philip Ward and Alistair Hawkyard]; *The Inventory of Henry VIII: Essays and Illustrations*, Vol 3 (2002) [with Philip Ward and Alistair Hawkyard]; *The Six Wives: The Queens of Henry VIII* (2003); *Henry: Virtuous Prince* (2008); *Henry: Model of a Tyrant* (2016)

STARKIE, Allan, Ph.D., American former adviser to Sarah, Duchess of York (q.v.), and also worked in Army Intelligence.
Fergie - Her Secret Love (1996)

STEEL, Anthony (Bedford) (1900-73), British historian of medieval England, was a fellow of Christ's College, Cambridge, and Principal of Cardiff University from 1949 to 1966.
Richard II (1941)

STENTON, Sir Frank (Merry) (1880-1967), British historian and authority on Anglo-Saxon England, was born at Manchester and read History at Keble College, Oxford, where he was elected an Honorary Fellow in 1947. He was

President of the Royal Historical Society from 1937 to 1945, Professor of History at Reading University from 1926 to 1946, and Vice-Chancellor from 1946 to 1950. He contributed the volume on *Anglo-Saxon England* to the Oxford History of England in 1943. His wife Doris Mary Stenton was also a renowned historian.
William the Conqueror (1908)

STEWART, Alan, British historian and writer on early modern literature and culture. He has been Professor of English and Comparative Literature at Columbia University in New York and International Director of the Centre for Editing Lives and Letters in London. He is co-general editor of the *Encyclopedia of English Renaissance Literature*.
The Cradle King: A Life of James VI and I (2003)

STOECKL, Agnes de (*née* Barron), (1874-1968), biographer. Born in Paris of Irish parents, she married Baron Alexander de Stoeckl in 1892 and was thereafter associated with the Russian court, becoming a lady-in-waiting to the Tsarina. Her husband was successively Chamberlain to the Tsar and Comptroller to Grand Duke George, until the Russian revolution forced them into exile. She was 78 before she took up writing, in order to escape, in her own words, 'the ennui of embroidery' (*The Times*, 31.1.1968), beginning with two volumes of memoirs, *Not All Vanity* and *My Dear Marquis*, and then branching out into historical biography, publishing her final title at the age of 92. She spent her last years as a friend of the royal family living on the estate of the Duke of Kent at Coppins, Iver, Buckinghamshire.
King of the French: A Portrait of Louis Philippe, 1772-1850 (1957); *Four Years an Empress: Marie-Louise, Second Wife of Napoleon* (1962)

STONE, J.M.
The History of Mary I, Queen of England (1901)

STRACHEY, (Giles) Lytton (1880-1932), British writer, critic and biographer, born in London. A founding member of the Bloomsbury Group, and for a while a regular reviewer for the *Spectator* and *Edinburgh Review*, he was noted for his somewhat iconoclastic biographical studies which combined sympathy and insight with gentle irreverence, as in his first major work, *Eminent Victorians*. Of his James Tatit Black Memorial Prize-winning study of Queen Victoria, Victorian Web observes that 'it is fascinating to see Strachey starting off here in his usual acerbic vein, mocking the public adulation of an elderly Queen, but then himself falling under the spell of her unchanged and unaffected "vitality, conscientiousness, pride, and simplicity."' Stricken with cancer at the end of his days, his last words were allegedly 'If this is dying, I don't think much of it'.
Queen Victoria (1921); *Elizabeth and Essex: A Tragic History* (1928)

STRATFORD, L.
Edward IV (1910)

STRICKLAND, Agnes (1796-1874), British biographer, was born in London, one of nine children, of whom all but one became published writers. Her first works were books of poetry, followed by children's works and then the royal titles for which she is best remembered. In fact the books which were ascribed to her were partly written and researched by her elder sister Elizabeth, who was also largely responsible for negotiating all business arrangements with their publisher. She however disliked the idea of being accorded publicity, and therefore willingly assented to Agnes being credited as sole author. Agnes was present at Queen Victoria's coronation, and was presented at Court in 1840. Her (or their) first royal biography was a two-volume work on the Queen, based mostly on inaccurate sources supplied by publisher Henry Colburn, and which the Queen reportedly disliked. Thereafter they used previously unpublished state and official records, contemporary letters and other private documents as far as possible, and travelled to various historic houses to examine manuscript sources. The Stricklands also visited many historic houses to examine documents. When Agnes went to Paris in 1844 François Guizot, French Ambassador to London and Foreign Minister, helped to grant her access to previously unseen archives in France. For their last work on the Stuarts, she travelled to Holland in 1869, where she was granted an interview with Queen Sophie. The initial 12-volume 'lives' was very successful, ran to several editions, and an abridged edition was published in 1867 for use in schools. According to the *Oxford Dictionary of National Biography*, the literary style of the books is weak, and their popularity can be ascribed largely to the trivial gossip and domestic details the writing contains. 'Yet in her extracts from contemporary authorities she amassed much valuable material, and her works contain pictures of the court, of society, and of domestic life not to be found elsewhere.' Elizabeth died in 1875, a year after Agnes.

Queen Victoria From Birth to Bridal, 2 vols (1840); *Lives of the Queens of England from the Norman Conquest*, 12 vols (1840–8); *The Letters of Mary Queen of Scots*, 3 vols (ed). (1842–3); *Lives of the Queens of Scotland and English Princesses Connected with the Regal Succession of Great Britain*, 8 vols (1851–9); *Lives of the Bachelor Kings of England* (1861); *Lives of the Tudor Princesses, Including Lady Jane Gray and Her Sisters* (1868); *Lives of the Last Four Princesses of the Royal House of Stuart* (1872)

STUART, Dorothy Margaret Stuart (*née* Dorothy Margaret Browne) (1889-1963), British poet and biographer, won a silver medal in the art competitions of the Olympic Games in 1924 for her song cycle. She also wrote literary and historical biographies, and history for children.

The King's Service (1935); *King George the Sixth* (1937); *The Daughters of George III* (1939); *Daughter of England: A New Study of Princess Charlotte of Wales and Her Family* (1951); *The Story of William the Conqueror* (1952); *Portrait of the Prince Regent* (1953); *Dearest Bess* (1955)

SULLIVAN, Michael John, American biographer and historian, and contributor to various journals.

A Fatal Passion: The Story of Victoria Melita, the Uncrowned Last Empress of Russia (1997)

SULZBERGER, C.L. (Cyrus Leo) (1912-93), American writer and journalist. Born in New York, he graduated from Harvard University, and joined the *New York Times*, of which his uncle Arthur Hays Sulzberger was publisher. He was its foreign correspondent for forty years, and he often took messages between foreign leaders including John Fitzgerald Kennedy, Nikita Khrushchev and Charles de Gaulle. He wrote several books on contemporary history, memoirs and fiction.

The Fall of Eagles (1977)

SUMMERS, Anthony (1942-), an Irish citizen, studied Modern Languages at Oxford University. He then became a freelance reporter for London newspapers, and then a reporter for and producer and editor for current affairs for BBC, where he was Assistant Editor of *Panorama*, and ITV, working on *World in Action*. After he left broadcasting he wrote several books of investigative non-fiction.

The File on the Tsar: The Fate of the Romanovs [with Tom Mangold (q.v.)] (1976)

SYMCOX, Geoffrey (Walter), BA, MA, PhD (1938-), British author and lecturer in Modern History at University of California, Los Angeles, from 1967 to 2004. *Victor Amadeus II: Absolutism in the Savoyard State, 1675-1730* (1983)

T

TAYLOR, Blaine (1946-), American author, historian and journalist. A former Vietnam war soldier and military policeman, he later became a political and crime newspaper reporter, and medical journalist. He was a US congressional aide on Capitol Hill, Washington DC, from 1991 to 1992.
Kaiser Bill: A New Look at Germany's Last Emperor, Wilhelm II, 1859-1941 (2014)

TAYLOR, I.A.
The Life of Queen Henrietta Maria (1905); *Christina of Sweden* (1909); *The Making of a King* (1910); *The Life of James IV* (1913)

TAYLOR, Lucy.
'Fritz' of Prussia: Germany's Second Emperor (1891)

THOMPSON, Andrew C., BA, MPhil, PhD, British historian, Official Fellow and Director of Studies in History at Queens' College, Cambridge.
George II: King and Elector (2011)

THOMPSON, Grace E, biographer, and novelist under the name Camilla Hope.
The First Gentleman of Europe: Being the Story of the Regent, Afterwards George IV (1931); *The Patriot King: The life of William IV* (1932)

THOMPSON, J.M. (James Matthew) (1878-1956), British historian and biographer, Tutorial Fellow in Modern History at Magdalen College, Oxford, and University Lecturer in French History.
Napoleon Bonaparte: His Rise and Fall (1951)

THORNTON, Michael, historian, biographer and journalist, has contributed to the *Daily Mail* and *Sunday Express*.
Royal Feud: The Queen Mother and the Duchess of Windsor (1985) UK/*Royal Feud: The Dark Side of the Love Story of the Century* (1985) US

TISDALL, E.E.P. (Evelyn Ernest Percy) (1907-77), was a Fleet Street journalist before turning to biography. After the Second World War he became headmaster of Dennington House School, near Barnstaple. His books on British and European royalty have been described as 'slightly sensational' and 'slightly hostile' (*Royalty Digest*, February 2002).
Queen Victoria's John Brown: The Life Story of the Most Remarkable Royal Servant in British History (1938); *The Wanton Queen* [Caroline, Consort of George IV] (19390; *She Made World Chaos: The Intimate Story of the Empress Frederick of Prussia* (1940); *Restless Consort: The Invasion of Albert the Conqueror* (1952); *Unpredictable Queen: The Intimate Life of Queen Alexandra* (1953); *Royal Destiny: The Royal Hellenic Ccousins* (1955); *The Dowager Empress* [Marie Feodorovna, Consort of Alexander III of Russia] (1957); *The Prince Imperial: A Study of his Life Among the British* (1959); *Queen Victoria's Private Life* (1961)

TOMALIN, Claire (*née* Claire Delavenay) (1933-), British biographer, born in London of a French father. She studied at Newnham College, Cambridge, and then became literary editor of the *New Statesman* and *Sunday Times*. Her first husband, Nick Tomalin, was killed in the

Yom Kippur War in 1973, and she subsequently married novelist Michael Frayn. She has also written biographies of Charles Dickens, Jane Austen and Thomas Hardy.
Mrs Jordan's Profession: The Story of a Great Actor and a Future King (1995)

TOMES, Jason, DPhil, MA, British biographer and political writer, read International Relations at Nuffield College, Oxford, and Politics, Philosophy, and Economics at Merton College, Oxford. He lectured in British history and politics in Poland at Warsaw University and Adam Mickiewicz University, Poznan, from 1993 to 1995, and taught Modern History and Politics for Boston University's Oxford Honours Studies Program from 1996 to 2008.
King Zog: Self-Made Monarch of Albania (2003).

TOUT, T.F. (Thomas Frederick), **FBA** (1855-1929), British historian, born in London, studied at Balliol College, Oxford, and became Professor of English and Modern Languages at St David's University College, Lampeter, later University of Wales. He was a contributor to the *Dictionary of National Biography*, and Professor of History at Owens College, Manchester, subsequently Manchester University, from 1890 to 1925, during which he published several works on 13th and 14th century history.
Edward I (1920)

TRAILL, H.D. (Henry Duff) (1842–1900), British author and journalist, born at Blackheath, London. Intending to pursue a medical career, he studied Natural Sciences at Oxford, but then read for the bar and was called in 1869. Two years later he was appointed Inspector of Returns for the Board of Education, and then became a writer, contributing to the *Pall Mall Gazette*, and *St James's Gazette*. He was successively on the staff of the *Saturday Review* and a leader-writer for the *Daily Telegraph*, Editor of the *Observer*

from 1889 until 1891, and first editor of *Literature* in 1897. He also wrote several historical and literary biographies, poems and plays, and edited the Centenary edition of the 30-volume *Works of Thomas Carlyle*.
William III (1888)

TREMLETT, Giles, British author, journalist and broadcaster. After graduating from Oxford University he lived in and wrote extensively about Spain. He has been Contributing Editor at the *Guardian* and Madrid Correspondent for *The Economist*, and contributed to several academic collections on Spanish history.
Catherine of Aragon: Henry's Spanish Queen (2010)

TREVOR, Meriol (1919-2000), British author, regarded as one of the most prolific Roman Catholic women writers of the 20th century. Born in Bath, she studied at St Hugh's College, Oxford. During the Second World War she worked in a day nursery, and then as the steerer of a barge on the Grand Union Canal. After being a relief worker in Italy for the United Nations Relief and Rehabilitation Administration, and as a result of her experience of Catholic culture, she was received into the Roman Catholic Church in 1950. In addition to biographies, she also wrote fiction, books for children and poetry.
The Shadow of a Crown: The Life Story of James II of England and VII of Scotland (1988)

TROYAT, Henri (Lev Aslanovich Tarasov) (1911–2007), Russian-born French author, biographer, historian and novelist, born in Moscow to parents of Armenian, Russian, German and Georgian heritage. His family fled Russia at the time of the revolution and they settled in Paris in 1920, where he earned a law degree. He published over a hundred books, novels and biographies.
Alexander of Russia [Alexander I] (1984)

TSCHUDI, Clara (1856-1945), Norwegian writer, born in Tønsberg, was best known for her lives of contemporary and historical women. A German translation of her biography of Empress Elizabeth was banned in Austria.

Augusta, Empress of Germany (1900); *Elizabeth, Empress of Austria and Queen of Hungary* (1901); *Maria Sophia, Queen of Naples: A Continuation of the Empress Elizabeth* (1905); *Eugenie: Empress of the French* (1906); *Ludwig the Second, King of Bavaria* (1908); *Napoleon's Mother* (1910); *Napoleon's Son* (1912)

TSCHUPPIK, Karl (1876-1937), Austrian journalist, columnist, journalist and editor, born in Bohemia. He wrote for various Viennese newspapers, notably *Prager Tagblatt*, of which he was editor and publisher from 1898 to 1917. An opponent of all forms of nationalism, and an advocate of an independent Austria, he clashed regularly with his employers, which contributed to his decision to move from Vienna to Berlin in 1926. Around this time he began writing and publishing biographies, but found himself increasingly at odds with the growing tide of German national socialism. Because of his Jewish blood, in 1933 his name appeared on the Nazis' 'black list' of authors accused of propagating 'harmful and undesirable literature', and his books were removed from libraries. That year he returned to Vienna to resume his career in journalism, but during his last few years most of his income came from books published in other European countries, in German and also translated into other European languages, including two (listed below) into English. They included biographies of Ludendorff and Maria Theresa and his last published title, *A Son of a Good Family*, a novel, and he would probably have written more fiction but for his sudden death from natural causes.

Franz Joseph I: The Downfall of an Empire (1930); *The Empress Elisabeth of Austria* (1930)

TURNBULL, Patrick (1908-?).
Eugenie of the French (1974)

TURNER, F.C.
James II (1949)

TYLER, Royall (1884-1953), American historian and
biographer. He was born in Quincy, Massachusetts, and
after being educated in England he studied at New
College, Oxford, and the University of Salamanca. He was
appointed by the British government to edit the Calendar
of State Papers relating to negotiations between England
and Spain during the era of Charles V, Holy Roman
Emperor, the first volume appearing in 1913, the last and
fifth in 1954, just after his death. He was a member of the
American delegation to the Paris Peace Conference in
1919, and appointed financial adviser to the Hungarian
government by the League of Nations in 1924. In the
Second World War he was based in Geneva, where he
undertook work for the American intelligence network,
then worked in Paris with the International Bank for
Reconstruction and Development, and then as European
Representative of the National Committee for a Free
Europe. In addition to his historical interests he was also
an expert on Byzantine art. His book on Charles V was
almost completed by the time of his death, and published
three years later.
The Emperor Charles the Fifth (1956)

V

VALLONE, Lynne, American author and academic. She was Chair of the Department of Childhood Studies, Rutgers University, Camden, New Jersey, and has written extensively on female culture and children's literature.
Becoming Victoria (2001)

VAN DER KISTE, John (1954-), British biographer, born at Wendover, read Librarianship at Ealing and has worked in public and college libraries. He has appeared on radio, was consultant for BBC TV's *The King, The Kaiser and The Tsar*, and has contributed articles and reviews to various national and local journals and newspapers. He has also published books on local history, true crime, music and fiction.
Frederick III, German Emperor 1888 (1981); *Queen Victoria's Family: A Select Bibliography* (1982); *Dearest Affie: Prince Alfred, Duke of Edinburgh* [with Bee Jordaan] (984); *Queen Victoria's Children* (1986); *Windsor and Habsburg: The British and Austrian Reigning Houses 1848-1922* (1987); *Edward VII's Children* (1989); *Princess Victoria Melita, Grand Duchess Cyril of Russia, 1876-1936* (1991); *George III's Children* (1992); *Crowns in a Changing World: The British and European Monarchies, 1901-36* (1993); *Kings of the Hellenes: The Greek Kings 1863-1974* (1994); *Childhood at Court 1819-1901* (1995); *Northern Crowns: The Kings of Modern Scandinavia* (1996); *King George II and Queen Caroline* (1997); *The Romanovs 1818-1959: Tsar Alexander II of Russia and his Family* (1998); *Kaiser Wilhelm II: Germany's Last Emperor* (1999); *The Georgian Princesses* (2000);

Dearest Vicky, Darling Fritz: Queen Victoria's Eldest Daughter and the German Emperor (2001); *Royal Visits to Devon and Cornwall* (2002); *Once a Grand Duchess: Xenia, Sister of Nicholas II* [with Coryne Hall] (2002); *William and Mary: Heroes of the Glorious Revolution* (2003); *Emperor Francis Joseph: Life, Death and the Fall of the Habsburg Empire* (2005); *Sons, Servants & Statesmen: The Men in Queen Victoria's Life* (2006); *A Divided Kingdom: The Spanish Monarchy from Isabel to Juan Carlos* (2007); *Alfred: Queen Victoria's Sercond Son* (2013); *The Prussian Princesses: Sisters of Kaiser Wilhelm II* (2014); *Prince Henry of Prussia, 1862-1929* (2015); *The Last German Empress: Empress Augusta Victoria, Consort of Emperor William II* (2015); *Princess Helena, Queen Victoria's Third Daughter* (2015); *Charlotte and Feodora: A Troubled Mother-Daughter Relationship in Imperial Germany* (2015)

VICKERS, Hugo (Ralph) (1951-), English writer, journalist and broadcaster, born in London, was educated at Strasbourg University. He was a TV studio guest for wedding of the Prince of Wales and Lady Diana Spencer in 1981 and the Princess's funeral sixteen years later, and subsequently a commentator on TV for other royal occasions including the Earl of Wessex's wedding to Sophie Rhys-Jones in 1999, the Queen Mother's centenary celebrations in 2000, and her funeral in 2002. He was appointed Chairman of the Jubilee Walkway Trust in October 2002.

Debrett's Book of the Royal Wedding [Charles and Diana, Prince and Princess of Wales] (1981); *The Private World of the Duke and Duchess of Windsor* (1995); *Alice, Princess Andrew of Greece* (2000); *Elizabeth, the Queen Mother* (2005)

VICKERS, Kenneth (Hotham), LLD (1881-1958), British historian and university administrator, was born at Naburn, near York. He left school at the age of fifteen, after contracting polio, which left him with a serious

weakness in one arm and one leg. He studied History at Exeter College, Oxford, becming Lecturer in History at University College, Bristol, then at Amstrong College, University of Durham, and in 1922 Principal of the University of Southampton until he retired in 1946. He published books on medieval and local history.
Humphrey, Duke of Gloucester (1907)

VOVK, Justin C. (Christopher), Canadian historian of Slovenian and English background, studying European history and political science at Redeemer University, Ontario. His work on documenting and cataloguing the royal houses of Europe since the beginning of the late modern period initially inspired him to compile a royalty encyclopedia and evolved into his first book. He also contributes to *European Royal History Journal.*
In Destiny's Hands: Five Tragic Rulers, Children of Maria Theresa (2009); *Imperial Requiem: Four Royal Women and the Fall of the Age of Empires* (2012)

VORRES, Ian (1924-2015), Canadian-Greek author and art collector, born in Athens, served with the American special forces behind German lines in the Second World War and fled to Canada at the end of the war. He graduated from Athens College, obtaining a diploma in Economics and Political Science from Queen's University in Ontario, Canada, and a higher education diploma in Philosophy and Psychology from the University of Toronto. After teaching for a while he worked as a journalist with the Canadian press, as art critic for the *Hamilton Spectator* and contributor to *The Globe and Mail* and *Saturday Night.* In 1962, he wrote an authorised biography of Grand Duchess Olga, the youngest child of Tsar Nicholas II of Russia, as she had emigrated to Canada and was glad to give him her assistance. In 1967, he was appointed Director of the Greek Pavilion at the Montreal

International Fair and was the only Canadian citizen director of a foreign country's pavilion at the exhibition. He returned to Greece to take over the family's import-export business. In 1983 he founded and opened the Vorres Museum of Contemporary Greek Art, Paiania, East Attica, Greece, to highlight Greek art and culture, with a collection of over six thousand pieces covering four thousand years of Greek history and art. From 1991 to 1998 he served as mayor in the Paiania municipality. In 2001, he received the honorary title of Doctor in Fine Arts from the American College in Greece.

The last Grand Duchess: Her Imperial Highness Grand Duchess Olga Alexandrovna (1964)

VULLIAMY, C.E. (Colwyn Edward) (1886-1971), Welsh biographer and novelist. As a young man he studied art under the painter Stanhope Forbes, and during the First World War he served with the army in France, Macedonia and Turkey. He wrote novels, crime fiction, some under the pseudonym Anthony Rolls, works of humour and biographies.

Royal George: A Study of George III, His Experiment in Monarchy, his Decline and Retirement (1937)

W

WAKE, Jehanne, British biographer, read Philosophy, Politics and Economics at Oxford University, and became one of the first generation of female graduate trainee investment bankers in the City of London. She also contributed to BBC radio and TV documentaries.
Princess Louise: Queen Victoria's Unconventional Daughter (1988)

WAKEFORD, Geoffrey (1910-95), British biographer, born in Barry, Glamorgan. He lost a foot in a tram accident at the age of six and was therefore exempt from military service. Joining the staff of the *Daily Mail* in 1940, he later briefly worked as news editor for the *Sunday Chronicle*, then rejoined the *Mail*, becoming Court Correspondent in 1961 until retiring nine years later.
His Royal Highness Charles, Prince of Wales (1962); *The Heir Apparent: An Authentic Study of the Life and Training of HRH Charles Prince of Wales* (1967); *Thirty Years a Queen: A Study of HM Queen Elizabeth the Queen Mother* (1968); *Three Consort Queens: Adelaide, Alexandra and Mary* (1971); *The Princesses Royal* (1973)

WALLER, Maureen, British biographer, studied medieval and modern history at University College London, and received a master's degree at Queen Mary College, London, in British and European history 1660--1714. She worked at the National Portrait Gallery, and as an editor at several London publishing houses, before publishing her first book, *1700: Scenes from London Life*.

Ungrateful Daughters: The Stuart Princesses Who Stole Their Father's Crown (2002); *Sovereign Ladies: The Six Reigning Queens of England* (2006)

WALTERS, John.
The Royal Griffin: Frederick, Prince of Wales, 1707-51 (1972)

WARD, Yvonne M., a historian with a doctorate from La Trobe University, Melbourne, Australia.
Censoring Queen Victoria: How Two Gentlemen Edited a Queen and Created an Icon (2014)

WARDROPER, John, British author, has contributed to *The Times*, *The Independent*, and *New Scientist*, and written extensively about 19th century caricature and satire.
Wicked Ernest: The Truth About the Man who was Almost Britain's King: An Extraordinary Life Revealed (2002)

WARNER, Kathryn, BA, MA, read Medieval History and Literature at the University of Manchester. She has contributed to the *English Historical Review*.
Edward II: The Unconventional King (2014)

WARNER, Marina, DBE, FRSL, FBA (1946-), British biographer, novelist, journalist, and historian, born in London, studied French and Italian at Lady Margaret Hall, Oxford. Noted particularly for non-fiction books on feminism, she has published studies of Zz'u-hsi, Empress Dowager of China, and Joan of Arc. She has contributed to The *London Review of Books, New Statesman, Daily Telegraph, Sunday Times* and *Vogue*. She was a professor in the Department of Literature, Film and Theatre Studies at the University of Essex from 2004 to 2014, and then took up a Chair in English and Creative Writing at Birkbeck College, University of London. She has been a visiting professor, given lectures and taught on the faculties of many

universities.   She was formerly married to William Shawcross (q.v.).   Her only contribution to British royal biography so far is an illustrated study of Queen Victoria's paintings and sketches, alongside a narrative text drawn partly from her journals.
Queen Victoria's Sketchbook (1979)

WARNICKE, Retha (Marvine), BA, MA, PhD (1939-), American historian and biographer, studied History at Indiana and then Harvard University.   She became a Lecturer at Arizona State University, becoming Assistant Professor, then Associate Professor and finally Professor. She was the Director of Graduate Studies at the History Department from 1987 to 1992, and Chair of the History Department from 1992 to 1998. A specialist in the Tudor court, she was noted for controversial theories over the life of Anne Boleyn, in particular challenging the work of Eric Ives (q.v.).
The Marrying of Anne of Cleves: Royal Protocol in Tudor England, (2000); *Mary, Queen of Scots* (2006); *Wicked Women of Tudor England: Queens, Aristocrats, and Commoners* (2012)

WARREN, W.L. (Wilfred Lewis) (1929–94), British historian, was educated at Exeter College, Oxford, and became Professor of Modern History at Queen's University, Belfast. He became renowned as a specialist in Norman and Angevin England.
King John (1961); *Henry II* (1973)

WARWICK, Christopher (1949-), British writer, biographer and broadcaster. A former consultant editor of *Majesty* magazine, he has contributed to the national press and to various television documentaries, been a ghost writer and television publicity writer. His media appearances include regular contributions to CTV, the Canadian news network, providing analysis and commentary for royal weddings, funerals and christenings and for The Queen's Golden and Diamond Jubilee celebrations.

Two Centuries of Royal Weddings (1980); *Princess Margaret* (1983); *King George VI and Queen Elizabeth* (1985); *Abdication* (1986); *Debrett's Queen Elizabeth II* (1986); *George and Marina: Duke and Duchess of Kent* (1988); *Queen Mary's Photograph Albums* (1989); *Princess Margaret: A Life of Contrasts* (2000); *Ella: Princess, Saint and Martyr* (2006); *Her Majesty* (2012)

WATKINS, Carl, British historian, Fellow of Magdalene College, Oxford, and specialist in medieval religious history.
Stephen (2015)

WATSON, Alfred E.T. (Edward Thomas) (1849-1922), British actor and journalist. He originally began his career on the stage but then turned to journalism. He worked for the *Evening Standard* for several years, and then became racing correspondent of *The Times* from 1908 to 1920. He was a friend of Edward VII and George V, and it was said that the latter 'seldom attended a meeting without discussing racing with him'. (*The Times*, 9.11.1922)
King Edward VII as a Sportsman (1911)

WATSON, J.N.P., British author, served in the army for many years, was with the airborne forces in the Suez campaign, and commanded an armoured reconnaissance squadron during the Cyprus revolt, as a result of which he was mentioned in despatches. He retired disabled in 1968 and took up a writing career, during which he contributed to Blackwood's Magazine and joined the editorial staff of *Country Life*.
Captain-General and Rebel Chief: The Life of James, Duke of Monmouth (1979)

WATSON, Sophia.
Marina: The Story of a Princess [Marina, Duchess of Kent]
(1994)

WATSON, Vera (1906-?).
*A Queen at Home: An Intimate Account of the Social and Domestic
Life of Queen Victoria's Court* (1952)

WEBSTER, Nesta H. (*née* Nesta Helen Bevan) (1876-
1960), British writer and historian. Throughout her career
she claimed that the Illuminati, a secret society, were
plotting world domination, and their subversive methods
and conspiracies had been responsible for the French
Revolution, the deaths of Louis XVI, Marie Antoinette of
France and Gustavus III of Sweden, the revolutions of
1848, the First World War, and the Bolshevik Revolution.
She was involved with several right-wing groups in Britain
including the British Union of Fascists, and claimed that
the persecution of the Jews in Nazi Germany was greatly
exaggerated.
Louis XVI and Marie Antoinette: Before the Revolution (1936);
Louis XVI and Marie Antoinette: During the Revolution (1937)

WEDGWOOD, C.V. (Dame Cicely Veronica, OM, DBE
(1910-97), British historian, born in Stocksfield,
Northumberland, read History at Lady Margaret Hall,
Oxford. A specialist in 17th century European history and
biography, she established her reputation with volumes on
the Thirty Years War, Oliver Cromwell and Cardinal
Richelieu. Her life of *William the Silent* was awarded the
1944 James Tait Black Memorial Prize for Biography (see
p. 246). Her best-remembered achievement was her
trilogy on Charles I. She published her books using the
initials C.V. because she considered that there was still
considerable prejudice against women being taken
seriously as historians, although she perhaps worried

unduly. According to fellow historian J.H. Plumb in the *Spectator*, she was 'a great craftswoman and a great writer'. In addition to writing she was also a journalist, lecturer and broadcaster. She contributed to *Time and Tide* on which she held editor posts from 1944 to 1952, the *Times Literary Supplement* and the *Spectator* among others, and was a Special Lecturer at University College, London from 1962 to 1991. She received honorary degrees from the universities of Sheffield and Glasgow and was a member of the Institute for Advanced Study, Princeton, from 1952 to 1966. Active in many societies, organisations and institutions, she was President of the Society of Authors from 1972 to 1977, served on the Arts Council, and the Advisory Council of the Victoria and Albert Museum, was a trustee of the National Gallery and a member of the Royal Commission on Historical Manuscripts.

William the Silent (1944); *The King's Peace, 1637–1641* (1955); *The King's War, 1641–1647* (1958); *The Trial of Charles I* (1964)

WEIGALL, Lady Rose (*née* Lady Rose Sophia Mary Fane) (1834–1921), British literary editor and social worker, was born at Hyde Park Terrace, London, youngest child of John Fane, Lord Burghersh, 11th Earl of Westmorland. Her mother was a niece of the Duke of Wellington. Her father was a British minister in Berlin and Vienna between 1841 and 1855 and she spent most of her formative years in Europe. She was encouraged to write her book on Princess Charlotte by Queen Victoria, partly as Prince Leopold, later King of the Belgians, had been a friend of the Earl of Westmorland. She and her husband, the renowned portrait painter Henry Weigall, whom she married in 1866, were involved in social and educational work for much of their lives. She became a member of the board of guardians and a regular workhouse visitor, and they arranged for a holiday home for London children to be built in their garden. She also edited three volumes of her mother's correspondence.

A Brief Memoir of the Princess Charlotte of Wales, with Selections from her Correspondence and Other Unpublished Papers (1874)

WEINTRAUB, Stanley (1929-), American historian and biographer, was born in Philadelphia, Pennsylvania. He attended West Chester State Teachers College and Temple University where he received his master's degree in English 'in absentia' as he was called up during the Korean War, receiving a commission as Army Second Lieutenant and serving with the Eighth Army. He then taught at Pennsylvania State University, where he was also Director of Penn State's Institute for the Arts and Humanistic Studies and became Evan Pugh Professor of Arts and Humanities, with Emeritus status on retirement in 2000.

Victoria: An Intimate Biography (1987); *Albert the Uncrowned King* (1997) UK; *Uncrowned King: The Life of Prince Albert* (1997) US; *The Importance of Being Edward: King in Waiting 1841-1901* (2000) UK; *Edward the Caresser: the Playboy Prince who Became Edward VII* (2001) US

WEIR, Alison, FRSA (1951-), studied history at the North Western Polytechnic of London and trained as a teacher. She later worked in Civil Service management, and then ran her own school for children with learning difficulties, before becoming a full-time writer. She described herself on her website as a writer of 'popular' history, while acknowledging that the term was sometimes used in a derogatory sense by academics.

Britain's Royal Families (1989); *The Six Wives of Henry VIII* (1991); *The Princes in the Tower* (1992), republished as *Richard III and the Princes in the Tower* (2014); *Children of England: The Heirs of King Henry VIII* (1996) UK/*The Children of Henry VIII* (1996) US; *Elizabeth the Queen* (1998) UK/*The Life of Elizabeth I* (1998); *Eleanor of Aquitaine, By the Wrath of God,*

Queen of England (1999) UK/*Eleanor of Aquitaine: A Life* (1999) US; *Henry VIII: King and Court* (2001) UK/*Henry VIII: The King and His Court* (2001) US; *Mary, Queen of Scots and the Murder of Lord Darnley* (2003); *Isabella, She-Wolf of France, Queen of England* (2005) UK/*Queen Isabella* (2005) US; *Katherine Swynford: The Story of John of Gaunt and His Scandalous Duchess/Mistress of the Monarchy: The Life of Katherine Swynford, Duchess of Lancaster* (2007); *The Lady in the Tower: The Fall of Anne Boleyn* (2009); *Traitors of the Tower* (2010); *Mary Boleyn: 'The Great and Infamous Whore'* (2011) UK/*Mary Boleyn: The Mistress of Kings* (2011) US; *The Ring and the Crown: A History of Royal Weddings, 1066-2011* [(co-written with Kate Williams, Sarah Gristwood and Tracy Borman] (2011); *Elizabeth of York: The First Tudor Queen* (2013) UK/*Elizabeth of York: A Tudor Queen and Her World* (2013) US; *The Lost Tudor Princess: The Life of Margaret Douglas, Countess of Lennox* (2015)

WELCH, Colin, *see* PONSONBY, Sir Frederick

WELCOME, John (real name John Needham Huggard Brennan) (1914-2010), Irish author, mostly of sporting novels, thrillers and books on horse racing, who was a lawyer by profession. Born in Ireland, he was sent to school in England and read Law at Exeter College, Oxford. After returning to Ireland he qualified as a solicitor, his legal career being interrupted by the Second World War and he was commissioned in the Royal Artillery. In 1942 his parents died in a house fire and he was allowed to return home and rescue the family legal practice. He began to write but through the demands of the legal profession he was obliged to do so under a pseudonym. He became Chairman of Wexford Racecourse, senior steward of the National Hunt Steeplechase Committee and a long-serving member of the Turf Club. In addition to writing books, he contributed

regularly to the *Irish Independent* and other newspapers on racing and as a book reviewer.
The Sporting Empress: The Story of Elizabeth of Austria and Bay Middleton (1975)

WELLMAN, Rita.
Eugenie: Star-Crossed Empress of the French (1941)

WHARFE, Ken, RVO (1960-), former Metropolitan police inspector attached to Royalty Protection New Scotland Yard. He was the personal protection officer to Diana, Princess of Wales from 1986 to 1994. His book, he claimed, was a truthful account intended to prevent the Princess's memory from being 'airbrushed' from history, but led to consideration that he should be stripped of his royal honour for betrayal of confidences and royal secrets, and condemnation from his colleagues in the Metropolitan Police.
Diana - A Closely Guarded Secret [with Robert Jobson (q.v.)] (2003)

WHEELER-BENNETT, Sir John, GCVO, CMG, OBE, FRSL (1902-75), was born in Keston, Kent. He was aged thirteen when a German plane dropped a bomb on his school at Westgate-on-Sea, leaving him with a stammer which was cured fifteen years later by Lionel Logue, the speech therapist who did the same for George VI. He worked in the publicity department of the League of Nations, Geneva, from 1923 to 1924, then as director of the Royal Institution of International Affairs Information Department, and as editor of the *Bulletin of International News* between 1924 and 1932. He lived in Germany between 1927–1934, witnessing at first-hand the fall of the Weimar Republic, and on his journeys around Europe meeting several statesmen and other notables including the ex-German Emperor William II. Some acquaintances later suggested that with his rather German features he was in fact a close relation of the former imperial head of state, to which he retorted that his mother 'never even met a Hohenzollern in her life' (Rose, *Kings, Queens and Courtiers*, 280). During the Second World War he worked in the United States as a lecturer on international relations at the University of Virginia., with the British Information Service in New York City, and as Assistant Director General of the Political Intelligence Department. After returning to Britain, he assisted the British Prosecution at the Nuremberg war trials. From 1946 to 1950 he taught International Relations at St Anthony's College and at New College, Oxford University. The British Foreign Office appointed him the British editor-in-chief of the edition *Documents on German Foreign Policy,* based on the captured archive of the German Foreign Office that had fallen into British and American hands in April 1945. On the recommendation of Sir Harold Nicolson, he was appointed official biographer of George VI in 1953, a task which took him five years. On publication, some readers remarked that 'its sombre style hardly reflected the sparkle of the author's conversation', though as his friend, publisher and Prime Minister Harold Macmillan noted, there was 'a gulf properly fixed between the frivolity of the spoken word and the decorum of the printed text'. (Rose, op cit, 280) From 1959 until his death, he was the first incumbent of a new post, Historical Adviser to the Royal Archives, Windsor.

King George VI: His Life and Reign (1958)

WHITAKER, James (1940-2012), English journalist well-known for his reporting of the British royal family for the tabloid press in the 1980s and 1990s. Born in Cheltenham, he worked for local newspapers before joining the *Daily Mail* in 1967, then successively the *Daily Express, The Sun, Daily Star* and *Daily Mirror*. Two books on the Prince and

Princess of Wales resulted. According to one obituary, he had a voice like 'a retired brigadier addressing a pair of deaf daughters', and when he was following Diana, Princess of Wales on her annual skiing holiday in the Alps, he wore a bright red ski suit, prompting her to call him 'The Big Red Tomato' (*Daily Telegraph*, 15.2.2012).
Settling Down (1982); *Diana Vs. Charles: Royal Blood Feud* (1995)

WHITE, Beatrice (Mary Irene), FRSL, FRHS (-1986), British biographer and author on English literature, was Professor Emeritus of London University and Vice-Principal of Westfield College, London University.
Mary Tudor (1935)

WHITELOCK, Dr Anna, PhD, FRHS, British historian and biographer, read History at Corpus Christi College, Cambridge, and then became a Reader in Early Modern History at Royal Holloway College, University of London, and director of the college's Centre for Public History. She has lectured on 16th and 17th political, social and cultural history, and contributed to and reviewed for the *Daily Telegraph*, *Guardian*, *Times Literary Supplement*, *BBC History* magazine, *History Today* and the *New York Times*. She has also appeared as a commentator on live television broadcasts for the BBC, Sky and ITV, and on royalty for British and international news channels, and as a presenter of or contributor to history programmes.
Mary Tudor: England's First Queen (2010) UK/*Mary Tudor: Princess, Bastard, Queen* (2010) US; *Elizabeth's Bedfellows: An Intimate History of the Queen's Court* (2013) UK/*The Queen's Bed* (2013) US

WHITING, Audrey (*née* Audrey Nener) (1927-2009), British journalist and biographer, born in Hull. She began her career as a reporter on the *Hull Daily Mail*, the *Yorkshire*

Evening Post, and joined the *Daily Mirror* in 1948. After marrying the editor, Jack Nener, she was transferred to the *Sunday Pictorial*, later the *Sunday Mirror*, where she was credited with doubling the circulation. She became the royal correspondent, according to her fellow members of staff, because at 6ft 2in she was the only one tall enough to see over the walls.

The Kents: A Royal Family (1985)

WHITTLE, Tyler (Michael Tyler-Whittle) (1927-), British author, served briefly in the Royal Marines in the Second World War, later became a regular contributor to TV and radio, and wrote fiction for adults and children as well as non-fiction, some under the name Mark Oliver.

The Last Kaiser: A Biography of William II (1977); *Victoria and Albert at Home* (1980)

WHITWORTH, Rex (Reginald Henry), CBE, CB, MBE (1916-2004), British soldier and historian, born at Overbury, Worcestershire. He read Modern History at Balliol College, Oxford, then joined the first Officer Cadet Training Unit and was commissioned into the Grenadier Guards in 1940. He saw active service with the 24th Guards Brigade in North Africa and Italy, and was subsequently appointed GSO2, 78 Division, in 1944, serving as an intelligence planning officer with Montgomery and the Eighth Army. He was Brigade Major, 24 Guards Brigade, from 1945 to 1946, and commanded the 1st Battalion Grenadier Guards from 1956 to 1957, then served at Supreme Headquarters Allied Command Europe, located at Versailles. He commanded the Berlin Infantry Brigade Group at the time the Berlin Wall was erected, in August 1961, throughout the Cuban missile crisis and during President Kennedy's visit to the city in June 1963. In 1964 he became Deputy Military Secretary at the Ministry of Defence in London, being

promoted to Major-General two years later, when he was appointed general officer commanding the Yorkshire and Northumbrian Districts until 1968. His final posting was as Chief of Staff, Southern Command, from 1968 to 1970. He was an usher at the state funeral of Sir Winston Churchill in 1965. On retirement he devoted himself to writing books on military history and biography. At the funeral of Lord Mountbatten in 1979 he was employed by the BBC, helping the commentary team to identify senior military figures as they appeared on screen.
William Augustus, Duke of Cumberland: A Life (1992)

WIEGLER, Paul (1878-1949) German journalist, editor and biographer.
William the First: His Life and Times (1929); *The Infidel Emperor and his Struggles against the Pope: A Chronicle of the Thirteenth Century* [Frederick III, Holy Roman Emperor] (1930)

WILKINS, W.H. (William Henry), BA, MA (1860–1905), English biographer, born at Compton Martin, Somerset. After working in a bank, he entered Clare College, Cambridge, then went into politics as a campaigner for immigration controls. He co-edited a short-lived monthly journal, *The Albemarle*, and published four novels, two in collaboration, under the pseudonym of De Winton. After he discovered unpublished correspondence between Sophia Dorothea of Celle, Consort of the future King George I, and her lover, Count Philip Königsmarck, at Lund University, Sweden, he turned to royal biography. A subsequent biography of Caroline Matilda of Denmark made use of material from Copenhagen, and for what proved to be his last work, he was granted access to the Fitzherbert Papers at Windsor Castle as well as papers belonging to her family.
The Love of an Uncrowned Queen, Queen Sophie Dorothea, Consort of George I, 2 vols (1900); *Caroline the Illustrious, Queen Consort of*

George II, 2 vols (1901); *Our King and Queen, the Story of their Life*, 2 vols (1903); *A Queen of Tears* [Caroline Matilda], 2 vols (1904); *Mrs. Fitzherbert and George IV*, 2 vols (1905)

WILKINSON, Clennell Anstruther, biographer.
Bonnie Prince Charlie (1932); *Coeur de Lion: A Biography of Richard I, King of England* (1933); *Prince Rupert the Cavalier* (1934)

WILKINSON, Josephine, British biographer, read History at Newcastle University. In addition to her own titles, she also edited a new version of the two-volume biography of Anne Boleyn (1884) by Paul Friedmann.
Richard III: The Young King to be (2009); *Mary Boleyn: The True Story of Henry VIII's Favourite Mistress* (2010); *Anne Boleyn* (2011) *The Princes in the Tower: Did Richard III Murder His Nephews, Edward V & Richard of York?* (2014); *Richard III: From Lord of the North to King of England* (2016)

WILLIAMS, Ethel Carleton.
Anne of Denmark (1970)

WILLIAMS, Kate, MA (1974-), British historian, read History at Oxford. She has appeared on radio and TV as a presenter of documentaries and commentator on royal events and historical material, and as a contributor to the *Daily Telegraph* and various historical journals.
Becoming Queen (2008) UK/*Becoming Queen Victoria* (2010) U); *The Ring and The Crown: A History of Royal Weddings 1066–2011* [with Alison Weir, Tracy Borman and Sarah Gristwood] (2011); *Young Elizabeth: The Making of Our Queen* (2012); *Josephine: Desire, Ambition, Napoleon* (2013)

WILLIAMS, Neville (John) (1924-77), historian and biographer, joined the Royal Navy during World War Two. He the read History at Oxford, and in 1950 became an Assistant Keeper at the Public Record Office, being appointed Deputy Keeper in 1970. Three years later he became Secretary of the British Academy. As a writer, his main period of interest was the Tudor era. He died suddenly in Nairobi while on a visit to the British Institute in Eastern Africa.

Elizabeth I, Queen of England (1971); *Henry VIII and his Court* (1971); *The Life and Times of Henry VII* (1973)

WILLIAMS, Susan, Senior Research Fellow at the Institute of Commonwealth Studies, School of Advanced Study, University of London. She has published widely on Africa, decolonisation and 20th century global power shifts.

The People's King: The True Story of the Abdication (2003)

WILLIS, G.M. (Geoffrey Malden).
Ernest Augustus, Duke of Cumberland and King of Hanover (1954)

WILLSON, D.H.
King James VI and I (1956)

WILSON, A.N. (Andrew Norman) (1950-) British writer and newspaper columnist, known for his biographies, novels, and works of popular history, was educated at New College, Oxford, and was destined for ordination in the Church of England. He was an occasional columnist for the *Daily Mail* and the *London Evening Standard*, and contributor to the *Times Literary Supplement, New Statesman, The Spectator* and *The Observer*.

Victoria: A Life (2014)

WILSON, Christopher (1946-), British journalist and author, born in Lancashire. He worked in newspapers, starting on his local weekly, *The Bedfordshire Times*, then for the *Daily Mail*, and the *Sunday Telegraph*. Moving to TV, he became ITV's first-ever environment correspondent and working as an on-screen reporter and presenter and making documentaries, mostly on environmental issues. He returned to Fleet Street as diplomatic correspondent of the *Daily Express* before taking over the paper's William Hickey column, and then wrote for *The Times*, the *Daily Telegraph*, and *Today* before becoming a full-time author. He has also appeared regularly on TV as an expert on the royal family, co-produced three major TV documentaries on royal figures, contributed to TV debates and documentaries on the British royals, and lectured on the subject.

A Greater Love: Charles and Camilla – The Inside Story of their Twenty-Three-Year Relationship (1994); *Dancing With The Devil: The Windsors and Jimmy Donahue* (2000); *The Windsor Knot: Charles, Camilla and the Legacy of Diana* (2003)

WILSON, Lawrence (Patrick Roy).
The Incredible Kaiser: a portrait of William II (1963)

WILSON, Mrs Northesk (*née* Flora Hayter) (1864-1959), British novelist and biographer. She was born in 1864 in Calcutta, India, and sent to England to be educated. Charles Northesk Wilson was her second husband, her first marriage having ended in divorce in 1895, two years before she remarried. She wrote several badly-received novels, published alternately under her own name and under the pseudonym Mrs Beresford, although there was apparently never a Mr Beresford. Her one biography, published under her married name, was written partly with the help of Serbian minister Chedomille Mijavotich (q.v.), who wrote and published his own account a little later. According to one review, the author 'seems to have put together this volume in breathless haste' (*Spectator*, 7.11.1903). In 1908 she eloped with Hugh Laurenson Ames, formerly a British Embassy attaché in Washington, and they left Britain for a lecture tour on America. Ames petitioned and received a fraudulent divorce from his wife

in London, enabling Hayter and Ames to marry in California. On their return to London they married again, and the other Mrs Ames petitioned for a divorce in 1912 on the grounds of desertion, bigamy, and adultery. It was granted as the American divorce was invalid. In 1913 Hayter and Ames pleaded guilty to bigamy and she was imprisoned for six months, after which Mr Wilson divorced her and she married Ames, legally, at last. She continued to write travel, general non-fiction and novels, until shortly before her death after she was hit by a motorbike.
Belgrade the White City of Death: Being the History of King Alexander and Queen Draga (1903)

WOLFFE, B. P. (Bertram Percy) (1922-88), British historian, studied History at Oxford, although interrupted by war service with the Royal Artillery in Africa and Italy during the Second World War. After completing his studies, he taught at Nottingham and Edinburg Universities and at Trinity College, Dublin, then became Reader in Medieval History at 'Exeter University from 1959 until his retirement in 1987.
Henry VI (1983)

WOMERSLEY, David (1957-), British historian, read English at Trinity College, Cambridge, held a Junior Research Fellowship at Pembroke College, Cambridge and then a Lecturership in the School of English at the University of Leeds, was a Tutorial Fellow in English at Jesus College, Oxford from 1984 until 2002, then became Thomas Wharton Professor of English Literature and took up a fellowship at St. Catherine's College.
James II: The Last Catholic King (2015)

WOODHAM-SMITH, Mrs Cecil, CBE (née Cecil Blanche Fitzgerald) (1896-1977), published three novels under the name Janet Gordon before turning to 19th

century history and biography. She was known for her meticulous attention to detail and only produced four works of non-fiction over a thirty-year period.
Queen Victoria, Vol. 1: Her Life and Times, 1819-1861 (1972)

WOOLMANS, Sue (*née* Sue Maillot), British biographer and sound engineer, born in Kent, contributor to *Royalty Digest* and *Atlantis*. For several years she was responsible for the annual *Royalty Digest* weekends at Ticehurst, founded by Paul Minet (q.v.).
25 Chapters of my Life: Grand Duchess Olga Alexandrovna (2009), ed. [with Paul Kulikovsky, Karen Roth-Nicholls]; *The Assassination of the Archduke: Sarajevo 1914 and the Murder that Changed the World* [with Greg King] (2013)

WORTHAM, H.E. (Hugh Evelyn) (1884-1959), British journalist and biographer, was born in Cambridgeshire and studied at King's College, Cambridge. He worked in Egypt from 1909 to 1919 as an editor, foreign correspondent and tutor to King Fuad. From 1934 until his death he wrote the 'Peterborough' column of the *Daily Telegraph*, in addition to biographies of General Gordon and Mustapha Kemal.
The Delightful Profession: Edward VII, A Study in Kingship (1931)

WRAXALL, Sir Frederic (Charles Lascelles), 3rd Baronet (1828–65), British biographer, born at Boulogne, was a biographer, historian, journalist and novelist. He studied at Oxford but left without graduating. He succeeded his uncle as Baronet in 1863, but died at Vienna two years later. In 1855 he served in the Crimean war as first-class assistant commissary, with the rank of Captain, in the Turkish contingent. In addition to biographies and military handbooks, he was also a regular contributor to the press, and published several translations from French and German literature. His work on the Queen Consort of

Holland is regarded as little more than a compilation of gossip. His final book, generally considered his best, claimed to have proved by original research the worthlessness of the evidence on which Caroline Matilda was divorced from Christian VII of Denmark after her alleged affair with Dr Struensee.

Memoirs of Queen Hortense [with Robert Wehran], 2 vols (1861); *The Life and Times of Caroline Matilda, Queen of Denmark and Norway*, 3 vols (1864)

WRIGHT, Constance (Choate) (1898-1987), American author and teacher, was born in New York. She wrote novels and several biographies.

Daughter to Napoleon: A Biography of Hortense, Queen of Holland (1962); *A Royal Affinity: The Lives of Frederick the Great and Wilhelmina of Bayreuth* (1967); *Louise, Queen of Prussia: A Biography* (1969)

Y

YERMILOVA, Larissa.
The Last Tsar (1996)

YOUNG, Sir George.
Poor Fred, The People's Prince (1937)

YOUSSOUPOV, Felix (1887-1967), Russian aristocrat, married to Princess Irina Alexandrovna, daughter of Grand Duchess Xenia, sister of Tsar Nicholas II. He was involved with and partly responsible for the murder of Rasputin, after which he and his wife left Russia, settling in France for the rest of their lives. His autobiography was reissued in 2014 with the subtitle *The Amazing Memoirs of the Man who Killed Rasputin*.
Lost Splendour (1953)

Z

ZAMOYSKI, Adam, MA (1949-), British-Polish biographer and historian. Born in New York City of parents who left Poland in 1939 after the invasion by Germany and Russia, he was brought up in England, and read History and Modern Languages at Queen's College, Oxford. His books include histories of Poland, and biographies of Chopin and Paderewski. He has regularly appeared on radio and TV and lectured widely throughout Europe, America and Australia.
The Last King of Poland [Stanislaus August] (1997)

ZEE, Henri van der (1934-2013), Dutch author, journalist and traveller. He initially planned to study medicine but took up journalism instead, accepting a job at *De Telegraaf*, becoming the paper's foreign correspondent in Paris. While in London he met and married journalist Barbara Griggs. From 1985 to 1996 he was based in Italy as Rome correspondent. In addition to royal biographies, he also wrote a highly acclaimed account of the German wartime occupation of the Netherlands.
William and Mary (1973); *1688: Revolution in the Family* (1988) [both with Barbara van der Zee]

ZEEPVAT, Charlotte (Maartje), MA, British author and historian of European royal history. She read Medieval and Modern History at University of Birmingham. She was the primary contributor to the monthly journal *Royalty Digest* from 1991 to 2005, and to its successor, *Royalty Digest*

Quarterly, as well as occasionally contributing to *The Independent* and to royal documentaries.

Prince Leopold: The Untold Story of Queen Victoria's Youngest Son (1998); *Romanov Autumn: The Last Century of Imperial Russia* (2000); *Queen Victoria's Family: A Century of Photographs 1840-1940* (2001); *The Camera and the Tsars: A Romanov Family Album* (2004); *From Cradle to Crown: British Nannies and Governesses at the World's Royal Courts* (2006)

ZIEGLER, Philip (Sandeman) (1929-), British biographer, born in Ringwood, Hampshire, and read Jurisprudence at New College, Oxford. He joined the Foreign Service, serving in Laos, Pretoria and Bogotá, and with the delegation to NATO in Paris. Retiring in 1967 to devote himself to writing, journalism and publishing, and at one stage planning to write novels, he became Editor-in-Chief at Collins from 1979 to 1980, and a contributor to *The Times*, *Daily Telegraph*, *The Spectator* and *The Listener*. In addition to royal biographies, he also wrote on the Black Death, and lives of Prime Ministers Lord Melbourne, Harold Wilson and Edward Heath.

King William IV (1971); *Crown and People* (1978); *Mountbatten, The Official Biography* (1985); *Diaries of Lord Louis Mountbatten 1920–1922: Tours with the Prince of Wales* (ed.) (1987); *Personal Diary of Admiral the Lord Louis Mountbatten, South-East Asia, 1943–1946* (ed.) (1988); *From Shore to Shore - The Final Years: The Diaries of Earl Mountbatten of Burma 1953–1979* (ed.) (1989); *Edward VIII, the Official Biography* (1990); *George VI: The Dutiful King* (2014)

ZWEIG, Stefan (1881-1942), Austrian novelist, playwright, journalist and biographer, born in Vienna, and studied Philosophy at the University of Vienna. A pacifist during the First World War, between the wars he lived in Salzburg. Being of Jewish blood he left Austria in 1934, moving to London and taking British citizenship. At the height of his career he was considered one of the most popular writers in the world. Fearing the advance of German troops, he and his second wife crossed the Atlantic in 1940, settling first in New York and then in Brazil, where they were found dead in their house after an apparent double suicide.

Marie Antoinette: The Portrait of an Average Woman (1932); *Maria Stuart* [Mary Queen of Scots] (1935)

ROYAL AUTHORS
OF MEMOIRS

ALEXANDER MICHAELOVICH, Grand Duke of Russia (1866-1933), married Grand Duke Xenia, sister of Tsar Nicholas II, in 1894. He and his wife drifted apart and both were able to leave Russia after the revolution for Europe but lived separately. He settled in Paris, where he wrote two volumes of memoirs, the second published posthumously.
Once a Grand Duke (1932); *Always a Grand Duke* (1933)

ALEXANDRA, Queen of Yugoslavia (1921–93) was born five months after the death of her father, King Alexander of Greece, to his morganatic widow, Aspasia Manos. Created Princess Alexandra of Greece and Denmark and granted the style of Her Royal Highness, she was educated in England and Paris. Moving to London, in 1944 she married her third cousin King Peter II of Yugoslavia at the Yugoslav Legation, with several of the British royal family and European royalty in temporary exile during the Second World War in attendance. After the birth of their son Crown Prince Alexander, King Peter was deposed, the marriage deteriorated, and she settled in Sussex for the rest of her life. Two books, a biography of her cousin Prince Philip and a memoir, were ghosted by Harold A. Albert (q.v.), also known as Helen Cathcart, and Joan Reeder of *Woman* magazine respectively. When the Duke of

Edinburgh was shown the manuscript of the book about him, he was annoyed at what he saw as his cousin's 'betrayal'. She was buried in the former private Greek royal residence at Tatoi in Greece, and in May 2013 her remains were transferred to Serbia for reburial in the crypt of the Royal Mausoleum at Oplenac at the same time as those of King Peter II and his mother, Queen Maria.

For a King's Love: The Intimate Recollections of Queen Alexandra of Yugoslavia (1956); *Prince Philip: A Family Portrait* (1961)

ALICE, Countess of Athlone (1883-1981), daughter of Leopold, Duke of Albany, fourth son of Queen Victoria, and the last survivor among the Queen's grandchildren. She was persuaded to write her memoirs by the diplomat and colonial administrator Sir Bede Clifford, a friend of hers for over forty years.

For my Grandchildren: Some Reminiscences (1966)

ALICE, Princess, Duchess of Gloucester (1901-2004), was born Alice Christabel Montagu Douglas Scott, daughter of John Montagu Douglas Scott, 7th Duke of Buccleuch and Queensberry, and was a descendant, in an unbroken male though illegitimate line, of King Charles II. She married Henry, Duke of Gloucester, their son of George V, in 1935. At her death, aged 102, she was the longest-lived member of the British royal family ever.

The Memoirs of Princess Alice, Duchess of Gloucester (1983); *Memories of Ninety Years* (1991)

ANDREAS of Saxe-Coburg and Gotha, Prince (1943-), was the only child of Prince Friedrich Josias of Saxe-Coburg and Gotha, a grandson of Charles Edward, the last reigning Duke of Saxe-Coburg and Gotha, and a cousin of King Carl XVI Gustav of Sweden. He was brought up partly in New Orleans after the divorce of his parents and then worked as a timber merchant in Hamburg for some

years.   He became head of the house of Saxe-Coburg Gotha on his father's death in 1998.   His memoirs were written with the assistance of Arturo E. Beéche (q.v.).
I Did It My Way (2015)

ANDREW of Greece and Denmark, Prince (1882-1944), fourth son of George I of Greece, and the father of five daughters and a son, Philip, who became Prince of Edinburgh on his marriage to the future Elizabeth II. He went into exile after the fall of the Greek monarchy in 1922, which followed defeat in the Graeco-Turkish War, and he later wrote an account of his role as a commander in the conflict.   According to the biographer of his wife Alice, 'while the book contains passages that are stylishly written, much of it is an apologia' (Vickers, *Alice, Princess Andrew of Greece*, 199).   Only a thousand copies were printed, and it is now considered one of the rarest of royal books.
Towards Disaster: The Greek Army in Asia Minor in 1921 (1935)

CECILIE, German Crown Princess (1886-1954), was wife of Crown Prince William (q.v.), who also wrote his memoirs. Their marriage broke down partly because of his infidelity and partly through their separation after he was exiled following the First World War, though they were never divorced.
The Memoirs of the Crown Princess Cecilie (1931)

CHRISTOPHER of Greece and Denmark, Prince (1888-1940), youngest son of George I of Greece.   His reminiscences concluded with his account of the restoration of the Greek monarchy in 1935 and the return of the bodies of King Constantine, Queen Sophie and Queen Olga from Florence and their reburial in Athens.
Memoirs (1938)

CYRIL VLADIMIROVICH, Grand Duke of Russia (1876-1938), son of Grand Duke Vladimir, son of Tsar Alexander II. He married his cousin Victoria Melita, divorced wife of Ernest, Grand Duke of Hesse and the Rhine, in 1905, a move which was considered scandalous and led to their temporary banishment from Russia. They were among the senior Romanovs who survived the Russian revolution, and settled in northern France. He proclaimed himself guardian of the imperial throne in 1924, an action furiously resented by other branches of the family.

My Life in Russia's Service – Then and Now (1939)

EDWARD VIII, Duke of Windsor (1894-1972), who abdicated the British throne after a reign of eleven months, put his name to a volume of memoirs in exile with the assistance of American journalist Charles J.V. Murphy (q.v.). According to Frances Donaldson (q.v.), the book came about because 'he wished to put history straight' as he always considered he had 'been deprived of his ordinary rights ever since he left the throne for reasons which were completely unworthy and totally unexpected' (Donaldson, *Edward VIII*, 397).

A King's Story (1951)

ELIZABETH of Yugoslavia, Princess, *see* BEECHE, Arturo E.

ERNEST, Duke of Saxe-Coburg Gotha (1818-93), elder brother of Albert, Prince Consort, succeeded his father, also Ernest, as Duke in 1844. After his brother's death, he identified himself increasingly with Prussia and the nationalist movement of Germany, which along with his unashamed infidelity to his wife estranged him from Queen Victoria and the rest of the family. Also renowned for his extravagance, he was frequently in debt, and saw the publication of his reminiscences as a possible solution to his financial problems.

Memoirs, 4 vols (1888)

EULALIA of Spain, Infanta (Maria Eulalia Francisca de Asís Margarita Roberta Isabel Francisca de Paula Cristina María de la Piedad), Duchess of Galliera (1864–1958) youngest child of Isabella II of Spain and Francis, Duke of Cadiz, and aunt of Alfonso XIII. Probably the most egalitarian member of her family, she became known for a series of partly autobiographical and very controversial books which were critical of foreign leaders as well as governments at home and abroad. Under the pseudonym '*Comtesse de Avila*', she wrote *Au fil de la vie*, published in 1911 and translated into English as *The Thread of Life*, expressing her views on education, the independence of women, the equality of classes, socialism, religion, marriage, and prejudice in general. Her nephew King Alfonso demanded that she suspend publication until he had seen it and granted her permission. She refused and went ahead regardless. In May 1915 she wrote an article about Emperor William II for *The Strand* Magazine, and published a second book shortly afterwards, again without seeking the approval of her uncle. Another memoir followed twenty years later, by which time the Spanish monarchy was in abeyance and the King had gone into exile.

The Thread of Life (1912); *Court Life From Within* (1915); *Courts and Countries After The War* (1925); *Memoirs of a Spanish Princess, H.R.H. the Infanta Eulalia* (1936)

FREDERICA, Queen of Greece (1917-81), Queen Consort of King Paul of Greece and daughter of Princess Victoria Louise of Prussia, Duchess of Brunswick (q.v.), wrote an account of her life from childhood to the death of her husband in 1964.

FREDERICK LEOPOLD of Prussia, Princess, formerly Princess Louise Sophie of Schleswig-Holstein-Augustenburg-Sonderburg (1866-1952), sixth child of Frederick VIII, Duke of Schleswig-Holstein, and younger sister of Augusta Victoria, German Empress, married Prince Frederick Leopold of Prussia in 1889. It was an unhappy marriage, and her refusal to obey the strict code of conduct imposed on members of the family in Germany often led to friction with her brother-in-law Emperor William II.
Behind the Scenes at the Prussian Court (ed. Desmond Chapman-Huston (q.v.)) (1939)

HAREWOOD, George Henry Hubert Lascelles, 7th Earl of (1923-2011), was the elder son of the 6th Earl of Harewood and Mary, Princess Royal, daughter of George V. His memoirs dealt in detail with family life, prisoner of war experiences, and his involvement with operatic affairs and patronage.
The Tongs and the Bones: The Memoirs of Lord Harewood (1981)

HERMINE, Empress, formerly Princess Hermine Reuss, widowed Princess von Schönaich-Carolath, (1887-1947), second wife of William II, former German Emperor, who she married in 1922. She always referred to herself as and used the title of Empress, although this was not strictly correct.
Days in Doorn (1928) UK/*An Empress in Exile: Days in Doorn* (1928) US

ILEANA of Roumania, Princess (1909-91), youngest daughter of King Ferdinand and Queen Marie (q.v.) of Roumania, was exiled from her homeland after the abdication of her nephew King Michael and the end of the

monarchy. She settled in the United States where she founded the Orthodox Monastery of the Transfiguration, Elwood City, Pennsylvania and became the Abbess. Her memoirs described her last years in Roumania.
I Live Again (1952)

LOUIS FERDINAND of Prussia, Prince (1907-94), second son of Crown Prince William (q.v.), and Crown Princess Ceciclie (q.v.), and head of the house of Hohenzollern after his father's death in 1951. He rejected a military career in Germany in favour of a life of business in America. A staunch opponent of the Nazi regime, he was not involved in the 20 July 1944 plot against Adolf Hitler, but because of his well-known hostility to the Führer, he was interrogated by the Gestapo and imprisoned in Dachau for a time. His reminiscences took their title from the epithet given him in America, and appeared with a foreword by the Pulitzer Prize-winning journalist and close friend, Louis P. Lochner.
The Rebel Prince (1952)

LOUISE of Prussia, Princess, later Princess Anton Radziwill (1770-1836), daughter of Prince Augustus Ferdinand of Prussia and Margravine Elizabeth Louise of Brandenburg-Schwedt. Her daughter Elise had a relationship with Prince William of Prussia, later first German Emperor, but they were not permitted to marry.
Forty-five Years of my Life (1912)

LOUISE of Tuscany, Princess, later Crown Princess of Saxony (1870-1947), daughter of Ferdinand IV of Tuscany. She married Prince (later King) Frederick Augustus of Saxony, and they had seven children, but after an increasingly fractious relationship with her father-in-law King George, he threatened to have her confined in a mental asylum for life. She fled from Dresden and was

divorced two months later. Having made a second and even more shortlived marriage, she wrote and published her memoirs in which she blamed her downfall on King George and his ministers, whom she claimed feared that when her husband ascended the throne, she would use her influence to have them dismissed from office.
My Own Story (1911)

MARIE, Queen of Roumania (1875-1938), daughter of Alfred, Duke of Edinburgh and of Saxe-Coburg Gotha, second son of Queen Victoria, and consort of Ferdinand, King from 1914 to 1927, was one of the most prolific of royal authors. She wrote fiction for adults and poetry, but is best remembered for her memoirs. When the first volume was published, critics were very enthusiastic; 'some faulted Marie for lack of historical depth and breadth, but most praised her lavishly for the portraits of her relatives and the vivid re-creation of a lost world' (Pakula, *The Last Romantic*, 399). Three volumes, in which she recounted her life from birth to the end of the First World War, were published during her lifetime. The manuscript of a fourth volume was thought for a long time to have been destroyed after her death by her son Carol II, but was later discovered in a file in the Romanian National Archives, Bucharest, in the mid-1990s by Diana Mandache (q.v.), who published it with a lengthy introduction and a Foreword by Dominic Lieven (q.v.)
The Story of my Life, 3 vols. (1934-5); *Later Chapters of my Life*, ed. Diana Mandache (2004)

MARIE-LOUISE, Empress of the French, later Duchess of Parma (1791-1847), daughter of Archduke Francis of Austria, later Francis II, Holy Roman Emperor. She married Napoleon, Emperor of the French, in 1810, and he abdicated in 1814. Published nearly forty years after

her death, her recollections cover life from birth to her husband's Russian campaign.
The Memoirs (1886)

MARIE LOUISE, Princess (1872-1956), younger daughter of Helena, Princess Christian of Schleswig-Holstein, third daughter of Queen Victoria. In the foreword to her memoirs, published a few months before her death, she recorded that 'writing what I can remember is like taking down a book that has lain on a shelf for many years – shut away behind a closed door'.
My Memories of Six Reigns (1956)

MARIE PAVLOVNA, Grand Duchess of Russia (1890-1958), daughter of Grand Duke Paul Alexandrovich of Russia, married Prince William of Sweden, Duke of Södermanland in 1908. They divorced six years later, and she married a commoner, Prince Sergei Putiatin, in 1917. They escaped Russia during the revolution to Europe, she divorced him in 1923 and settled in the United States, publishing her memoirs while she lived in New York City. She moved to Argentina in 1942, returned to Europe in 1949 and died in Germany. *Things I Remember* (1930) UK/*Education of a Princess: A Memoir* (1931) US; *A Princess in Exile* (1932)

NICHOLAS of Greece and Denmark, Prince (1872-1938), third son of King George I of Greece, wrote two volumes of memoirs while in exile after the fall of the Greek monarchy in 1922. After the restoration of 1935 he returned to his homeland where he died two years later.
My Fifty Years (1926); *Political Memoirs, 1914-1917: Pages from my Diary* (1928)

PAUL (Paul-Philippe), Prince of Hohenzollern-Roumania (1948-), is son of Carol Lambrino and Hélène Nagavitzine.

His father was the son of King Carol II of Rumania and Zizi Lambrino.
King Carol II: A Life of my Grandfather (1988)

PETER II of Yugoslavia, King (1923-70), was King from 1934 to 1945 when the monarchy was overthrown, and spent the rest of his life in the United States. His consort Queen Alexandra (q.v.) also published her memoirs a year later. At a reception to mark a new edition of his book, his son and heir, Crown Prince Alexander, said that readers would 'find in it a clear picture of the true face of the personae about which it speaks and see the huge difference between the communist's decades-long brutal propaganda against my father and what he truly was.' (http://www.royalfamily.org/presentation-of-a-kings-heritage-the-memoirs-by-king-peter-ii-of-yugoslavia/ accessed July 2015)
A King's Heritage: The Memoirs (1955)

PILAR of Bavaria, Princess (Maria del Pilar Eulalia Antonia Isabella Ludovika Franziska Josepha Rita Euphrasia von Wittelsbach) (1891-1987), daughter of Prince Ludwig Ferdinand of Bavaria, and Infanta Maria del la Paz of Spain, and thus a cousin of King Alfonso XIII.
Don Alfonso XIII, A Study of Monarchy [with Desmond Chapman-Huston (q.v.)] (1931)

STEPHANIE, Princess of Belgium (1864-1945), daughter of Leopold II of the Belgians, married Crown Prince Rudolf of Austria-Hungary in 1881 and, eleven years after he committed suicide at Mayerling, Cunt Elemer Lonyay, a Hungarian nobleman. It is believed that she lost large sums of money through gambling and doomed business ventures in the 1920s and that she saw publication of her

life story as a solution to her debts. They were published outside Austria as *Ich Sollte Kaiserin Werden.*
I Was To Be Empress (1937)

VICTORIA, Queen (1819-1901) published two books based on her life in the Scottish Highlands. The first, edited by Arthur Helps, Dean of the Privy Council, was initially printed for private circulation in 1867, and covered visits and expeditions from 1842 to 1861, as well as 'tours in England and Ireland, and yachting excursions'. Several readers persuaded her to give permission for general publication. Although her elder children and members of her household voiced grave misgivings about its appearance, it proved an instant success, with 10,000 copies sold within three months. A second volume appeared sixteen years later, and was dedicated to her 'Loyal Highlanders and especially to the memory of my devoted personal attendant and faithful friend JOHN BROWN'. Significantly, her name did not appear on the front cover or the title page, as this was presumably thought superfluous. Selections from her letters and journal were published posthumously in three series of three volumes each, the first, edited by A.C. Benson and Viscount Esher, covering 1837 to 1861 (1907), the second and third edited by G.E. Buckle, the first of these covering 1862 to 1885 (1926-8), the second 1886 to 1901 (1930). Esher also edited a parallel series, *The Girlhood of Queen Victoria*, covering the years 1832-40, in two volumes (1912). *Leaves from the Journal of Our Life in the Highlands from 1848 to 1861* (1868); *More Leaves from the Journal of Our Life in the Highlands from 1862 to 1882* (1884)

VICTORIA LOUISE of Prussia, Duchess of Brunswick (1892-1980), was the youngest child and only daughter of William II, German Emperor. She was inspired to write her reminiscences, with assistance from unnamed

collaborators, largely as she considered it a duty to give posterity 'a faithful picture' of her father. The one-volume English edition was translated from German, compiled and edited by Robert Vacha from three books originally published in Hanover between 1965 and 1974.
The Kaiser's Daughter (1977)

VICTORIA of Prussia, Princess, later Princess Adolf of Schaumburg-Lippe, later Frau Zoubkoff (1866-1929), second daughter of German Emperor Frederick III and sister of William II (q.v.). In the preface to her autobiography, written in response to an approach from a British publisher and based mainly on her personal diaries, she stressed that she did not intend to venture into the political situation before, during or since the First World War, as 'it may be that I lived too much in the midst of things to be quite impartial about them'. The book, published a few months before her death, was described by an anonymous reviewer as 'somewhat naïve' and 'mostly personal and domestic' (*The Times*, 7.6.1929).
My Memoirs (1929)

WILHELMINA, Queen of the Netherlands (1880-1962), ascended the throne in 1890 at the age of ten and reigned for 57 years, spanning both World Wars. She abdicated in favour of her daughter Juliana in 1948 on the grounds of ill-health. Her memoirs were originally published in the Netherlands in 1959.
Lonely But Not Alone (1960)

WILLIAM II, German Emperor (1859-1941), wrote three books, two of them reminiscences, in exile in Doorn after his abdication and the end of the German empire in 1918. The first volume, published in German as *Ereignisse und Gestalten in den Jahren 1878-1918*, was widely criticised as an unconvincing attempt at justification of his role and vindication of his policy. Rudolf von Valentini, his former chief of the civil cabinet, remarked that the most shocking aspect of the book was its untruthfulness 'with which he stands things on their head in order to place himself in the best light' (Röhl, *Wilhelm II, Into the Abyss of War and Exile, 1900-1941*, 1215-6). The second, an account of his childhood and youth and concluding with the death of Frederick III, *Aus meinem Leben 1859-1888*, is generally regarded as a better work and more charitable in his portrayal of members of his family. A third book, *My Ancestors* (1929), was in his own words 'a general impression of the personalities of my forefathers'. There is speculation that some of his output at least may have been partly ghostwritten by his friend Friedrich Rosen, diplomat, politician and German envoy in The Hague for some years.

My Memoirs, 1878-1918 (1922); *My Early Life* (1926)

WILLIAM, German Crown Prince (1882-1951), eldest son of William II, German Emperor, and head of the house of Hohenzollern after his father's death in 1941. In the preface to his reminiscences, published less than four years after the end of the German Empire, he declared that he would write 'the pages that shall recall and arrange the past, shall bring me out of this turmoil into calmness and serenity'. His wife Cecilie (q.v.), from whom he was estranged soon after the end of the First World War, also published her memoirs.

The Memoirs of the Crown Prince of Germany (1922)

WINDSOR, Wallis Warfield, Duchess of (1896-1986), married the former King Edward VIII, Duke of Windsor (q.v.) in 1937. Her memoirs, published five years after those of her third husband, were like his ghost-written, probably by Charles J.V. Murphy (q.v.), and according to a biographer, 'facts were remorselessly rearranged in what

amounted to a self-performed face-lift...reflecting in abundance its author's politically misguided but winning and desirable personality' (Charles Higham, *The Duchess of Windsor: The Secret Life*, 452-3).
The Heart Has Its Reasons (1956)

THE JAMES TAIT BLACK MEMORIAL PRIZE FOR BIOGRAPHY

The James Tait Black Memorial Prizes, Britain's oldest literary awards, were founded in 1919 by Mrs Janet Coats Black in memory of her husband, James Tait Black, a partner in A. & C. Black Ltd, publishers. Only works of fiction and biographies written in English and first published in Britain in the 12-month period prior to the submission date are eligible for the award.

The following royal biographies have been awarded the prize:

1921 *Queen Victoria* (Lytton Strachey)
1934 *Queen Elizabeth* (J.E. Neale)
1941 *King George V* (John Gore)
1944 *William the Silent* (C.V. Wedgwood)
1964 *Victoria R.I.* (Elizabeth Longford)
1969 *Mary Queen of Scots* (Antonia Fraser)

In 1942 the prize was awarded for *Henry Ponsonby: His Life from his Letters* (Arthur Ponsonby), a biography of Queen Victoria's Private Secretary.

The author

John Van der Kiste has written over sixty books, including historical and royal biographies, works of local history, true crime, music, fiction and plays. He has reviewed records and books for various national, local and independent publications and websites, and is a contributor to the *Oxford Dictionary of National Biography*. He lives in Devon.

For a complete list of his other titles currently available, please see Amazon.co.uk/Amazon.com